sweet miniatures

# sweet miniatures

## THE ART OF MAKING BITE-SIZE DESSERTS

completely revised and expanded by **FLO BRAKER**

photographs by MICHAEL LAMOTTE

line illustrations by LAURA HARTMAN MAESTRO

CHRONICLE BOOKS
SAN FRANCISCO

## acknowledgments

How lucky I am to be able to take a second look at one of my favorite projects. The revision was just as sweet as the first round.

How fortunate I've been to work with such a dynamic team of professionals. To Andrew Baker who was always ready, willing, and able to give his time, energy, and wisdom to this updated version, thank you. My deepest appreciation to Bill LeBlond at Chronicle Books for his staunch support of *Sweet Miniatures,* and many thanks to his editorial assistant Stephanie Rosenbaum; hugs to Jane Dystel, my literary agent whose meticulous attention to detail, boundless enthusiasm, and hard work make her the best; my sincere gratitude and admiration go to photographer Michael Lamotte and assistant Bill Checkvala at the Michael Lamotte Studio; stylist par excellence Sara Slavin; computer wizards Adrienne and Mark Armstrong; designer Frances Baca; and illustrator Laura Hartman Maestro. Without your talents and imaginations, I could not have done it—again.

Thank you to Elaine Gonzalez, Nick Malgieri, and Alice Medrich (my chocolate gurus), Roger Kelly, Nancy Kux, Evie and Larry Lieb, Karl Reich, Shirley Rosenberg, and Amy Whitelaw who tested recipes tirelessly, or gave invaluable advice, or took time to think out of the "oven"—or all of the above.

Heartfelt thanks to friends of the original *Sweet Miniatures* whose positive responses inspired me to consider republication.

**FLO BRAKER**

**For my honey, our children, and our grandson, Joshua, always with love**

Text copyright © 2000 by Flo Braker.

Photographs copyright © 2000 by Michael Lamotte.

Illustrations copyright © 2000 by Laura Hartman Maestro.

Library of Congress Cataloging-in-Publication Data available.

ISBN 0-8118-2446-2

Printed in the United States of America.

Distributed in Canada by Raincoast Books
9050 Shaughnessy Street
Vancouver, British Columbia V6P 6E5

10 9 8 7 6 5 4 3 2

Chronicle Books LLC
85 Second Street
San Francisco, California 94105

www.chroniclebooks.com

Prop styling: Sara Slavin
Food styling: Flo Braker
Assistant Photographer: Bill Checkvala
Book design: Frances Baca
Typeset in: Clarendon and New Century Schoolbook

# table of contents

introduction . . . . . . . . . . . . . . . . . . . . . . . . . . . . . . 7

**PART I**

good things come in small packages . . . . . . . . . . . 11

    equipment for sweet miniatures . . . . . . . . . . . . . . 15

    ingredients for miniatures . . . . . . . . . . . . . . . . . . 24

    the essentials of wonderful-tasting miniatures . . . . 27

**PART II**

miniature cookies . . . . . . . . . . . . . . . . . . . . . . . . . 31

    shortbread miniatures . . . . . . . . . . . . . . . . . . . . . 47

    chewy miniatures . . . . . . . . . . . . . . . . . . . . . . . . 91

    crispy miniatures . . . . . . . . . . . . . . . . . . . . . . . . 111

    spicy miniatures . . . . . . . . . . . . . . . . . . . . . . . . 137

    chocolate miniatures . . . . . . . . . . . . . . . . . . . . . 161

**PART III**

miniature pastries . . . . . . . . . . . . . . . . . . . . . . . . 199

    tartlet miniatures . . . . . . . . . . . . . . . . . . . . . . . 203

    flaky miniatures . . . . . . . . . . . . . . . . . . . . . . . . 233

**PART IV**

miniature cakes . . . . . . . . . . . . . . . . . . . . . . . . . . 277

    cake miniatures . . . . . . . . . . . . . . . . . . . . . . . . . 281

**PART V**

miniature sweets . . . . . . . . . . . . . . . . . . . . . . . . . 309

    miniature sweets . . . . . . . . . . . . . . . . . . . . . . . . 317

**PART VI**

planning ahead . . . . . . . . . . . . . . . . . . . . . . . . . . 337

    making miniatures ahead, 1–100 dozen . . . . . . . . 339

    quick miniatures reference . . . . . . . . . . . . . . . . . 345

    freezing and storing . . . . . . . . . . . . . . . . . . . . . 352

index . . . . . . . . . . . . . . . . . . . . . . . . . . . . . . . . . . . 357

table of equivalents . . . . . . . . . . . . . . . . . . . . . . . 366

# introduction

I baked every day, and no matter what I baked, I always focused on making it in miniature

My fascination with cookies, pastries, cakes, and candies in miniature started in childhood. My maternal grandmother made frequent business trips to New York and she always came back to Indiana with at least one box of cookies and small pastries from Schrafft's, the well-known tearoom. These were called Little Gems. Before these, I'd only seen candy this small. Each time I ate one of the tiny treats, I secretly dreamed of duplicating one or even creating my own someday.

Growing up, and as a young wife and mother, I often read biographies of world-renowned artists, such as Van Gogh and Rembrandt, with envy. After each book I was inspired to try the artist's medium—in the hopes that I possessed latent artistic talent.

But it was only as my interest in baking grew that my dreams became reality. Because of my fascination with every facet of baking, I baked every day, and no matter what I baked, I always focused on making it in miniature. And so, baking and candy making in miniature became my favorite creative outlet, my hobby. It made no difference whether these miniatures were cookies, pastries, cakes, or candies—tiny confections packed with a luscious chocolate cream, tart lemon curd, crisp florentines, pungently spicy gingersnaps, or juicy strawberries obsessed me. Like popping corn, new miniatures kept coming. Finally, I'd found my art form.

For years I've studied the details and designs of cakes, candies, and pastries everywhere—name a city anywhere in the world and if I've been there, I'll bet my favorite rolling pin that something sweet intrigued me. Wherever I go I carry a camera, notebook, pen, and measuring tape, all ready to record whatever catches my eye or my taste buds from the simplest sugar cookie to the most elaborate, fresh flower-topped wedding cakes. Searching out pastry and candy shops from New York to Berkeley, from London to Tokyo, even after 40-plus years, I am still filled with a rush of pleasure when I enter a first-rate one. But I find inspiration in places other than food shops, always imagining from other art forms how to apply what I see to miniature shapes and sizes—for example, jewelry at the Victoria and Albert Museum, fashion on Bond Street, architecture at the Vatican, and art at the Louvre.

Soon a crossroad came in my life. My family could not eat fast enough the candies, cakes, cookies, and pastries that I made daily. My production exceeded their consumption, and so the timing seemed perfect to begin baking professionally. I began Occasional Baking, a dessert catering business.

I never anticipated that the majority of the orders would be for the miniatures. People liked them assorted on trays to adorn their tables before serving. They loved everything about them—the textures, crispy or tender; the flavors, spicy or sweet; and, of course, the size. As business grew, I was encouraged to expand the miniature repertoire, which had become my trademark.

One observation I made during my catering career also holds true when I entertain in my home. No matter how much I fuss over a cake or a special dessert, when I accompany it with a tray of miniatures, the miniatures get the attention every time. Guests love to look at them, but after tasting a few—small bites of spice, tangy citrus with fresh fruit, creamy caramel and flaky pastry, bittersweet chocolate and jam, buttery coconut, pecans and tender pastry, spongy cake and honey, nutty meringue and semisweet chocolate—they become even more enthusiastic, eager to sample each variety.

After three years of business experience and hundreds of educational baking errors, I decided to teach what I had learned about the subject of baking and candy making. Of all my classes, the ones on the miniatures were in greatest demand. Some popular miniatures—Drei Augen (page 56), Lemon Meringue Tartlets (page 219), and Sweet Cheese Puffs (page 236)—became my signature miniatures.

My most beloved recipes are in this book. You will find how I make them, and what works for me. What I wish for you is to enjoy them as much as I have. But the best reward for me would be if this book inspired you to invent your own memorable miniatures.

# good things come in small packages

Some miniatures are elegant,
others are cute, whimsical,
or just plain stunning

Miniatures have special appeal. A tray of assorted miniature cookies, pastries, and cakes offers a dazzling array of shapes, colors, flavors, and textures. Imagine a display of miniatures in all their variety. Some are round and some square. They are a delicious golden brown or brightly colored. Taste a few. Some are rich, others sweet, tart, or spicy. Their textures may be soft, chewy, crisp, crumbly, short, crunchy, or flaky.

We are attracted to miniatures. Something makes us thrill to see a familiar object scaled down to an unusually small size. And a close look at our tray reveals that each morsel is not just little, but is, in fact, a complete tiny cookie, pastry, or cake with careful, authentic decorations that give it a distinct personality. Some miniatures are elegant, others are cute, whimsical, or just plain stunning.

Before you eat a miniature, you fall in love with it. After all, it's all yours. Who would ask you to share something so small and perfect? It's never necessary to cut or alter the shape of a miniature before it is safely in your mouth.

The trim size of miniatures makes them desserts that are quite a bit less intimidating than a slice of cake or a scoop of ice cream. You can easily choose to have a portion of any size, from a single bite-sized gem to one—or two—of each of a large assortment.

Making miniatures is enjoyable and rewarding. They are not difficult to prepare and offer a great change from making cakes, pastries, and pies. Baking slip-ups don't count, because the miniatures are so tiny that mistakes don't really show. It's easy to stick one in your mouth and test the taste without anyone knowing. Miniatures perfume the air while they bake with their intense and mouth-watering aromas.

Yes, I love everything about miniatures. I associate them with good will and happiness. And so, after many happy years baking miniatures, I offer a variety of recipes, some old favorites, some new. Whether you bake them to serve alone or to ornament other desserts, for a catered affair, a restaurant, a crowd at a tailgate party, a wedding, anniversary, or birthday reception, a small dinner party, or a brunch, for holiday gifts for family or friends, or when just plain relaxing with colleagues or visiting old friends, you will help perpetuate the happiness that goes with miniatures.

These recipes are straightforward, requiring no tricky techniques to guarantee their success. In consideration of our busy lives, I have given specific information, step by step, for handling, shaping, baking, decorating, and storing with each of my recipes. In this way, you can plan your miniature making ahead according to your schedule. I have also included many shortcuts that will help you to spend time efficiently in the kitchen, to streamline your baking and ensure the best miniature results every time.

# equipment for sweet miniatures

Part of the fun in miniature making is that you do not need a lot of esoteric or expensive equipment. Although the equipment I recommend is basic, it does facilitate miniature making so preparation is smoother and less time-consuming.

## BEFORE YOU BAKE

Scales For consistent results in miniature making, a scale is invaluable for weighing dry ingredients. I prefer one that is easy to read, with markings in ounces and grams, and that can accommodate a bowl on top for holding up to 2 pounds of flour or sugar.

Food Thermometers The candy thermometer tracks the stages of cooking sugar syrups, such as for buttercreams and candies. I prefer the type which has the thermometer attached to a 12-x-1¾-inch stainless steel strip with a clip for the saucepan. When melting or tempering chocolate, I check the temperature of the chocolate or the water in the pan under the bowl of chocolate frequently with an instant-read meat/yeast thermometer since it shows results quickly.

Electric Mixers and the Food Processor Electric mixers are invaluable for making buttercreams, doughs, batters—even flaky puff pastry. If you use a hand mixer instead of a more powerful heavy-duty mixer with the balloon whisk, dough hook, or paddle attachments, you'll need to adjust the speed given in my recipes. For instance, when a recipe says to use medium-low speed, set a hand mixer at medium.

I use the food processor when I want to make doughs quickly and easily without adding a lot of air to them (Miniature Tartlet Pastry, page 205) or to crush the praline into tiny golden crumbs to flavor buttercream for the Swiss Japonais (page 107).

**The Microwave Oven** I find this appliance very handy for simple tasks like melting chocolate (see page 313) and butter, and softening brown sugar. Tempering chocolate (see Express Method in Seven Easy Steps, page 315) takes only 30 minutes when using the microwave.

**Nut Grinders** Nuts have a high oil content and become stale or rancid quickly, so I always grate or chop them as I need them.

**How to Measure Nuts** When you're measuring whole, chopped, or finely ground nuts for a miniature recipe, pour or scoop them from the package, your hand, a serving spoon, or a metal spatula into a dry measuring cup. Do not pack them. Strange as it may seem, because you do not pack the nuts, a given volume of whole or large pieces of nuts will yield what appears to be the same volume of chopped nuts. Nougatine Cones (page 124) is a good example. The recipe calls for 4 ounces, or ¾ cup, of hazelnuts, chopped medium-fine. You will find that the nuts still measure ¾ cup after you chop them.

When a recipe lists a nut as an ingredient, I give the weight first, then the cup measurement before chopping or finely grinding as a matter of convenience, since you usually buy nuts in packages marked in ounces.

**Finely Ground Nuts** The Mouli grater, the rotary grater you hold in your hand while you turn the handle, is fine for small amounts of nuts. For larger quantities, use a grater that attaches to the edge of a tabletop. A wooden pusher keeps the nuts against the stainless steel drum while you turn the handle.

You can use a food processor or an electric herb and spice mincer, but I recommend you grate only a few ounces of nuts at a time to prevent their high fat content from causing the finely ground nuts to become oily.

**Coarsely Chopped Nuts**  Chop the nuts on a chopping block with a chef's knife, or use a food processor with brief on/off pulses until you have the desired size.

**Finely Chopped Nuts**  When I want nuts chopped somewhere between fine and coarse, as in the Black Walnut Genoise Wafers (page 116), the Pecan Strudel (page 260), and the Toffee Butter Crunch (page 319), I use a nut mill. When chopped nuts are part of the bulk of the recipe, such as in the filling for the Pecan Strudel, rather than present simply for their texture and flavor, I use a nut mill for chopping them. Since this piece of equipment allows for no variation in speed, intensity, or length of time of chopping, the nut granules it produces will be the same proportion of slightly larger to slightly smaller pieces every time. This ensures that a given weight of nuts yields the same volume of chopped nuts every time. Chopping nuts with a chef's knife is less quick and accurate. With a nut mill the nuts go in the top hopper, you turn the handle, and the chopped nuts fall into the glass container below.

**Citrus Zesters**  There are a variety of tools available for grating citrus fruit (including a box grater and a small hand tool called the zester), but the one that produces fine, delicately thin shreds of zest while removing hardly any pith with the zest is a long and narrow lightweight stainless-steel strip that looks very much like a carpenter's rasp. The ultra-fine zest dissolves into the boiling syrup (Raspberry Jellies, page 334) so that only the zest's flavor remains.

## PAPER PRODUCTS

**Waxed Paper**  I keep a roll of waxed paper in every corner of my kitchen. Rolling cookie doughs between two sheets of paper into circles or rectangles before refrigerating to firm them is a technique I strongly endorse (Drei Augen, page 56).

**Aluminum Foil**  Aluminum foil's flexibility and strength make it easy to mold it to fit into cardboard boxes to line them before storing miniatures. When I roll up small pieces of foil to make springlike shapes that fit between spaces to cushion cookies from rattling, and thereby breaking, the foil's strength and flexibility are again important. I choose foil to line cardboard boxes as well as to layer between cookies in airtight metal tins because foil won't absorb the butter from the miniatures. I line baking sheets with foil when I want cookies, such as the Florentine Squares (page 114), to be released in perfect form when cool and firm.

**Parchment Paper**  Lining baking sheets with parchment paper promotes even baking of many types of cookies. Parchment paper is reusable. Also, you can fashion paper cones from parchment as well as mark circles on it with pencil to make forms for piping the meringue mixture for Swiss Japonais (page 107). Rather than use waxed paper, you can roll out miniature cookie doughs between two sheets of parchment. Then it's easy to mark the paper with pencil to identify doughs with names and dates before refrigerating.

**Plastic Wrap**  Wrapping cylinders of dough in plastic prevents their drying when refrigerated. For longer storage in the refrigerator or freezer of several dough circles, stack on one baking sheet, overwrapping with sturdy plastic wrap to prevent drying out.

**Baking Cup Paper Liners**  Pack fluted bonbon cups with miniature cookies or cakes for serving trays or gift boxes. Cupcake liners 1⅜ inches across the bottom with ¾-inch sides are useful for baking Dutch Chocolate Minicakes (page 198).

## SHAPING MINIATURES

**Straight Wooden Pin**  The rolling pin that is easiest for me to roll is a 16-inch-long straight pin, about 2 inches in diameter, without handles.

**Springerle and Waffle Rollers**  Both these rollers form decorative patterns when rolled over dough.

**Pastry and Cookie Cutters**  Sets of round cutters in graduated sizes, plain and fluted, are useful. An assortment of shapes is nice to have. Always look for them in heavy tinned steel since sturdy cutters don't bend easily and sharp ones cut doughs, especially pastry doughs, cleanly.

A set of four Japanese cutters, each one a different shape (one is a flower), can be used to cut out shapes in dough or marzipan, as in Lemon Sunflowers (page 86) and Chocolate Coins (page 183).

**Cookie Stamps**  Designs from clay or glass stamps can be stamped into the dough to emboss it before baking. Roll dough such as Almond Teardrops dough (page 72) into balls, roll the balls of dough in sugar, and stamp. If stamp gets sticky, wash and dry thoroughly before reusing.

**Ice Cream Scoops**  Most scoops are numbered for the number of scoops per quart of ice cream. I use scoops #70 (capacity is 2½ teaspoons) and #100 (capacity is 1½ teaspoons) for dropping cookie doughs and batters for miniature cookies and cakes. A tiny scoop, not numbered, whose capacity is 1 teaspoon is ideal for depositing dollops of cookie dough or forming truffles.

**Plastic Lids and Rubber Inserts**  Make your own stencils from disposable plastic lids and rubber jar inserts to create reusable designs, as for Chocolate Fringe Cups (page 132) and Chantilly Fans (page 134).

**Krumkake Iron** For the wafer-thin Miniature Krumkake (page 126) that I roll into small cone shapes, I prefer a cast-iron krumkake iron, though electric ones are available. Both irons imprint a pattern on the cookies.

**Wooden Dowels and Cornets** With a small household hand saw, I cut wooden dowels, ⅜ inch in diameter, into 6-inch-long sticks to roll up cookies while warm and flexible (Crispy Corkscrews, page 128). I use a wooden cornet to roll cookies warm from the oven when I want them cone-shaped (Nougatine Cones, page 124, and Miniature Krumkake, page 126).

**Wooden Decorative Molds** Doughs can be pressed into designs in wooden forms to imprint them (Speculaas, page 152).

**Spritz** A metal cylinder fitted with plates with a variety of cutout designs can be filled with dough to shape it into decorative forms.

## BAKING MINIATURES

### Baking Pans

**Baking Sheets** I use baking sheets for baking most miniature cookies, pastries, and cakes, such as the Genoise Sheet Cake (page 283). But I also find them invaluable for holding a stack of cookie circles or cakes in the refrigerator or freezer. The two sizes that I use the most are 12-x-15½-inch and 14-x-17-inch sheets, both with a 45-degree-angle ½-inch rim on all four sides, open at the corners. When I want to remove cookies quickly while warm and flexible without fear of sticking, I use Teflon-coated baking sheets (Tuiles, page 113, and Cigarettes, page 122). And the rectangular jelly-roll pan (10 x 15 x 1 inch) is perfect for glazing miniatures, since drips are contained in the pan (Hedgehogs, page 174, and Parisers, page 289).

**Nonstick Pan Liners** Reusable rubberized silicone mats, Silpat or Exopat, or Super Parchment (a flexible, ultrathin reusable 13-x-17-inch sheet) provide a nonstick surface for sheet pans so that sticky candies (Golden Caramels, page 326, and Five-Spice Marshmallows, page 332) and many baked goods release easily.

**Miniature Muffin Pans** For miniatures such as and Dutch Chocolate Minicakes (page 198) and Sweet Cheese Puffs (page 236), the heavy-gauge aluminum pan with 12 individual cups, each measuring 1¼ inches across the bottom, 1⅞ inches across the top, and ¾-inch deep, is perfect.

**Tartlet Pans** To give shape to the Miniature Tartlet Pastry (page 205) and form it into an assortment of small individual tarts, I've collected over the years from cookware shops across the country—even the world—a variety of heavy-gauge miniature tin containers with plain, fluted, or swirled sides. No matter what the shape—barquette, round, square, or oval—I prefer them to measure no more than 1½ inches to 2¼ inches across. It's nice to own at least 2 dozen of each shape, but if one shape is a particular favorite, you might want more. For example, I can fit 4 dozen 1½-inch round Swedish tartlet tins, close together, on one 12-x-15½-inch baking sheet. Owning this number is convenient, allowing me to bake more at once.

**Madeleine Pan** For the Sweet Seashells (page 64), I press dough into the 20 tiny shell molds in a mini madeleine pan.

## AFTER YOU BAKE

**Cooling Racks** Most miniature cookies, cakes, and pastries must be ventilated. Extra-large sturdy cooling racks, rectangular in shape, are best for miniatures. You can easily fit a batch on the rack without overlapping or crowding.

For glazing, I prefer cooling racks with wires close together to form a grid. These racks keep miniatures steady and prevent them from tilting or slipping through the wires.

Storage Containers Whenever I store miniatures, my goal is to fit them as snugly as possible to avoid breakage, with as little room as possible between the miniatures and the lid of the container to prevent a lot of stale air from penetrating the miniatures.

Airtight metal containers are best for cookies that must remain crisp or age and mellow. To prevent miniatures sensitive to humidity, such as Nougatine Cones (page 124), from absorbing moisture at room temperature, I keep them in a canister called a Krispy Kan. The lid has a removable glass knob filled with nontoxic blue crystals that absorb moisture. When the crystals turn light lilac, it's time to place the knob in a hot oven to reactivate them. Many times I place this removable knob in another airtight metal container that has a more convenient shape for storing miniatures.

Sturdy plastic containers are useful when I want to ensure that moist or chewy cookies remain that way. These containers are airtight and perfect for freezing such pastries as the Sweet Cheese Puffs (page 236).

## DECORATIVE UTENSILS

Pastry Tips Buttercream and whipped cream look very attractive after they have been piped through a pastry tip. In addition, many times piping a dough, batter, or filling is the fastest and easiest way to accomplish the work of miniature making. Even though I have a drawer full of different sizes and shapes, I use just a few plain open tips (¼ and ½ inch) and a few open and closed star tips the most often. There are instances when the wider end of a tip (for example, the ½-inch plain open tip, Ateco # 6) is convenient for cutting out shapes in cakes (Parisers, page 289) or dough (Hedgehogs, page 174).

**Pastry Bags** I always have 12-inch, 14-inch, and 16-inch lightweight flexible nylon pastry bags as well as 12-inch and 18-inch disposable decorating bags on hand. Whereas the nylon bags are easy to clean and reusable, the disposable ones save time by eliminating clean-up. Fill the bag no more than two-thirds full, and twist the upper third tightly to prevent the mixture from coming out the top portion as you pipe.

**Handmade Paper Cones** These disposable cones are great for piping small amounts of jelly, buttercream, royal icing, chocolate, and ganache. If you do not have precut triangular paper for paper cones, cut a 22-inch square from parchment paper. Fold it diagonally, and cut into two triangles. Hold a triangle in one hand with the longest side at the bottom and the thumb of your other hand in the center. Manipulate it into a cone shape so that the long side becomes the tip and the point of the triangle (opposite the long side) becomes the opening of the cone. Fold the top of the point into the cone to hold it together. Fill the cone half full, fold the tops of the two sides toward the middle, and fold the top down to enclose the mixture. Cut the tip to the desired opening before piping.

# ingredients for miniatures

Good-tasting and fresh ingredients are essential and easy to acquire

Almost all the ingredients for the miniature recipes are straightforward and easy to acquire. Where I recommend using a more esoteric item, such as rice flour for the Shortbread Cameos (page 49), there will be a note in the recipe describing it and suggesting where to find it.

When you shop for baking ingredients, the most important criteria are that the items be good-tasting and fresh. Once you get them home, store them as well as possible so as to maintain their freshness and quality and thus keep them tasting their best. Here are some brief guidelines on selecting and storing ingredients, based on what works for me in my kitchen.

I have on hand at all times the ingredients to bake several different recipes. Many of these baking ingredients go in the pantry, while in my upright freezer I've dedicated four shelves to assorted bags of nuts, one shelf to butter, with a few bags of coffee beans off to the side—everything securely wrapped. I have eggs, heavy cream, milk, cheese, and a variety of fruits in the refrigerator, and everything else I need is in kitchen cabinets or drawers.

U.S. grade AA unsalted butter smells and tastes sweet since it is made from the highest-quality fresh cream. I keep a small amount of it in the refrigerator, always drawing from my ample supply in the freezer. Since butter easily picks up flavors from other foods in the refrigerator, it's a good idea to wrap securely any opened portions.

Only buy grade AA eggs that are stored in refrigerated cases at the supermarket. And always store them in their cartons in the refrigerator to avoid salmonella-contaminated eggs.

Heavy cream, sometimes called heavy whipping cream, has at least 36 percent milkfat. It is available pasteurized and ultrapasteurized. I prefer pasteurized, since a cooked taste can sometimes be detected in ultrapasteurized cream.

Observe dates on packages and cartons for reference to freshness for butters, eggs, heavy creams, and even packages of nuts, and also for pasteurized whole milk, buttermilk, sour cream, small curd cottage cheese, mascarpone cheese (an unripened Italian dessert cheese made from fresh cream), and cream cheese. For baking, I prefer a cream cheese with a gum arabic stabilizer. This variety is consistently less watery and gives great results after baking. Use the type without a stabilizer for no-bake recipes or spreading on English muffins or bagels.

Buy small amounts of spices, because they become stale or lose their punch rapidly. Also, buy small amounts of extracts and keep them tightly capped in a cool place. I mark the date of purchase on spices and extracts and even on chocolate and nuts, so that the oldest always get used first.

When it comes to chocolate, I always use the real thing. Whether to use bittersweet or semisweet is a matter of taste preference. Bittersweet is usually less sweet, with a higher content of chocolate liquor—the nonalcoholic liquid made from the nibs of cocoa beans that is the basis of all chocolate—than semisweet. Milk chocolate has less chocolate liquor than dark chocolate and has milk solids added.

When buying white chocolate, which the U.S. Standard of Identity does not consider a pure chocolate since it contains no chocolate liquor, buy a brand that has no fats other than cocoa butter and butterfat. If you buy chocolate in bulk, overwrap it with heavy-duty aluminum foil. Store all chocolate varieties in a dark, cool, dry place. Semisweet and bittersweet chocolate keep longer than white or milk.

Unsweetened cocoa powders come in two forms: alkalized ("Dutched," to reduce bitterness and give it a darker color) or nonalkalized ("natural," which is lighter in color than alkalized, but bolder and fruitier in flavor). Either type is fine in my miniature recipes.

Always keep nuts well wrapped, whether in an airtight tin at room temperature or in storage bags in the freezer. Thaw them before using in a recipe. Choose jams and jellies based on your personal preferences. Store sugars, especially light and dark brown sugars, and flours in covered containers at room temperature.

Always store a can of solid vegetable shortening in the refrigerator. This keeps it fresh for making shiny homemade chocolate glazes, such as Dark Chocolate Satin Glaze (page 104). Since I use a lot of almond paste, I also refrigerate a large can of it to keep it fresh for an indefinite amount of time. I use store-bought marzipan when I don't have time to make my own. Always keep it well wrapped in the refrigerator so that it does not dry out.

The world of fruits, fresh and dried, is always changing. Every season a new fruit or variety appears in the produce repertoire. Dried fruits are available year-round, and even dried cherries and cranberries are more widely distributed now.

# the essentials of wonderful-tasting miniatures

Baking miniatures is fun and need not be complicated. Here are the essentials for smooth and easy miniature making.

Read the recipe carefully before you bake.

➤ Assemble all ingredients and equipment before you begin.

➤ Allow enough time for ingredients to reach room temperature when recipe specifies.

Trust your own judgment.

➤ When baking miniatures, if they test done before the time given in the recipe, remove them from the oven. Each recipe in this book tells you what to look for in a properly baked miniature and specifies a baking time. Remember, baking times are only approximate because of temperature variations in ovens.

➤ If you don't have time to decorate a miniature as recommended in the recipe, choose a more simple decoration, or serve unadorned.

➤ If you miscalculate in measuring the ingredients or the baking time, taste the dough or the baked miniature. If the flavor is OK, it's OK. Perhaps your mistake invented a new recipe.

Measure accurately.

➤ Use a scale or stainless steel cups for dry ingredients, Pyrex cups for liquids.

Follow procedures in the recipe closely.

➤ To form smooth, homogeneous cookie doughs and cake batters, add the flour gradually.

➤ If a recipe specifies that the mixture must be baked immediately after making, be prepared to do so. For example, see Chocolate Macaroons (page 163).

Prepare baking sheets, molds, and pans as the recipe specifies to ensure successful results.

➤ Lining baking sheets with parchment paper, which is reusable, prevents cookies from burning on the bottom and promotes even baking. It is quick and eliminates baking sheet clean-up.

➤ Greasing baking sheets increases spreading of cookie doughs and batters during baking, while greasing and flouring sheets inhibits spreading.

Set oven racks and temperature as each recipe specifies.

➤ Unless the recipe specifies otherwise, always bake in the lower third of the oven to allow the heated air to circulate evenly around the baking pan or sheet.

➤ When using two baking sheets simultaneously, adjust two racks to divide the oven into thirds. Rotate the baking sheets from front to back and from one shelf to the other halfway through baking.

➤ Preheat the oven for at least 15 minutes.

➤ Incorrect baking temperatures, whether too high or too low, ruin the taste and textures of all miniatures. Each recipe specifies the temperature for optimum results.

➤ Notice that many recipes in this book recommend oven temperatures lower than those in similar recipes from other sources. For example, my Shortbread Cameos (page 49) bake at 300 degrees F and are slower to finish than most other shortbreads, which usually bake at 350 degrees F. Lower temperatures prevent all cookies, tartlets, and pastries from browning too quickly and promote uniform baking.

➤ Notice that the Genoise Sheet Cake (page 283), a thin, flexible cake, bakes at 450 degrees F, which is quite hot for cakes. In this case, the hotter temperature bakes the cake more quickly and ensures a moist interior without the cake being overly dry and crisp throughout.

Bake a batch of miniature cookies or pastries on a cool baking sheet.

➤ Miniature doughs and batters set on hot sheets begin to spread or even bake before all the cookies or pastries are in place. Allow baking sheets hot from the oven to cool on a rack 10 to 15 minutes before baking another batch.

➤ If your supply of baking sheets is limited, set miniatures on parchment paper cut to fit the baking sheet while the sheet is cooling. Once the sheet is cool to the touch, slip it under the paper and set it in the oven.

Before baking a large batch, bake one miniature cookie or pastry as a sample to gauge spreading distance and cooking time in your oven.

➤ It takes only a few minutes to test-bake one miniature. Then you can adjust the oven temperature, recipe, or baking sheet without wasting an entire batch.

➤ Keep in mind that cookies brown quickly once they begin to change color, so watch them closely. It is especially easy to burn chocolate doughs because of their dark color.

➤ Overbaking dries cookies and spoils delicate flavors such as those of butter, spices, and chocolate.

Follow the cooling and storing procedures each recipe specifies for best flavor and texture.

➤ In general, place baking sheets, molds, and pans on a wire rack to cool 10 minutes before handling miniature cookies, tartlets, pastries, and cakes.

➤ If miniatures are still fragile after 10 minutes, wait until they are cooler to avoid breaking or distorting their form.

➤ If cookies or pastries are already a bit too golden, to avoid further baking on the hot-from-the-oven baking sheet, lift the parchment paper with the cookies or pastries from the sheet onto a rack.

➤ Cool miniatures completely before storing.

PART II

# miniature cookies

Cookies are delicious
fun without taking a lot
of time, effort, or skill

Making cookies is the most popular form of baking. Anyone can make them. They're delicious fun without taking a lot of time, effort, or skill. You can bake any size, shape, flavor, or texture. The variety is endless.

## MIXING MINIATURE COOKIE DOUGHS

I've discovered from years of cookie making that whether cookies are crisp, soft, chewy, brittle, sandy, short, or dense depends on a multitude of factors: the recipe's ingredients, their ratio to one another, the cookies' size and shape, baking methods, oven temperatures, and baking time.

But there is perhaps one factor that is most crucial to cookie making. I discovered it more than two decades ago, when I experienced two baking mishaps.

I cannot recall when I made my first batch of chocolate chip cookies—but I'll never forget the time I baked my most unusual batch. As always, I began making my favorite chocolate chip recipe using the electric mixer. While I was beating the butter with the sugar, the phone rang. When I returned to the kitchen five minutes later, the machine was still in motion and the mixture was fluffy white. I added the egg, then the remaining ingredients, and dropped the dough on the baking sheets.

When the cookies baked sooner than I expected, I got my first indication that these were not my normal chocolate chip cookies. When I removed them from the oven, I saw that they were puffy, almost domelike. I picked one up. It was light in my hand—and in my mouth. The extra beating time had somehow modified the cookies.

The next incident occurred while I was making tartlets from a not-too-sweet cookie recipe. (See Miniature Tartlet Pastry, page 205.) I thought this recipe was ideal because it baked miniature tartlet shells firm enough to hold creamy fillings yet tender from the first bite.

I had always made the recipe dough by hand or in the food processor, but that one time I switched to the electric mixer for no reason other than to change the routine. The dough appeared smooth and homogeneous, as usual, but after the tartlets had baked and cooled in their tins, they were impossible to remove without breaking. Instead of firm and tender, they were fragile and crumbly.

The chocolate chip caper and my fateful mistake with the miniature pastry dough led me to this most important truth about cookie making: How you mix the ingredients together determines the final consistency of the dough or batter and, ultimately, the texture of the cookies after baking.

There are three basic techniques for preparing cookie doughs or batters: the simple mixing method, the creaming mixing method, and the whipping mixing method.

Understanding these methods helps me when I need to be sure that the recipes that I bake repeatedly will consistently produce what I want each time, when I want to duplicate cookies' results frequently, and even when I want to make a cookie from a recipe new to me or to improve an old one.

When you understand these simple methods, you'll be able to produce the results you want, improve and improvise your cookie making—and even correct cookie errors.

## SIMPLE MIXING METHOD

The simple mixing method is just as its name implies: Ingredients need merely be mixed together. It's the easiest and most straightforward method. You do not need to incorporate any air or work the mixture until light and creamy.

- To mix ingredients together to form smooth, homogeneous mixtures, it's important to add the ingredients in the order the recipe specifies. If the recipe calls for a fat, such as butter, it's important that it be at room temperature.

- Stir ingredients together using a rubber spatula or a wooden spoon in a bowl.

- To mix ingredients together with an electric mixer, use low to medium-low speed.

This is the simplest way to make cookie doughs. Ingredients need merely be stirred together to combine them completely into a smooth, homogeneous mixture.

Since the simple mixing method is exactly as it says, it works well in combining ingredients for recipes that call for little or no fat and need not begin with an airy base. Soft batters such as Miniature Krumkake (page 126) that are moistened by sour cream, stiff batters such as Macaroon Trios (page 99) that are nut-paste or ground-nut mixtures bound and moistened by egg whites, stiff doughs such as Pains d'Amande (page 143), and soft batters such as Nougatine Cones (page 124) that begin as a warm, syrupy mixture are examples. Ingredients are usually stirred together with a rubber spatula or wooden spoon in a bowl or mixed together on low to medium-low speed with an electric mixer.

## CREAMING METHOD

The creaming method is used in cookie recipes that contain an abundance of fat. Fat's job in a recipe is both to absorb dry and liquid ingredients and to trap air. A recipe using the creaming method usually begins with the phrase "cream the butter with the sugar," since it is the manipulation of the fat that causes it to incorporate air bubbles.

All recipes that use this method share in common a generous amount of fat, usually butter. Room-temperature butter is beaten with sugar (OK by hand, but easier by machine) to incorporate air, and then egg and liquid, if called for in the recipe, are beaten in before adding dry ingredients. Having the ingredients at similar temperatures makes it easier to combine them to form a smooth, homogeneous mixture.

➤ To cream properly, begin with room-temperature butter. Butter that is too firm requires more beating, which incorporates more air.

➤ Sometimes it's quicker to use a hand mixer than a heavy-duty mixer. To beat or cream the butter with the sugar using a rotary hand mixer, cream room-temperature butter with the sugar at medium to medium-high speed just until the mixture is smooth. When a mixture's volume is small, as in the buttercream for the Cognac Wafers (page 120), the ability afforded by a hand-held mixer to reach any part of the bowl or the bottom of a deep bowl is invaluable.

➤ To cream with a heavy-duty electric mixer, using the paddle, flat beater, or dough hook, begin at medium-low speed until the butter is smooth.

Within this group of recipes there are two basic types of creaming. The difference lies in how long and how vigorously the butter (or other fat) is creamed, which determines the amount of air incorporated during mixing. One method involves a minimum amount of air and thus less creaming, and the other involves more air, and thus more creaming. The creaming method used affects the baked cookies' texture (dense, delicate, or crumbly) and the way the cookies leaven and spread during baking (becoming thin, puffy, flat, and/or retaining their shapes).

Do not be confused by the difference between these two types of creaming. My chocolate chip cookie incident illustrates the distinction beautifully. The recipe I used started with the words "Combine the butter with the sugars until creamy." But when I inadvertently left the mixture beating for five minutes, I truly *creamed* the mixture until light and fluffy and ended up with airy, rounded cookies.

Many recipes can be made successfully starting with either a smooth and creamy mixture, pale yellow in color, or a very light and fluffy white one. The amount of mixing you choose to do depends on the degree of density or airiness you desire in your baked cookies. I have designed the recipes in this book so that if you follow my instructions exactly, you will bake what I think are the best miniature cookies. But with an understanding of the creaming methods, you may freely adjust the beating of your cookie doughs to come up with cookies that suit your taste exactly.

When you want cookies to retain their shape and bake densely—for example, with firm doughs that contain an abundance of butter but no liquid ingredients, such as Shortbread Cameos (page 49) and Drei Augen (page 56), and stiff doughs that contain a great deal of butter with small amounts of egg or other liquids, such as the Miniature Tartlet Pastry (page 205)—the minimal creaming method is useful. It also works well for cookie batters like Almond Confetti (page 88) that you want to spread thinly in the oven and bake to a delicate texture. Too much air in either type of batter and you get a crumbly texture, so only a small amount of creaming is needed.

Cookies made without incorporating a lot of air, especially those with an abundance of butter, that you slice, cut out, pipe, imprint, or mold retain their shape well during baking. Any cookie made with the minimal creaming method bakes denser than one made differently, and it can sometimes have a chewy texture as well.

The vigorous creaming method, which produces a lighter, creamier mixture, is usually recommended for dropped cookies, to support the raisins, nuts, and/or chocolate chips, and piped cookies, to make piping through a pastry bag easier.

Doughs that are creamed until light and airy can be shaped in many ways. You can pipe, roll, mold, and/or drop them, or even spread them thinly on baking sheets to make crisp wafers as in Ladies' Wafers (page 118), Cigarettes (page 122), Crispy Corkscrews (page 128), Champagne Biscuits (page 130), Chocolate Fringe Cups (page 132), and Chocolate Pistachio Cigarettes (page 192).

## HAND VS. MACHINE

When a cookie recipe specifies "Combine ingredients until creamy," "Cream the butter until creamy," or "Cream together the butter and the sugar," you are using the creaming mixing method. When making these cookies, you can use the minimal creaming method or the vigorous one to control just how much air you incorporate into the dough to make the cookies exactly the texture you prefer. Here's my guide to a spectrum of creaming methods that has evolved as baking technology has changed:

➤ Mixing by hand, the technique our grandparents used when making many sweet, short doughs, incorporates the least amount of air possible. On a work surface, rub or cut small pieces of fat into dry ingredients to completely coat them. This intimate blending of the fat with the flour "shortens" the flour and prevents the proteins in the flour from forming a strong bond before you add the liquid and gather the dough together. Almost no air is incorporated.

➤ To add slightly more air, mix the fat and sugar by hand with a wooden spoon. You can regulate aeration according to the stamina of your arm muscles.

➤ The next method uses the food processor, which aerates less than any other machine and simulates the hand method best, especially when you place chilled fat, in chunks, on top of the dry ingredients in the food processor bowl before processing.

➤ Using the electric mixer and beating the fat with the paddle or flat beater, or even the dough hook, is the lightest and airiest end of the spectrum, since any electric mixer is capable of mixing in a lot of air. But as with any technique, how vigorously and how long you beat does influence the amount of aeration.

The amount of air incorporated into a cookie dough is not a question of right or wrong. The only thing that matters is your personal preference for a texture to serve a certain purpose, such as in my tartlet dough example, or simply the mood of your appetite, such as in my chocolate chip cookie example.

## WHIPPING MIXING METHOD

The whipping method is for cookie recipes containing a lot of eggs, some sugar, and little or no fat. In these recipes, the eggs are responsible for holding air bubbles, so the method begins the same way as the one used for genoise, chiffon, or angel food cake—whipping the eggs (whole, whites, or yolks) and sugar together to trap air bubbles and expand the mixture before other ingredients are added.

Each of my recipes specifies the proper stage to which the eggs should be whipped. Stages are marked by visual clues, such as soft or thick peaks. It's the air bubbles trapped in the whipped eggs, along with the eggs' moisture, that transform into steam during baking and expand, leaven, and give the cookies their characteristic textures.

Chewy Springerle (page 149), dense chewy Hahnpfeffernüsse (page 147), crunchy Black Walnut Genoise Wafers (page 116), fragile crispy Chantilly Fans (page 134), and crunchy crispy Tuiles (page 113) and Cognac Wafers (page 120) are a diverse assortment of cookies with a wide variety of textures, shapes, and forms that use the whipping method.

➤ Use fresh eggs for best results and flavor.

➤ To whip properly, begin with room-temperature eggs and/or butter.

➤ To whip with a rotary hand mixer, begin at medium speed.

➤ To whip with a heavy-duty electric mixer, preferably with a whisk attachment, begin at medium-low speed.

You can modify cookies' textures from spongy to crispy by changing the amount of eggs or other liquids in the recipe to make soft to runny batters, as in Cognac Wafers (page 120) and Chantilly Fans (page 134). Any airy, spongy mixture in this group is susceptible to deflating if over-mixed, so dry ingredients, such as ground nuts and flour (Japonais, page 107), and liquid ingredients, such as melted chocolate (Chocolate Macaroons, page 163) or melted butter (Genoise, page 283), must be carefully folded in.

### SHAPING MINIATURE COOKIE DOUGHS

Please keep in mind that the benefit of mixing ingredients together correctly is that it makes a smooth dough that forms shapes easily. It's nice to shape cookies uniformly in order to promote more even baking so each cookie will taste its best.

A variety of cookie shapes creates an assortment that gives character, personality, and eye appeal to a tray of cookies. The dough's consistency, depending on the proportions of the ingredients it contains, dictates what methods you can use to shape it. Follow shaping procedures as each recipe specifies. Place all the cookies on baking sheets of the same size and thickness for uniform baking.

It's easy to classify or categorize cookies by shape. There are at least six types, each one distinct from the others: dropped, piped, rolled, hand-shaped, refrigerator, and bar. Doughs vary in their shaping versatility. For example, it's possible to mold, pipe, slice, or roll one dough (Butter Dough in Chocolate Shadows, page 194), while another dough can only be dropped (Almond Confetti, page 88). In order to produce an infinite variety of shapes and sizes, here's what you need to know.

## ROLLED DOUGH

Many cookie doughs made with a minimum of egg and a good deal of flour are firm enough to roll out easily.

➤ Make the dough, then roll it out between sheets of waxed paper rather than in flour. Rolling these doughs in flour changes the butter-flour balance, which can alter the cookies' delicate flavor and texture. When you roll dough between sheets of waxed paper, the scraps are always reusable. Gather the scraps into a flat disk to roll out between two waxed paper sheets again.

➤ Some spice doughs, such as Lebkuchen Circles (page 156), benefit from rolling out in flour. The amount of honey or molasses in a spice dough can make it too sticky to roll between waxed paper sheets. Rolling out the dough in flour does not affect its tasty bite of spice after baking.

➤ When rolling out the dough, there is a natural tendency to roll thicker in the middle. To compensate for this, don't roll the rolling pin off the edges. Roll with even pressure, or it will be difficult to maintain a uniform thickness.

➤ When cutting out shapes, dip the cookie cutter in unflavored vegetable oil rather than in flour to ensure that the cutter lifts out easily. Repeat whenever necessary to prevent dough from sticking to the cutter.

➤ The chilled dough should not be too firm or too soft to cut out shapes easily. It's easy to compensate: Either leave it in the refrigerator longer or remove from the refrigerator sooner.

➤ If you need a special shape of cutter, make it. Form shapes in household paraffin, then mold tin or strips of heavy-duty aluminum foil around the wax.

- ➤ To cut out shapes from the dough, begin at the edges and work to the center. Cut shapes close together to keep scraps at a minimum.

- ➤ Lift shapes to a baking sheet with a metal spatula to avoid changing their form.

## BAR DOUGH

Some doughs, usually made with egg, are soft enough to spread or pat into a baking pan. Bar cookies are convenient to bake since the whole batch goes into the oven at once.

- ➤ After making the dough, divide it into several pieces and scatter them over the baking pan. With floured fingertips, pat the dough to extend the portions to cover the pan as evenly as possible.

- ➤ It's easy to determine the quantity of bar cookies from the pan size the recipe indicates, even before baking: Decide on a standard measurement as an appropriate portion for each bar cookie. For example, if the portion is 1½ x 1½ inches, first divide the length of the pan by 1½ inches, disregarding any fraction in your result. Do the same calculation with the width of the pan, and multiply the two resulting numbers to find the number of cookies the recipe will yield.

- ➤ Bake only until the cookies test done. If underbaked, they taste doughy, and if overbaked, they are hard and crisp. Cut portions while slightly warm, unless the recipe specifies otherwise.

## DROPPED DOUGH

Dropped cookie doughs are softer than doughs for rolling because they contain more eggs and/or other liquid, or less flour. Dropped cookies are not just chocolate chip and oatmeal types; many crisp types begin as dropped cookies. Black Walnut Genoise Wafers (page 116) and Nougatine Cones (page 124) are excellent examples.

➤ Usually dropped cookie dough is formed and baked right after it is made. You can refrigerate the dough, covered, for several hours before baking. Chilling doughs that contain double-acting baking powder, baking soda, and/or cream of tartar does slow their chemical reaction during baking. Doughs that contain baking soda or cream of tartar do not store as well as those with baking powder. Once moistened, baking soda reacts to ingredients such as buttermilk, brown sugar, honey, molasses, unsweetened chocolate and cocoa powder, and even cream of tartar on contact and releases carbon dioxide so that the dough loses some of its potency by baking time.

➤ Chilling dropped cookie dough can help the cookies to maintain their shapes without spreading too much while baking. If this is the case, drop mounds of dough on parchment-lined baking sheets and refrigerate before baking to firm them up. Because the cold baking sheet might warp in the hot oven, causing the cookies to bake unevenly, lift the parchment paper onto another baking sheet just before baking.

➤ To form dropped cookies easily, dip 2 teaspoons into cold water before filling one with dough. Use the back of the other teaspoon to push the dough onto the baking sheet.

➤ To shape uniform mounds of dropped dough, an ice cream scoop is handy for depositing batter on the baking sheets quickly and easily. Use a size 40 scoop, with a capacity equivalent to 1 mounded tablespoon, for standard chocolate chip cookies. For smaller, daintier dropped cookies, use a size 70 scoop, with a capacity equivalent to a scant 2½ teaspoons.

➤ You can form cylinders or logs of dropped dough and chill to bake at another time.

## HAND-FORMED DOUGH

Like the dough for rolled cookies, this dough is firm enough to mold or twist into shapes.

➤ If the dough sticks to your fingers, chill it until you can handle it more easily before shaping.

➤ To aid in molding doughs more evenly, begin by pinching off tea-spoonsful of dough and shaping them in the palms of your hands into smooth forms similar to the desired shape. For example, the Chevron Twists (page 70) begin with pencil-shaped ropes before the final formation; Autumn Acorns (page 80) begin as small dough balls before being formed into acorn shapes; and Miniature Tartlet Pastry (page 205) begins as small dough balls so that the dough can be pressed more evenly into tartlet tins.

➤ To flatten balls of dough on a baking sheet uniformly at once: Evenly space dough balls on the sheet, flour the underside of another baking sheet with similar or identical dimensions, and press down gently but firmly on balls. Carefully lift off the top baking sheet.

## PIPED AND PRESSED-SPRITZ DOUGH

These types are merely a fancier form of dropped cookies. The dough must be soft and pliable enough to pass through a pastry tip or cookie press without too much pressure but have enough body to hold a distinct form after shaping.

➤ A pastry bag works just as well as a cookie press for making spritz-type cookies.

➤ Piping forms to hold their shapes during baking requires a room-temperature dough on the stiff side. If the dough is too cold, it will be crumbly.

➤ Doughs or batters that are soft, sticky, or runny are easier and quicker to deposit on a baking sheet from a pastry bag than from a spoon. This method also eliminates the temptation to lick clean the finger that pushed the dough off the spoon onto the baking sheet.

➤ Fill the pastry bag or cookie press half full each time.

➤ Doughs made by the creaming mixing method are fluffier and easier to pipe than doughs made by the blending mixing method.

## REFRIGERATOR DOUGH

Making refrigerator doughs is great for enabling you to bake cookies when you want them at their best—fresh. Make the dough now and bake it later.

➤ Many doughs adapt well to being shaped into cylinders, wrapped in plastic, refrigerated for from 4 hours up to 3 days, and then sliced to make uniform cookies quickly, easily, and efficiently. Shortbread Cameos (page 49) or logs, such as Daddy Long Legs (page 84), are excellent examples.

➤ Patch different doughs together, such as the Apricot Medals dough (page 58) and the White Blossom Circles chocolate dough (page 188), into a cylinder or log to create a variety of shapes, patterns, and flavors.

## A WORD ABOUT COOKIE CATEGORIES

It's popular to categorize cookies by their mixing or shaping methods. For my book, I've chosen to categorize miniature cookies in chapters according to their dominant flavor or texture, since the taste and chew of cookies after the first bite is critical to me.

# shortbread miniatures

shortbread cameos . . . . . . . . . . . . . . . . . . . . . .49

harlequins . . . . . . . . . . . . . . . . . . . . . . . . . . .51

little gems . . . . . . . . . . . . . . . . . . . . . . . . . . .53

java sticks . . . . . . . . . . . . . . . . . . . . . . . . . . .54

drei augen . . . . . . . . . . . . . . . . . . . . . . . . . . .56

apricot medals . . . . . . . . . . . . . . . . . . . . . . . .58

pineapple pockets . . . . . . . . . . . . . . . . . . . . . .60

chocolate chip swirls . . . . . . . . . . . . . . . . . . . .62

sweet seashells . . . . . . . . . . . . . . . . . . . . . . . .64

cocos . . . . . . . . . . . . . . . . . . . . . . . . . . . . . .66

peanut butter petal cookies . . . . . . . . . . . . . . .68

chevron twists . . . . . . . . . . . . . . . . . . . . . . . .70

almond teardrops . . . . . . . . . . . . . . . . . . . . . .72

macadamia crescents . . . . . . . . . . . . . . . . . . . .74

cornmeal batons . . . . . . . . . . . . . . . . . . . . . . .76

maple butterballs . . . . . . . . . . . . . . . . . . . . . .78

autumn acorns . . . . . . . . . . . . . . . . . . . . . . . .80

mimosa rosettes . . . . . . . . . . . . . . . . . . . . . . .82

daddy long legs . . . . . . . . . . . . . . . . . . . . . . .84

lemon sunflowers . . . . . . . . . . . . . . . . . . . . . .86

almond confetti . . . . . . . . . . . . . . . . . . . . . . .88

pistachio buttons . . . . . . . . . . . . . . . . . . . . . .90

# shortbread cameos

➤ **Makes 8 dozen 1⅓-x-1¾-inch oval cookies**

Rice flour is the secret to achieving the subtly sandy texture that sets this great shortbread apart. Because ingredients are few, be sure to use the best-tasting butter possible to effect a clean, rich flavor.

1. Dough: In a medium bowl, blend the flours and salt briefly with a wire whisk; set aside. In the large bowl of an electric mixer, cream the butter at medium-low speed until smooth, about 1 minute. Beat in the sugar at medium speed until creamy; add the vanilla until blended, scraping down the sides of the bowl. Lower speed, and gradually add the flours, mixing only until mixture is thoroughly combined.

2. Divide the dough in quarters, rolling each portion into a cylinder about ¾ inch in diameter. Wrap in plastic and refrigerate until firm, for at least 4 hours or up to 3 days; or freeze, well wrapped, up to 1 month.

3. Adjust rack to lower third of oven and preheat oven to 300 degrees F. Line two large cool baking sheets with parchment paper.

4. Remove one cylinder of dough at a time from refrigerator. Using a sharp knife, cut slices, on an exaggerated diagonal, ¼ inch thick and space them about ½ inch apart on the baking sheets.

5. Decoration: Sprinkle the sugar over cookies lightly and evenly. Bake, one sheet at a time, for 12 to 15 minutes, or until the cookies are no longer shiny and feel firm (lightly touch a few). Do not allow cookies to color. Using a metal spatula, transfer the cookies to a wire rack until cool.

6. Stack in an airtight metal container and store at room temperature up to 1 week.

CONTINUED ➤

## DOUGH

1¾ cups (245 grams)
   unsifted all-purpose flour

⅓ cup unsifted rice flour

⅛ teaspoon salt

7 ounces (1 stick plus 6
   tablespoons) unsalted butter,
   room temperature

½ cup (100 grams)
   granulated sugar

1 teaspoon pure vanilla extract

## DECORATION

1 cup (200 grams)
   granulated sugar

## BAKING NOTES

To create the cookie's distinctive texture, some recipes use a combination of cornstarch and all-purpose flour while others use powdered instead of granulated sugar. I prefer using granulated sugar with a combination of rice flour and all-purpose flour to give the most authentic texture.

Note that rice flour—the nonglutenous variety necessary for this recipe—is available at health food stores. You don't want to use sweet rice flour, the glutenous variety sold in Asian markets, which has a sticky characteristic and is not desirable for any type of baking.

STEP 4

Pearl sugar (sometimes known as sparkling sugar), a larger-grain sugar than granulated sugar and a favorite choice for decorating Scandinavian cookies, may be sprinkled on top of these cookies for additional sparkle and crunch. Just combine ½ cup pearl sugar with ½ cup granulated sugar to decorate these. You'll find pearl sugar at most confectionery or baking supply stores.

## VARIATION NOTE

To give these cookies a fresh, spicy flavor, add 2 teaspoons finely grated lemon zest, 1 teaspoon freshly ground black pepper, and 1 teaspoon grated fresh ginger. Do not sprinkle with granulated sugar for decoration. After baking, place baking sheet on a wire rack until cookies are cool. To decorate, brush each cookie with a thin coating of Sugar Glaze: Mix ½ cup unsifted powdered sugar with 4 teaspoons water until smooth. Return cookies to a 140-degree-F preheated oven until glaze is set and dry, about 10 minutes.

# harlequins

➤ **Makes about 4 dozen 1½-inch cookies**

These simple but delicious cookies, scented with orange and lemon zest, are made elegant by an easy two-glaze decorative finish I learned at the Richemont Professional School in Lucerne, Switzerland. To achieve a sweet-and-sour flavor, brush half of each cookie with apricot jam and the other half with red currant jelly before painting a shimmery soft sugar glaze over it all.

1. Dough: In the large bowl of an electric mixer, cream the butter at medium-low speed until it is smooth, about 1 minute. Beat in the sugars and salt at medium speed until creamy. Add the egg yolk, then the citrus zests and vanilla, mixing just until mixture is well combined and slightly fluffy, scraping down the sides of the bowl. Lower mixer speed, and gradually add the flour, mixing only until mixture is thoroughly combined.

2. Divide the dough in thirds, and roll out each portion of dough between two sheets of waxed paper to form a circle 10 inches in diameter and ⅛ inch thick. Leaving the dough circles between the waxed paper, stack them on a baking sheet and refrigerate until firm, for at least 2 hours or up to 3 days; or freeze, well wrapped, up to 1 month.

3. Adjust rack to lower third of oven and preheat oven to 325 degrees F. Line two large cool baking sheets with parchment paper.

4. Remove one dough package at at time from the refrigerator. Peel off top waxed paper sheet, replace it loosely on top, and flip the entire package over. Peel off and discard the second sheet of waxed paper.

CONTINUED ➤

## DOUGH

8 ounces (2 sticks) unsalted butter, room temperature

⅓ cup (30 grams) unsifted powdered sugar

⅓ cup (65 grams) granulated sugar

⅛ teaspoon salt

1 egg yolk

½ teaspoon each finely grated lemon and orange zest

½ teaspoon pure vanilla extract

2 cups (280 grams) unsifted all-purpose flour

## DECORATIVE GLAZES

Jelly Glaze

⅔ cup strained apricot jam

⅔ cup red currant jelly

Sugar Glaze

½ cup (50 grams) unsifted powdered sugar

4 teaspoons water

Additional powdered sugar

5. Using a 1½-inch cutter of any shape, cut out shapes in the dough and set them about ½ inch apart on the baking sheets. Bake, one sheet at a time, for 12 to 15 minutes, or until cookies are no longer shiny, just ivory-colored, and feel slightly firm (lightly touch a few). Place baking sheet on a wire rack until cookies are cool.

6. Jelly Glaze: Keep the oven rack in the same position; preheat oven to 140 degrees F. Place the apricot jam and currant jelly in two small saucepans. Simmer on low heat for 2 minutes to evaporate some liquid before decorating cookies. Cool just until warm.

7. Brush warm apricot jam over half of one cookie's surface. With a clean brush, paint the other half with the currant jelly. Paint the remaining cookies, setting them as you finish about ¼ inch apart on one large clean baking sheet.

8. Sugar Glaze: Mix the sugar and water together until smooth. With a clean pastry brush, paint a thin coating of glaze over the jelly-glazed cookies. The glaze's consistency should be thin enough that a transparent film covers the jellies. Adjust the consistency by adding 1 teaspoon water at a time if it is too thick or more sugar if it is too thin. Place cookies in preheated oven until glaze is set and dry, about 10 minutes. Place baking sheet on a wire rack to cool for 5 minutes; then, lift cookies with a metal spatula to a rack to cool.

9. Stack undecorated cookies in an airtight metal container and store at room temperature up to 10 days. Store decorated cookies in one layer in a covered foil-lined cardboard container, such as a cake box, at room temperature up to 3 days.

# little gems

➤ **Makes 11 dozen 1½-inch cookies**

Buttery and sandy-textured, these are one of my favorite cookies, and not just because they're my mother's recipe. One bite and the secret is out. The pecan halves on top hide a dot of jam. Since the recipe yields a generous amount, they're easy to make, and their flavor is enhanced with time. These fragrant morsels are ideal for stacking in handsome airtight metal containers to present as gifts.

1. Adjust rack to lower third of oven and preheat oven to 325 degrees F. Line two large cool baking sheets with parchment paper.

2. In the large bowl of an electric mixer, cream the butter at medium-low speed until smooth, about 1 minute. Beat in the sugar at medium speed until creamy. Add the egg yolks, one at a time, then the vanilla, beating until well combined and slightly fluffy, scraping down the sides of the bowl. Lower mixer speed, and add the flour, mixing only until thoroughly combined.

3. With your palms, shape the dough, 1 level measuring teaspoon at a time, into balls and drop ½ inch apart on a baking sheet. Using the end of a wooden spoon dipped in flour, gently make a small shallow indentation in the center of each cookie. Place a scant ⅛ teaspoon strawberry preserves in each indentation, and top with a pecan half, gently pressing so it will adhere and hide the preserves.

4. Bake, one sheet at a time, for 13 to 15 minutes, or just until the cookies are ivory-colored and pale golden on the bottom. Transfer cookies to a wire rack to cool.

5. Stack in an airtight metal container and store at room temperature up to 10 days.

## DOUGH

12 ounces (3 sticks) unsalted butter, room temperature

1 cup (200 grams) granulated sugar

2 egg yolks

2 teaspoons pure vanilla extract

3 cups (420 grams) unsifted all-purpose flour

## DECORATION

½ cup strawberry preserves

8 ounces (about 2 cups) whole pecan halves

# java sticks

➤ **Makes 6 dozen 1½-inch sticks**

. . . . . . . . . . . . . . . . . . . . . . . . . . . . . . . . . . . .

These light, tender butterfingers, enhanced by flecks of walnuts, feature the fragrances of coffee and white chocolate in a superb-tasting cookie.

1. Adjust rack to lower third of oven and preheat oven to 325 degrees F. Line two large cool baking sheets with parchment paper.

2. Dough: Put the flour, salt, sugar, walnuts, and cocoa powder in a food processor. Process just to blend the ingredients. Add the butter and coffee powder mixture and process with on/off bursts just until the mixture forms a ball.

3. Place half the dough in a 16-inch pastry bag fitted with a ½-inch plain decorating tip (such as Ateco #6). Pipe the dough into sticks 1½ inches in length and about 1 inch apart on baking sheets. To cut off the dough at the end of each piped stick, press the decorating tip down toward the baking sheet. (Piping is more efficient if you anchor the parchment paper to the baking sheet by smearing a dab of dough in each corner of the baking sheet under the paper.) Fill the pastry bag with the remaining dough and pipe it into sticks.

4. Bake, one sheet at a time, for 8 to 11 minutes, or until the cookies no longer appear shiny and are pale tan or taupe in color. (Sticks' width spread to about an inch.) Place baking sheet on a wire rack.

5. Decoration: Melt the chocolate in a bowl set over 110-degree-F water. Put the walnuts on a baking sheet.

## DOUGH

1½ cups (210 grams) unsifted all-purpose flour

⅛ teaspoon salt

½ cup (100 grams) granulated sugar

1 ounce (¼ cup) walnuts

¼ cup unsweetened cocoa powder

6 ounces (1½ sticks) unsalted butter, room temperature

1 teaspoon instant coffee powder dissolved in 1 teaspoon pure vanilla extract

## DECORATION

6 ounces white chocolate, finely chopped

4 ounces (1 cup) walnuts, finely chopped

6. Dip both long edges of each cookie in chocolate, then dip them into the walnuts. To ensure that the nuts adhere to the chocolate, press them with fingertips; place each cookie on a clean baking sheet as you finish. Set sheet of cookies in a cool room or refrigerate a few minutes just to firm the chocolate.

7. Stack undecorated cookies in an airtight metal container and store at room temperature up to 10 days. Store decorated cookies in a single layer in a covered foil-lined cardboard container, such as a cake box, at room temperature up to 3 days.

# drei augen

➤ **Makes about 3 dozen 1½-inch sandwiches**

. . . . . . . . . . . . . . . . . . . . . . . . . . . . . . . . . .

In Germany, where they are traditional, *Drei Augen*, which translates as "three eyes," are topped with circles of dough in which three holes have been cut to reveal a jelly center. Consisting of shortbread with ground nuts and spice, these cookies taste delicious freshly baked. After a few days, the spicy, nutty flavors emerge even richer. These were among the most often requested miniatures from my catering baking business in the early 1970s.

1.  Dough: In a medium bowl, blend the flour, ground nuts, and cinnamon briefly with a wire whisk; set aside. In the large bowl of an electric mixer, cream the butter at medium-low speed until smooth, about 1 minute. Beat in the sugar at medium speed until well combined and slightly fluffy, scraping down the sides of the bowl. Lower mixer speed, gradually add the dry ingredients, and mix just until the mixture is thoroughly combined.

2.  Divide the dough in thirds. Roll out each portion of dough between two sheets of waxed paper to form a circle 11 inches in diameter and ⅛ inch thick. Leaving the dough circles between the sheets of waxed paper, stack them on a baking sheet and refrigerate until firm, for at least 2 hours or up to 3 days; or freeze, well wrapped, up to 1 month.

3.  Adjust rack to lower third of oven and preheat oven to 325 degrees F. Line two large cool baking sheets with parchment paper.

4.  Remove one dough package at a time from refrigerator. Peel off top sheet of waxed paper, replace it loosely on top, and flip the entire package over. Peel off and discard the second sheet of waxed paper.

## DOUGH

2⅓ cups (325 grams)
  unsifted all-purpose flour

3 ounces (½ cup) unblanched
  almonds, finely ground

1 teaspoon ground cinnamon

10 ounces (2½ sticks) unsalted
  butter, room temperature

⅔ cup (130 grams)
  granulated sugar

## DECORATION

1 cup (100 grams) unsifted
  powdered sugar

1 cup red currant jelly

5. Using a 1½-inch round cutter, cut out circles in the dough. Using the narrow end of a ⅜-inch plain pastry tip (such as Ateco #3) as a cutter, cut out three small holes in each circle. Space the cookies ½ inch apart on a baking sheet. Bake for 13 to 15 minutes, or until the cookies are pale golden, no longer appear raw or shiny, and feel slightly firm (lightly touch a few). Place baking sheet on a wire rack to cool 5 minutes. Lift the cookies from the parchment with a metal spatula to a rack to cool.

6. Repeat with the other two portions of dough, cutting out holes in only one-quarter of these circles in order to sandwich the cookies later. Keep in mind that when there is a mixture of cookies with and without holes, the cookies with holes bake faster. Remove them from the oven with a metal spatula to a wire rack. Return the baking sheet to the oven until the remaining cookies are done.

7. Decoration: Using a sieve, dust the powdered sugar just over the tops of the cookies with holes.

8. In a small saucepan, boil the currant jelly for 2 minutes to evaporate some of its liquid. Cool just until warm. Spoon about ¼ teaspoon jelly on each plain circle, baked-bottom side up. Center a sugared circle on top of a jellied bottom, and gently press so the jelly fills in the three holes. Repeat with the remaining cookies.

9. Stack undecorated cookies in an airtight metal container and store at room temperature up to 10 days. Store decorated cookies in a single layer in a covered foil-lined cardboard container, such as a cake box, at room temperature up to 3 days.

# apricot medals

➤ Makes 4 dozen 1¾-inch pairs

This sophisticated cookie sandwich, made from buttery short dough, sparkles from a light brushing of sugar glaze and an orange crystal-clear apricot jam center.

1. Dough: In a medium bowl, blend the flour and salt briefly with a wire whisk; set aside. In the large bowl of an electric mixer, cream the butter at medium-low speed until smooth, about 1 minute. Add the sugar very gradually, beating at low speed to prevent it from flying out of the bowl, and scraping down the sides of the bowl. Gradually blend in the dry ingredients and mix just until thoroughly combined.

2. Divide the dough in half, and roll one portion of dough at a time between two sheets of waxed paper into a circle 10 inches in diameter and ⅛ inch thick. Leaving the dough circles between the waxed paper, stack on a baking sheet and refrigerate until firm, for at least 2 hours or up to 3 days; or freeze, well wrapped, up to 1 month.

3. Adjust rack to lower third of oven and preheat oven to 300 degrees F. Line two large cool baking sheets with parchment paper.

4. Remove one dough circle package at a time from refrigerator. Peel off top sheet of waxed paper, replace it loosely on top, and flip the entire package over. Peel off and discard the second sheet of waxed paper.

5. With a 1½-inch scalloped round cutter, cut out circles in the dough. Using the narrow end of a ½-inch plain decorating tip (such as Ateco #6) as a cutter, cut out a hole in the center of each cookie. Put scalloped circles ½ inch apart on baking sheets. If the dough softens, making it difficult to transfer cutouts, refrigerate dough on its waxed paper until it is firmer.

## DOUGH

1¾ cups (245 grams) unsifted all-purpose flour

⅛ teaspoon salt

8 ounces (2 sticks) unsalted butter, room temperature

⅔ cup (60 grams) unsifted powdered sugar

## DECORATION

Sugar Glaze

½ cup (50 grams) unsifted powdered sugar

4 teaspoons water

½ cup strained apricot jam

6.  Bake for 11 to 13 minutes, or until cookies no longer appear raw or shiny and feel slightly firm (lightly touch a few). Do not allow cookies to color. Place baking sheet on a wire rack to cool 5 minutes. Then lift cookies from parchment with a spatula to a rack to cool.

7.  Repeat with the other portion of dough. Do not cut holes in these scalloped circles.

8.  Keep the oven rack in the same position; lower oven temperature to 140 degrees F. Put the cookies with holes on a clean baking sheet.

9.  Sugar Glaze: Mix the sugar and water together until smooth. With a pastry brush, spread a very thin layer of glaze on each of the cookies with holes. Return cookies to oven until the glaze is set and dry, about 5 to 10 minutes.

10. In a small saucepan, boil the apricot jam gently for 2 minutes. Cool just until warm. Spoon about ½ teaspoon jam on each plain cookie, baked-bottom side up. Center a glazed circle on top of a jellied bottom, and gently press so the apricot jam fills the hole. Repeat with the remaining cookies.

11. Stack undecorated cookies in an airtight metal container and store at room temperature up to 10 days. Store decorated cookies in a single layer in a covered foil-lined cardboard container, such as a cake box, at room temperature up to 3 days.

# pineapple pockets

➤ Makes 4 dozen 1½-inch cookies

. . . . . . . . . . . . . . . . . . . . . . . . . . . . . . . . . . . .

A flattened cone of butter dough with a pineapple filling laced with the pleasant taste of caramel creates an unusually scrumptious cookie.

1. Dough: In the large bowl of an electric mixer, cream the butter at medium-low speed until smooth, about 1 minute. Beat in the sugars and salt on medium speed until creamy. Add the egg yolk, then the vanilla, beating just until well combined and slightly fluffy, and scraping down the sides of the bowl. Lower mixer speed, gradually add the flour, and mix just until thoroughly combined.

2. Divide the dough in half, and roll out one portion of dough at a time between two sheets of waxed paper to form a circle 11 inches in diameter and ⅛ inch thick. Leaving the dough circles between the sheets of waxed paper, transfer them to a baking sheet and refrigerate until firm, for at least 2 hours or up to 3 days; or freeze, well wrapped, up to 1 month.

3. Pineapple Filling: In a 3-cup heavy-bottomed saucepan, combine the water and the sugar over low heat. Stir occasionally, washing down any sugar crystals clinging to the sides of the pan with a brush dipped in cold water, until the sugar is dissolved. Increase heat to medium-high and cook, without stirring, until the sugar syrup becomes thicker and amber in color, about 8 minutes. Remove from heat, and pour in the crushed pineapple with its juice all at once. Be careful, as the mixture will foam up. Stir the mixture with a wooden spoon to distribute the heat and blend the ingredients together. Return to stove and cook over medium-high heat 4 minutes more, or until mixture is golden and syrupy. Turn off heat, stir in the butter. Pour the mixture into a small bowl and set aside until completely cool.

## DOUGH

6 ounces (1½ sticks) unsalted butter, room temperature

¼ cup (50 grams) granulated sugar

½ cup (50 grams) unsifted powdered sugar

⅛ teaspoon salt

1 egg yolk

1 teaspoon pure vanilla extract

1⅔ cups (235 grams) unsifted all-purpose flour

## PINEAPPLE FILLING

2 tablespoons water

⅓ cup (65 grams) granulated sugar

One 8-ounce can crushed pineapple in unsweetened juice

½ tablespoon unsalted butter

4. Adjust rack to lower third of oven and preheat oven to 325 degrees F. Line two cool baking sheets with parchment paper.

5. Remove one dough circle package at a time from refrigerator. Peel off top sheet of waxed paper, replace it loosely on top, and flip the entire package over. Peel off and discard the second sheet of waxed paper.

6. Using a 2-inch round cutter, cut out circles in the dough. Place the circles on cool baking sheets and spoon ½ teaspoon filling slightly off center on each. Fold over one edge of the dough, then overlap the opposite side to partially cover the filling: The cookie should look like a flattened cone with some filling showing at the wider end. Bake, one sheet at a time, for 12 to 14 minutes, or until edges are light golden. Place baking sheet on a wire rack to cool for 5 minutes. Then lift cookies from parchment with a spatula to a rack to cool.

7. Stack cookies in an airtight metal container, separating the layers with strips of aluminum foil to keep them from sticking together, and store at room temperature up to 10 days.

**VARIATION NOTE**

**Apricot Pockets**  Substitute Apricot-Pistachio Filling (page 242) for the Pineapple Filling.

STEP 6

# chocolate chip swirls

➤ **Makes about 10 dozen 1½-inch round cookies**

. . . . . . . . . . . . . . . . . . . . . . . . . . . . . . . . . .

These swirl-shaped cookies are like the traditional chocolate chip—the only change is their appearance and the addition of orange zest.

1. In a food processor, process the flour, sugars, and salt to blend. Add the butter pieces, all at once, and process with on/off bursts until the mixture has the consistency of cornmeal. Whisk the egg with the vanilla and zest in a small bowl. Add the mixture to food processor or bowl and with the motor running, pour the egg mixture down the feed tube, and process just until the ingredients form a ball.

2. Divide the dough in half and transfer one-half of the dough to a bowl. Stir in the cocoa and chocolate chips. Roll out one portion at a time between two sheets of waxed paper into a 16-x-8-inch rectangle ⅛ inch thick. Leaving the dough rectangles between the sheets of waxed paper, stack on a baking sheet, and refrigerate until firm, for at least 2 hours or up to 3 days.

3. Remove the dough rectangles from refrigerator. Peel off top sheet of waxed paper from each dough half. Brush the plain dough *very* lightly with water. Using the waxed paper, lift the chocolate chip dough and place it face down directly onto the plain dough. With fingertips, press the two together to seal. Remove top sheet of waxed paper and trim the edges even with a pastry wheel or chef's knife. Cut in half crosswise to form two 8-x-8-inch pieces, then cut each 8-inch square in half lengthwise to form four 4-x-8-inch pieces. When the dough is just pliable (but still cold), roll up each dough rectangle (begin with the long side) into a cylinder; discard the waxed paper. Wrap each portion in plastic wrap; refrigerate until firm, for at least 2 hours or up to 3 days.

2½ cups (350 grams) unsifted all-purpose flour

½ cup (100 grams) granulated sugar

½ cup (100 grams) packed light brown sugar

¼ teaspoon salt

8 ounces (2 sticks) unsalted butter, room temperature and cut into ½-inch slices

1 large egg

1 teaspoon pure vanilla extract

4 teaspoons (1 orange) finely grated orange zest

2 tablespoons unsifted cocoa powder

1 cup (6 ounces) mini chocolate chips

4. Adjust rack to lower third of oven and preheat oven to 350 degrees F at least 15 minutes before baking. Line two large cool baking sheets with parchment paper. To bake, slice one roll at a time into ¼-inch-thick rounds with a sharp knife. Bake for 10 to 13 minutes, or until the cookies are no longer shiny on top and the bottoms are light brown.

5. Store stacked in airtight plastic containers at room temperature up to 10 days.

# sweet seashells

➤ **Makes 4 dozen 1⅛-x-1¾-inch shell-shaped cookies**

After using what seemed like tons of flour, I discovered that potato starch was the key ingredient to these delicious sandy-textured shortbread cookies. You'll never taste the potato starch in the finished product, but it does heighten the cookies' buttery taste since it gives the illusion that there's more butter in the recipe than there actually is.

1. Adjust rack to lower third of oven and preheat oven to 325 degrees F.

2. Dough: In a medium bowl, blend the flour, potato starch, and salt briefly with a wire whisk; set aside. In the large bowl of an electric mixer, cream the butter at medium-low speed until smooth, about 1 minute. Beat in the sugar, then the vanilla, just until well combined and slightly fluffy, scraping down the sides of the bowl. Lower speed, gradually add the dry ingredients, and mix just until the mixture is thoroughly combined.

3. For each cookie, pinch off a piece of dough measuring 1 teaspoon in size. Shape into a ball with your palms, drop into ungreased tiny metal shell molds (20 shells in a pan), and press evenly into the molds with a fingertip.

4. Bake for 13 to 15 minutes, or until cookies no longer appear shiny and are pale golden in color. Remove pans to a wire rack to cool for 10 minutes. Tilt the pans slightly and tap them gently to loosen the cookies. Carefully lift each cookie from its mold to a wire rack, fluted side up. Decorate while warm.

## DOUGH

¾ cup (105 grams) unsifted all-purpose flour

⅓ cup (65 grams) potato starch

⅛ teaspoon salt

4 ounces (1 stick) unsalted butter, room temperature

¼ cup (50 grams) granulated sugar

1 teaspoon pure vanilla extract

## DECORATION

⅓ cup strained apricot jam

5. Decoration: In a small saucepan, heat the jam just to warm and liquefy it. Using a small pastry brush, coat each cookie with a thin layer of jam. Dry on the rack until the glaze is no longer sticky to the touch, about 1 hour.

6. Stack the undecorated cookies in an airtight metal container and store at room temperature up to 10 days. Store the decorated cookies in one layer in a covered foil-lined cardboard container, such as a cake box, at room temperature up to 3 days.

### VARIATION NOTE

For a sweet-and-sour flavor, brush the Sugar Glaze (page 51) directly over the apricot jam.

# COCOS

➤ **Makes 12 dozen 1¼-inch cookies**

. . . . . . . . . . . . . . . . . . . . . . . . . . . . . .

If you're looking for the best coconut cookie, one that melts in your mouth, your search has ended. I discovered this shortbread version at Gayle's Bakery and Rotisserie in Capitola near Santa Cruz, along the northern California coast. The owners, Joe and Gayle Ortiz, graciously released the recipe for this book.

1. In a medium bowl, blend the flour, salt, and 7 ounces coconut briefly with a wire whisk; set aside. In the large bowl of an electric mixer, cream the butter at medium-low speed until smooth, about 1 minute. Beat in the sugar at medium speed until creamy. Add the egg yolk, beating until well combined and slightly fluffy, and scraping down the sides of the bowl. Lower speed, and gradually blend in the dry ingredients just until thoroughly combined.

2. Divide the dough into 8 equal portions. Roll each portion back and forth in the 2 ounces coconut, on the work surface, into cylinders 9 inches long and 1 inch in diameter. Wrap in plastic and refrigerate until firm, for at least 4 hours or up to 1 week; or freeze, well wrapped, up to 1 month.

3. Adjust rack to lower third of oven and preheat oven to 325 degrees F. Line two large cool baking sheets with parchment paper.

1½ cups (210 grams) unsifted all-purpose flour

⅛ teaspoon salt

7 ounces (2½ cups) unsweetened medium-shred coconut

11 ounces (2¾ sticks) unsalted butter, room temperature

1 cup (200 grams) granulated sugar

1 egg yolk

2 ounces (⅔ cup) unsweetened medium-shred coconut

4. Using a serrated knife, and sawing the dough gently to make a clean cut, slice ¼-inch-thick rounds. Space 1 inch apart on baking sheet. Bake, one sheet at a time, for 8 minutes or until light golden around the edges. Place baking sheet on a wire rack to cool 5 minutes. Then lift the cookies from parchment with a spatula to a rack to cool.

5. Stack cookies in an airtight metal container and store at room temperature up to 1 week; or freeze up to 1 month.

### BAKING NOTE

The best unsweetened medium-shred coconut is available at health food stores and specialty food markets.

# peanut butter petal cookies

➤ **Makes 6 dozen 1½-inch 5-petal flower cookies**

. . . . . . . . . . . . . . . . . . . . . . . . . . . . . . . . . . . . . . .

A spritz press is a fun way to form a batch of cookies quickly. These tender, crisp peanut butter "flowers" are dotted with a "stamen" of dark chocolate ganache.

1. Adjust rack in lower third of oven and preheat oven to 325 degrees F. Have nearby one large cool ungreased baking sheet.

2. Dough: Stir the flour and salt to combine in a small bowl; set aside. Beat the butter, peanut butter, and granulated and brown sugars in a large bowl until very creamy and well blended. Beat in the egg yolk and vanilla. Gradually add the flour mixture.

3. While the dough is soft, pliable, and at room temperature, follow the manufacturer's directions for inserting the design plate (the 5-petal one is used for these cookies) and filling the cookie press. When filling the metal cylinder with dough, pack it firmly.

4. Holding the press perpendicular to the baking sheet, press out the cookies (each about 1 level measuring teaspoon of dough), spacing them about 1 inch apart. As you press out the dough, it will stick to the ungreased sheet making it easier to form each cookie. If desired, sprinkle the sanding or pearl sugar over top of cookies.

5. Bake for 9 to 11 minutes or just until the cookies' edges are barely golden.

## DOUGH

2 cups plus 2 tablespoons unsifted all-purpose flour

¼ teaspoon salt

8 ounces (2 sticks) unsalted butter, softened

⅓ cup creamy peanut butter

⅓ cup (65 grams) granulated sugar

⅓ cup (65 grams) packed light brown sugar

1 egg yolk

1 teaspoon pure vanilla extract

½ cup sanding sugar or pearl sugar (optional)

## DARK CHOCOLATE GANACHE

2½ ounces semisweet or bittersweet chocolate, finely chopped

3 tablespoons heavy cream

6. Dark Chocolate Ganache: Place the chocolate in a medium bowl. In a small saucepan, heat the heavy cream just until boiling. Pour the cream over the chocolate and let sit 30 seconds. Whisk together until smooth and creamy. Set the mixture aside at room temperature just until it cools a bit and begins to thicken.

7. Using a small handmade paper cone, pipe a tiny dot of ganache in the center of each cookie. Cool completely before stacking between sheets of aluminum foil in an airtight metal container in a cool place for up to 1 week.

# chevron twists

➤ **Makes 7 dozen 1½-inch twists**

. . . . . . . . . . . . . . . . . . . . . . . . . . . . .

These cookies are a simpler version of the traditional pretzel shape. After tasting the buttery cookie with the maple pecan filling, you'll agree the flavors are natural companions.

1. Adjust rack to lower third of oven and preheat oven to 300 degrees F. Line two cool baking sheets with parchment paper.

2. Dough: In the large bowl of an electric mixer, cream the butter at medium-low speed until smooth, about 1 minute. Beat in the sugars and salt on medium speed until creamy. Add the egg yolk, and then the vanilla, beating just until well combined and slightly fluffy, and scraping down the sides of the bowl. Lower mixer speed, gradually add the flour, and mix just until thoroughly combined.

3. Shape the dough, 1 teaspoon at a time, into balls with your palms, and drop 1 inch apart on baking sheets. Then, with fingertips, roll each ball back and forth on the work surface into a pencil-like rope about 4 to 5 inches long and ¼ inch in diameter. Place back on the baking sheet, and twist each rope of dough into a loop, overlapping the ends, and curve the two ends. The cookie should resemble the letter "e" in lowercase script.

4. Bake, one sheet at a time, for 10 to 13 minutes, or until firm when lightly touched and pale golden in color. Place baking sheet on a wire rack to cool for 5 minutes. Then lift the cookies from parchment with a spatula to a rack to cool.

## DOUGH

6 ounces (1½ sticks) unsalted butter, room temperature

¼ cup (50 grams) granulated sugar

½ cup (50 grams) unsifted powdered sugar

⅛ teaspoon salt

1 egg yolk

1 teaspoon pure vanilla extract

1½ cups plus 2 tablespoons (235 grams) unsifted all-purpose flour

## MAPLE PECAN FILLING

3¾ ounces (scant 1 cup) pecans, toasted

1 tablespoon unsalted butter, room temperature

1 teaspoon pure maple syrup

5. Maple Pecan Filling: Finely grind the nuts in a food processor. Add the butter and maple syrup and blend until smooth. Using a 14-inch pastry bag fitted with a ¼-inch plain decorating tip (such as Ateco #2), pipe a small dot of filling in the center hole of the loop of each "e."

6. Stack the unfilled cookies in an airtight metal container and store at room temperature up to 10 days, or freeze up to 1 month. Store the filled cookies in one layer in a covered foil-lined cardboard container, such as a cake box, at room temperature up to 3 days.

STEP 5

# almond teardrops

➤ **Makes 5 dozen 1½-inch cookies**

. . . . . . . . . . . . . . . . . . . . . . . . . . . . . . . . . .

Almonds, ground like flour, give these cookies an extra-nutty flavor. Each teardrop-shaped cookie is brushed with an egg yolk glaze and topped with a split blanched almond before baking.

1. Dough: In a medium bowl, blend the flour, ground nuts, and salt briefly with a wire whisk; set aside. In the large bowl of an electric mixer, cream the butter at medium-low speed until smooth, about 1 minute. Beat in the sugar at medium speed until creamy. Add the egg, lemon zest, and almond extract, beating just until well combined and slightly fluffy, and scraping down the sides of the bowl. Lower speed, gradually add the dry ingredients, and mix just until the mixture is thoroughly combined.

2. Divide the dough in half. Roll one portion of dough at a time between two sheets of waxed paper to form a circle 11 inches in diameter and ¼ inch thick. Peel off top waxed paper sheet and roll a rolling pin with a waffle pattern over the dough once. Exert just enough pressure to flatten dough to ³⁄₁₆ inch thick. If dough sticks to the pin, lightly flour dough's surface. Replace waxed paper on top, and place on a baking sheet, waffle design up. Refrigerate until firm, for at least 2 hours or up to 3 days.

3. Adjust rack to lower third of oven and preheat oven to 325 degrees F. Line two large cool baking sheets with parchment paper.

4. Decoration: In a small bowl, blend the egg yolk with the cream until smooth; set aside. Put the almonds and water to cover in a small saucepan and bring to a boil. Remove from heat; let stand for 1 minute to soften. Remove the nuts, one by one, and, using the tip of a small paring knife, split them in half along their natural seams.

## DOUGH

1½ cups (210 grams) unsifted all-purpose flour

3 ounces (½ cup) blanched almonds, finely ground

⅛ teaspoon salt

5 ounces (1¼ sticks) unsalted butter, room temperature

½ cup (100 grams) granulated sugar

1 large egg

1 teaspoon finely grated lemon zest

¼ teaspoon almond extract

## DECORATION

1 egg yolk

2 teaspoons heavy cream

2 ounces (about 40) blanched almonds

5. Remove one dough circle at a time from refrigerator and peel off top sheet of waxed paper; discard the waxed paper. Using a pastry brush, lightly coat the waffle-patterned dough with the egg wash.

6. Pinch the wide end of a ½-inch plain decorating tip (such as Ateco #6) into an oval shape resembling a teardrop to make a cutter. Using the cutter, cut out shapes in the dough. Space the cutouts ½ inch apart on baking sheets. Put an almond half, rounded side up, on each cookie. Bake, one sheet at a time, until the cookies appear set and ivory-colored, about 12 to 15 minutes. Place baking sheet on a wire rack to cool for 5 minutes. Then lift cookies from parchment with a spatula to a rack to cool.

7. Stack in an airtight metal container and store at room temperature up to 10 days; or freeze up to 1 month.

# macadamia crescents

➤ **Makes 5 dozen 1½-inch crescents**

These not-overly-sweet cookies, traditionally shaped into crescents, were inspired by a recipe from my longtime friend and former baking colleague Jack Lirio. Besides savoring these cookies' nutty flavor, you will be reminded by their texture of the best short crust you ever tasted.

1. Dough: In a medium bowl, blend the flour, ground nuts, and salt briefly with a wire whisk; set aside. In the large bowl of an electric mixer, cream the butter at medium-low speed until smooth, about 1 minute. Beat in the granulated sugar at medium speed until well combined and slightly fluffy, scraping down the sides of the bowl. Lower speed, gradually add the nuts and flour, and mix just until the mixture is thoroughly combined.

2. Refrigerate the dough, tightly covered, in a bowl. Chill for about 1 hour or until it is partially firm but not solid, to make handling easier.

3. Adjust rack to lower third of oven and preheat oven to 325 degrees F. Line two cool baking sheets with parchment paper.

4. Divide the chilled dough into several portions, each about ¼ cup. With floured fingertips, roll each portion back and forth on the work surface to shape ropes about ½ inch in diameter. If dough is difficult to shape, lightly flour the work surface. Cut each roll into uniform 1-inch lengths. With fingertips, shape into crescents with slightly tapered ends, and space ½ inch apart on the baking sheets.

5. Bake, one sheet at a time, for 12 to 15 minutes, or until the cookies are no longer shiny and their shape is set. Place baking sheet on a wire rack. Sift the powdered sugar over cookies while warm.

### DOUGH

1¾ cups (245 grams)
unsifted all-purpose flour

5 ounces (1 cup) macadamia
nuts, finely ground to yield about
1½ cups (see Baking Notes)

⅛ teaspoon salt

8 ounces (2 sticks) unsalted
butter, room temperature

⅓ cup (65 grams)
granulated sugar

### DECORATION

2 cups (200 grams)
unsifted powdered sugar

6. When completely cool, lift cookies with a metal spatula to an airtight metal container, arranging them in one layer. Store up to 1 week at room temperature; or freeze up to 1 month.

## BAKING NOTES

Unsalted macadamia nuts, available in health food stores and some supermarkets, are best in this recipe.

For variety, substitute black walnuts or unblanched almonds for the macadamias.

See How to Measure Nuts (page 16). Because the nuts provide structure as well as flavor in this recipe, it is important to measure the ground nuts.

# cornmeal batons

➤ **Makes 7 dozen 1½-inch sticks**

. . . . . . . . . . . . . . . . . . . . . . .

Dip these plump, buttery cookie sticks into a cornmeal streusel before baking. These not-too-sweet treats are terrific as a snack with coffee or tea.

1. Streusel: In a medium bowl, combine the dry ingredients and lemon zest. With fingertips, work in the butter until the mixture resembles coarse crumbs. For a more uniform and delicate-looking streusel, push the mixture through a sieve with a rubber spatula into another bowl. Cover and refrigerate until firm, at least 2 hours.

2. Dough: In the large bowl of an electric mixer, cream the butter at medium-low speed until smooth, about 1 minute. Beat in the sugar and salt at medium speed until creamy. Add the egg white, zest, and vanilla, beating just until fluffy, and scraping down the sides of the bowl. Lower speed, gradually add the flour, and mix just until thoroughly combined.

3. Refrigerate the dough in a bowl, tightly covered, for 1 hour or until it is partially firm but not solid.

4. Adjust rack to lower third of oven and preheat oven to 325 degrees F. Line two cool baking sheets with parchment paper.

5. With fingertips, toss the chilled streusel around gently to break up any large lumps; don't overwork.

6. Divide the chilled dough into several portions, each about ¼ cup, and with floured fingertips roll each back and forth on a lightly floured work surface to shape ropes about ½ inch in diameter.

## STREUSEL

½ cup (70 grams) unsifted all-purpose flour

⅓ cup yellow cornmeal

⅓ cup (65 grams) granulated sugar

1 teaspoon finely grated lemon zest

3 ounces (6 tablespoons) unsalted butter, room temperature, cut into ½-inch slices

## DOUGH

8 ounces (2 sticks) unsalted butter, room temperature

½ cup (100 grams) granulated sugar

⅛ teaspoon salt

2 tablespoons (about 1 large) egg white

2 teaspoons finely grated orange zest

1 teaspoon pure vanilla extract

2 cups (280 grams) unsifted all-purpose flour

## EGG WASH

1 egg yolk

2 teaspoons heavy cream

7. Egg Wash: In a small bowl, blend the egg yolk with the cream for an egg wash. Using a small pastry brush, lightly coat the top of each cylinder with the egg wash. Cut each roll into 1½-inch lengths to yield uniformly shaped sticks. Dip each stick's glazed side in the streusel, then place on a baking sheet ½ inch apart.

8. Bake, one sheet at a time, for about 13 to 15 minutes, or until the cookies appear set and no longer shiny and are light golden on the bottom. Do not allow to color on top. Place baking sheet on a wire rack to cool for 5 minutes. Then lift cookies from parchment with a spatula to a rack to cool.

9. Stack cookies in an airtight metal container and store at room temperature up to 1 week; or freeze up to 1 month.

# maple butterballs

➤ **Makes 4 dozen 1¼-inch pairs**

Butter, brown sugar, vanilla, maple syrup, and heavy cream harmonize perfectly in a cookie. For gift giving at holiday time, put the butterballs in paper candy cases.

1. Adjust rack to lower third of oven and preheat oven to 325 degrees F. Line two large cool baking sheets with parchment paper.

2. Dough: In the large bowl of an electric mixer, cream the butter at medium-low speed until smooth, about 1 minute. Beat in the sugar and salt at medium speed until creamy. Add the egg, then the vanilla, beating just until well combined and slightly fluffy, and scraping down the sides of the bowl. Lower speed, gradually blend in the flour, and mix just until thoroughly combined.

3. Using a 12-inch pastry bag fitted with a ½-inch plain decorating tip (such as Ateco #6), pipe bulbs ½ to ¾ inch in diameter and ½ inch apart on baking sheets. (Piping is easier if you anchor the parchment to the baking sheet with a dab of dough in each corner under the paper.) Using a damp pastry brush, tap cookies to flatten the point left from piping.

4. Bake, one sheet at a time, for 10 to 12 minutes, or until firm when lightly touched and tan in color. Place baking sheet on a wire rack to cool for 5 minutes. Then lift the cookies from parchment with a spatula to a rack to cool.

5. Maple Cream Filling: In a 1½-quart heavy-bottomed saucepan, gently boil the maple syrup and cream over medium heat until reduced by half, about 20 minutes. Turn off heat, stir in the butter. Cool until filling is lukewarm and its consistency is like honey, about 30 minutes.

### DOUGH

8 ounces (2 sticks) unsalted butter, room temperature

¾ cup (150 grams) packed light brown sugar

⅛ teaspoon salt

1 large egg

1 teaspoon pure vanilla extract

2 cups (280 grams) unsifted all-purpose flour

### MAPLE CREAM FILLING

⅔ cup pure maple syrup

⅔ cup (5 ounces) heavy cream

1 ounce (2 tablespoons) unsalted butter

6. Spoon or pipe ¼ to ½ teaspoon filling on half of the cookies, flat side up. Center the remaining cookies on top of the filled bottoms, gently pressing the pairs together.

7. Stack undecorated cookies in an airtight metal container and store at room temperature up to 10 days; or freeze up to 1 month. Store decorated cookies in one layer in a covered foil-lined cardboard container, such as a cake box, at room temperature up to 3 days.

# autumn acorns

➤ **Makes 7 dozen 1½-inch cookies**

. . . . . . . . . . . . . . . . . . . . . . . . . . . .

Rich, tender cookies are given a flavor and visual boost by ground hazelnuts and cinnamon. Teaspoons of dough are molded into balls and pinched on one end to create an acorn shape. The rounded end is dipped into an egg-and-nut mixture to form the acorn's cap.

1. Dough: In the large bowl of an electric mixer, cream the butter at medium-low speed until smooth, about 1 minute. Beat in the sugar and salt until well combined and slightly fluffy, scraping down the sides of the bowl. Lower speed, gradually add the flour, and mix just until thoroughly combined.

2. Adjust rack to lower third of oven and preheat oven to 325 degrees F. Line two large cool baking sheets with parchment paper.

3. With your palms, shape the dough, 1 teaspoon at a time, into balls. Pinch them so that each ball is pointed at the bottom to form an acorn shape, and place ½ inch apart on the baking sheet. Place baking sheet in the refrigerator for 15 minutes or just until dough is firm.

4. Decoration: In a bowl, whisk the egg until smooth. In another bowl, whisk the ground nuts, sugar, and cinnamon briefly just to blend. Dip just the larger rounded end of each acorn-shaped cookie into the beaten egg, then into the crumb mixture, returning each cookie to the baking sheet, ½ inch apart.

## DOUGH

8 ounces (2 sticks) unsalted butter, room temperature

½ cup (100 grams) granulated sugar

¼ teaspoon salt

2⅓ cups (330 grams) unsifted all-purpose flour

## DECORATION

1 large egg

1 ounce (2 tablespoons) hazelnuts, finely ground

2 tablespoons (25 grams) granulated sugar

⅛ teaspoon ground cinnamon

5. Bake, one sheet at a time, for 12 to 15 minutes, or until the cookies no longer appear shiny and feel slightly firm when lightly touched. Do not allow them to color. Place baking sheet on wire rack to cool for 5 minutes. Then lift cookies from parchment with a metal spatula to a wire rack to cool.

6. Stack cookies in an airtight metal container, separating layers with sheets of aluminum foil to keep cookies snug and the topping in place, and store at room temperature up to 10 days; or freeze up to 1 month.

# mimosa rosettes

➤ **Makes 3 dozen 1½-inch cookies**

. . . . . . . . . . . . . . . . . . . . . . . .

Shortbread dough, subtly orange-flavored, takes on an elegant look when piped into spirals and embellished with a candied mimosa in the center to resemble a flower.

1. Adjust rack to lower third of oven and preheat oven to 350 degrees F. Line a large cool baking sheet with parchment paper.

2. Dough: Sift the flour, baking powder, and salt on a sheet of waxed paper; set aside. In the large bowl of an electric mixer, cream the butter at medium-low speed until smooth, about 1 minute. Beat in the ¾ cup powdered sugar very gradually until creamy. Add the egg yolk, liqueur, vanilla, and zest, beating until light and fluffy, and scraping down the sides of the bowl. Lower speed, gradually blend in dry ingredients, and mix just until thoroughly combined.

3. Anchor parchment paper with a dab of dough under each corner. Using a pastry bag fitted with an open star decorating tip (such as Ateco #8), pipe soft dough onto the baking sheet. Hold the pastry tip perpendicular to the baking sheet and ½ inch above it, and pipe rosette shapes equivalent to 1½ teaspoons dough each, spaced ¾ inch apart. Each time you finish piping a rosette, twist the pastry tip in the center of the spiral. This action stops the flow of dough and makes it easy to lift the dough away from the rosette shape. Center a candied mimosa on each rosette.

## DOUGH

1½ cups (210 grams) unsifted all-purpose flour

¼ teaspoon baking powder

⅛ teaspoon salt

6 ounces (1½ sticks) unsalted butter, room temperature

¾ cup (75 grams) unsifted powdered sugar

1 egg yolk

1 tablespoon Grand Marnier liqueur

1 teaspoon pure vanilla extract

1 teaspoon finely grated orange zest

3 dozen candied mimosa

## DECORATION

¼ cup (25 grams) unsifted powdered sugar

4. Bake for 11 to 13 minutes, or until the cookies no longer appear raw or shiny, are pale golden, and feel slightly firm (lightly touch a few). Place baking sheet on a wire rack to cool for 5 minutes. Then lift cookies from parchment with a spatula to a rack to cool.

5. Decoration: Sift the ¼ cup powdered sugar over them lightly before serving.

6. Stack cookies in an airtight metal container and store at room temperature up to 10 days; or freeze up to 1 month.

# daddy long legs

➤ **Makes 8 dozen 2-inch cookies**

Here's a great cookie to eat while sipping a cup of coffee. This crisp, crunchy cookie is made with a minimum of butter and a good deal more sugar than is used in most cookie doughs. Add a lot of nuts and you have not only an additional crunch but an intense flavor.

1. In the large bowl of an electric mixer, cream the butter at medium-low speed until smooth, about 1 minute. Beat in the sugar at medium speed until well combined and slightly fluffy, scraping down the sides of the bowl. Add the eggs, one at a time, mixing until well combined. Lower speed, add the nuts all at once, then add the flour gradually. Mix just until thoroughly combined.

2. Divide the dough into four equal portions. With your floured finger-tips, form each portion of dough into a rectangular brick 10 inches long, 2 inches wide, and ¾ inch high. Wrap each in plastic and refrigerate until firm, for at least 4 hours or up to 3 days; or freeze, well wrapped, up to 1 month.

3. Adjust rack to lower third of oven and preheat oven to 350 degrees F. Line two large cool baking sheets with parchment paper.

4. Remove one brick of dough at a time from the refrigerator. Using a sharp knife, cut ⅜-inch-thick slices and place them, cut side down, ½ inch apart on baking sheet. Bake, one sheet at a time, for just 8 minutes. The cookies' surface will be dull, not shiny. Remove baking sheet from oven and turn cookies over with a metal spatula. Return to oven and bake about 7 to 10 minutes more, or until pale golden and crisp. Remove cookies with a metal spatula to a wire rack to cool.

5 ounces (1 ¼ sticks) unsalted butter, room temperature

1 cup (200 grams) granulated sugar

2 large eggs, room temperature

10 ounces (2 cups) hazelnuts, toasted

2 ¼ cups (315 grams) unsifted all-purpose flour

5. Stack cookies in airtight metal containers and store at room temperature up to 10 days.

## BAKING NOTE

Resting and chilling the dough are especially important steps in this recipe. In order to cut the dough neatly to retain chunks of nuts in each slice, you must let the dough rest and firm in the refrigerator. Resting allows time for the nuts to absorb moisture from the dough, thereby softening them for cutting. Chilling makes it easier to slice the dough precisely.

# lemon sunflowers

➤ **Makes 6 dozen 1½-inch cookies**

For me, these snappy, crisp, flower-shaped cookies flavored with caramel, lemon, and butter are irresistible. Caramelized sugar fills the cookie centers to give a stained glass effect.

1. Caramelized Sugar: Line a baking sheet with aluminum foil; set near the stove. In a 1½-quart heavy-bottomed saucepan over low heat, melt the sugar, stirring occasionally. Wash down any crystals clinging to the sides of the pan with a brush dipped in cold water. When sugar is dissolved, increase the heat to medium-high and cook the melted sugar without stirring until it becomes amber in color, about 8 minutes. Pour the bubbling syrup onto the foil. Cool until firm, about 1 hour.

2. Dough: Sift the flour with the baking powder on a sheet of waxed paper; set aside. In the large bowl of an electric mixer, cream the butter at medium-low speed until smooth, about 1 minute. Beat in the sugar at medium speed until creamy. Add the egg, yolk, and lemon zest just until well combined and slightly fluffy, scraping down the sides of the bowl. Lower speed, gradually add the dry ingredients, and mix just until thoroughly combined.

3. Divide the dough in half. Roll each portion of dough between two sheets of waxed paper to form a circle 11 inches in diameter and ⅛ inch thick. Stack circles on a baking sheet and refrigerate until firm for at least 2 hours or up to 3 days; or freeze, well wrapped, up to 1 month.

4. Adjust rack to lower third of oven and preheat oven to 325 degrees F. Line two large cool baking sheets with parchment paper.

## CARAMELIZED SUGAR

½ cup granulated sugar

## DOUGH

2¼ cups (315 grams) unsifted all-purpose flour

¼ teaspoon baking powder

6 ounces (1½ sticks) unsalted butter, room temperature

1 cup (200 grams) granulated sugar

1 large egg

1 egg yolk

4 teaspoons finely grated lemon zest

5. Break the caramelized sugar into pieces. Pulverize in a food processor into golden powder crystals; set aside.

6. Remove one dough package at a time from refrigerator. Peel off top sheet of waxed paper, replace it loosely on top, and flip the entire package over. Peel off and discard the second sheet of waxed paper.

7. Using a 1½-inch scalloped round cutter, cut out circles and space ½ inch apart on baking sheets. Using the narrow end of a ½-inch plain decorating tip (such as Ateco #6) as a cutter, cut out a hole from the center of each cookie. Spoon about ½ teaspoon of the sugar crystals into each hole and lightly pat in place.

8. Bake, one sheet at a time, for 10 minutes, or until edges are a delicate brown and the sugar crystals are shiny and have melted to their original amber color. Cool the cookies on the baking sheet until the caramelized sugar is firm.

9. Stack in an airtight metal container, separating layers with strips of aluminum foil to prevent rattling and sticking, and store at room temperature up to 3 days. For controlling moisture in container, see the paragraph on the nontoxic blue crystals, page 22.

### BAKING NOTE

These cookies are as crisp as the Daddy Long Legs (page 84). When a cookie recipe has a lot of sugar in relation to the amount of butter, the cookies will be crisp.

### SHAPING NOTE

To form the cookies, use a flower-shaped cookie cutter. The one I use is from a set of Japanese cutters sold in housewares departments and cookware stores.

# almond confetti

➤ **Makes 5 dozen 1 ½-inch wafers**

These sweet, delicate cookies are like potato chips—you can't eat just one. Not only are they easy to make, they have a captivating almond-and-vanilla flavor with an unexpected tang from sour cream in the recipe.

1. Adjust rack to lower third of oven and preheat oven to 325 degrees F. Unwrap one end of a chilled stick of unsalted butter and rub it over two large cool Teflon-coated baking sheets to apply a thin film of fat.

2. In a small bowl, briefly blend the flour and the salt with a wire whisk; set aside. In the large bowl of an electric mixer, cream butter at medium speed until creamy, about 1 minute. Beat in the sugar until light and very fluffy. Add the sour cream, vanilla, and almond extract, blending well. Gradually add the flour mixture, then the nuts, combining thoroughly.

3. Drop level teaspoons of the batter on baking sheets, spacing them 1 inch apart. A quick method is to pipe the soft batter from a 16-inch pastry bag fitted with a ⅝-inch plain decorating tip (such as Ateco #8). Pipe mounds about 1 inch in diameter. The decorating tip's size is large enough for the nut pieces to flow through easily.

4. Bake, one sheet at a time, for 11 to 14 minutes, or until the cookies' edges and undersides are golden brown and the centers are ivory. Cool the cookies on the baking sheet for only 2 minutes to firm slightly. Then, with a metal spatula, transfer cookies to a wire rack to cool.

5. Repeat baking process with any remaining batter.

6. Stack cookies in an airtight metal container and store at room temperature up to 1 week.

¼ cup (35 grams) unsifted all-purpose flour

⅛ teaspoon salt

4 ounces (1 stick) unsalted butter, softened

½ cup (100 grams) granulated sugar

½ cup (5 ounces) sour cream

½ teaspoon pure vanilla extract

⅛ teaspoon almond extract

4 ounces (¾ cup) unblanched almonds, coarsely chopped (see Baking Note)

## BAKING NOTE

Because the nuts provide structure as well as flavor in this recipe, it is important to measure the chopped nut pieces as accurately as possible. With a food processor, through variations of brand, speed, blade, timing, and force, you can grind a given weight of nuts into widely varying volumes of chopped nuts. A nut mill grinds nuts into the same volume every time, so for this recipe use a nut mill to chop the nuts to yield a rounded ¾ cup. See How to Measure Nuts (page 16).

# pistachio buttons

➤ **Makes about 8 dozen 1½-inch round cookies**

Here's a gussied-up version of a thumbprint cookie. Pistachios, white chocolate, and chewy dried apricots replace traditional soft jam filling.

I prefer using kitchen scissors to a knife to cut the dried apricots. I find the scissors make it easy to cut the apricots into narrow strips, then cut the strips crosswise into a small dice.

1. Adjust rack to lower third of oven and preheat oven to 350 degrees F. Line two large cool baking sheets with parchment paper.

2. Dough: Place the flour, pistachios, sugar, and salt in food processor; process just to blend ingredients. Add the butter in pieces, then process with on/off bursts until the mixture has the consistency of cornmeal. Whisk the egg and extracts in a small bowl. With the motor running, pour the egg mixture down the feed tube and process just until ingredients form a ball.

3. With your palms, shape the dough, 1 level measuring teaspoon at a time, into balls and set ½ inch apart on the baking sheet. Gently make an indentation in the center of each ball, pressing down almost to the bottom without breaking through the dough.

4. Bake for 12 minutes, or just until the cookies are ivory-colored and pale golden on the bottom. Transfer cookies to a wire rack to cool.

5. Filling: In a small saucepan, melt the butter and white chocolate, stirring just until chocolate is almost completely liquid. Place ⅛ to ¼ teaspoon white chocolate butter in each indentation. Sprinkle the chopped pistachios and apricots over chocolate. Allow 30 minutes to set.

6. Stack in an airtight metal container and store at room temperature up to 1 week.

## DOUGH

2 cups (280 grams)
  unsifted all-purpose flour

1½ ounces (⅓ cup)
  shelled raw pistachios

¾ cup (150 grams)
  granulated sugar

⅛ teaspoon salt

8 ounces (2 sticks)
  unsalted butter, chilled

1 large egg

¼ teaspoon each pure
  lemon and almond extract

## FILLING

6 tablespoons (3 ounces)
  unsalted butter

4 ounces pure white
  chocolate, finely chopped

4 ounces (1 cup) raw shelled
  pistachios, finely chopped

3 ounces (about 6 large whole)
  dried apricots, finely chopped
  and mixed with pistachios

# chewy miniatures

gianduja cubes . . . . . . . . . . . . . . . . . . . . . . . . . . . . . .93

meringue bubbles . . . . . . . . . . . . . . . . . . . . . . . . . .95

panforte di siena . . . . . . . . . . . . . . . . . . . . . . . . . .97

macaroon trios . . . . . . . . . . . . . . . . . . . . . . . . . . . .99

glazed almond weave . . . . . . . . . . . . . . . . . . . . . . .101

viennese triangles . . . . . . . . . . . . . . . . . . . . . . . . .103

pecan diamonds . . . . . . . . . . . . . . . . . . . . . . . . . . .105

swiss japonais . . . . . . . . . . . . . . . . . . . . . . . . . . . .107

# gianduja cubes

➤ Makes 2 dozen 1½-inch cubes

Gianduja (pronounced john-doo-ya), a creamy mixture of toasted ground almonds and hazelnuts and chocolate, is often used in French, Italian, and Swiss confectionery. In this recipe, a thin layer is spread over a thin sheet of dacquoise before it is cut into small squares. Gianduja's rich flavor and creamy texture contrast wonderfully with the dacquoise, which is simply a crisp, nutty meringue.

1. Adjust rack to lower third of oven and preheat oven to 350 degrees F. Line a 12-x-15½-x-½-inch baking sheet with aluminum foil, leaving a 2-inch overhang at each short end of the pan. Grease the foil, then flour it, tapping out excess flour.

2. Dacquoise: Combine the ground nuts and ¼ cup sugar with the flour in a small bowl; set aside.

3. Using an electric mixer, preferably with a whisk attachment, whip the egg whites in a large bowl at medium speed until foamy, about 30 seconds. Add the ⅓ cup sugar and continue whipping until soft glossy peaks form, about 2 to 3 minutes. Add the almond extract toward the end of whipping. Sprinkle the nut mixture over the meringue and fold the two together just until incorporated.

4. Spread the batter evenly over the baking sheet. Bake for 20 to 25 minutes, or until light brown and crisp. Remove from the oven. With a thin-bladed knife, release the edges of the dacquoise sticking to the baking sheet. Pull up on the foil overhangs to loosen the foil from the bottom of the baking sheet. Using a small paring knife, trim top edges of the dacquoise to make the surface level.

CONTINUED ➤

## DACQUOISE

3 ounces (½ cup) unblanched almonds, toasted and finely ground

¼ cup (50 grams) granulated sugar

1 tablespoon unsifted all-purpose flour

½ cup (about 4 large) egg whites

⅓ cup (65 grams) granulated sugar

½ teaspoon almond extract

## GIANDUJA FILLING

2 ounces semisweet chocolate, finely chopped

2 ounces unsweetened chocolate, finely chopped

2 ounces (⅓ cup) blanched almonds, toasted

2 ounces (⅓ cup) hazelnuts, toasted and most skins removed

½ cup (50 grams) unsifted powdered sugar

## DECORATION

¼ cup (25 grams) unsifted powdered sugar

24 hazelnuts, toasted and skins removed

5. Place a second baking sheet on top of the dacquoise, invert the dacquoise on it, lift off top baking sheet, and carefully peel the foil from the dacquoise.

6. Gianduja Filling: Melt the chocolates in a bowl set over water approximately 120 degrees F. In the bowl of a food processor, whirl the nuts with the sugar to form a thick paste, about 4 minutes. Add the chocolate to the nut paste, and process just until mixture is combined and smooth. Spread evenly over the dacquoise in a very thin layer.

7. Before the creamy topping sets up, using a ruler and a paring knife, cut the gianduja-topped dacquoise into nine strips 1½ inches wide and 11½ inches long. Using a long metal spatula, lift the dacquoise strips to form three stacks of three strips each on a clean baking sheet. If a strip breaks, merely fit together like pieces of a puzzle. Breaks will not be apparent when you serve the finished pastries. Crumble dacquoise trimmings into crumbs and sprinkle them over the stacks.

8. Set stacks, on the baking sheet, in the refrigerator for 10 minutes only, so the layers stick firmly together and absorb moisture from the filling to make cutting easier and neater.

9. Decoration: Lightly sift the powdered sugar over the strips. Cut into 1½-inch squares, cutting straight down through the layers with a sharp knife and wiping the knife clean after each slice. Press a whole hazelnut on top of each square.

10. Serve at room temperature the same day they are baked.

# meringue bubbles

➤ **Makes 4 dozen 1¼-inch cookies**

You taste chocolate right away when you bite into these, but the appearance of a snowy white meringue "kiss" shape atop a short tender cookie gives no clue. A creative baker can have fun with these cookies: Rather than a kiss, pipe the chocolate-flecked meringue into any shape on the cookie bases—hearts, butterflies, rosebuds, leaves, latticework, even a family coat of arms.

1. Dough: In the large bowl of an electric mixer, cream the butter at medium speed just until smooth, about 1 minute. Beat in the sugar and salt until well combined and slightly fluffy, scraping down the sides. Lower speed, gradually add the flour, and mix just until thoroughly combined.

2. Divide the dough in half. Roll out each portion of dough between two sheets of waxed paper to form a circle 6 inches in diameter and ¼ inch thick. Leaving the dough between the waxed paper, transfer circles to a baking sheet and refrigerate until firm, for at least 2 hours or up to 3 days; or freeze, well wrapped, up to 1 month.

3. Adjust rack to the *center* of the oven and preheat oven to 350 degrees F. Line two large cool baking sheets with parchment paper.

4. Remove one dough package at a time from refrigerator. Remove top waxed paper sheet, and lay it loosely back on the dough. Turn the dough over and peel off and discard the second sheet of waxed paper.

CONTINUED ➤

## DOUGH

4 ounces (1 stick) unsalted
　butter, room temperature

¼ cup (50 grams)
　granulated sugar

⅛ teaspoon salt

1 cup plus 2 tablespoons
　(160 grams) unsifted
　all-purpose flour

## MERINGUE

¼ cup (about 2 large)
　fresh egg whites

½ cup (100 grams)
　granulated sugar

½ teaspoon pure vanilla extract

1½ ounces semisweet
　chocolate, finely grated

5.  Using the wide end of a ½-inch plain decorating tip (such as Ateco #6) as a cutter, cut out circles of dough. If they stick to the decorating tip, use a chopstick or wooden spoon handle to gently push through the decorating tip to release the circles of dough. Place the circles ½ inch apart on a baking sheet. Partially bake the cookies, one sheet at a time, for 6 to 8 minutes only, or until just set. Set the baking sheet on a wire rack to cool. Reduce the oven temperature to 225 degrees F.

6.  Meringue: When the cookies are cool, place all of them on one baking sheet lined with parchment, leaving about ¼ inch between cookies. Using an electric mixer, preferably with a whisk attachment, whip the egg whites in a large bowl on medium-low speed until surface is frothy. Increase speed to medium, then pour in half the sugar and whip until soft white peaks form, about 30 seconds. While continuing to whip, slowly add the remaining sugar and the vanilla and continue whipping until the egg whites form stiff, shiny peaks, about 1½ minutes.

7.  Using a rubber spatula, fold the grated chocolate into the meringue. Immediately scoop all of the meringue into a 16-inch pastry bag fitted with a ½-inch plain decorating tip (such as Ateco #6). Pipe a bulb of meringue onto each cookie in a candy "kiss" shape. The bottom of the meringue "kiss" should be the diameter of the cookie circle. Bake the Meringue Bubbles for an additional 60 minutes, until the meringue is firm to the touch. Place the baking sheet on a wire rack to cool. Lift cookies from parchment when cool.

8.  These are best eaten the same day. To store, place them in an airtight metal container for up to 1 week.

# panforte di siena

➤ **Makes 2 dozen 1½-inch squares**

· · · · · · · · · · · · · · · · · · · · · · · · · ·

An Italian confection, panforte, meaning "strong bread," originated in Siena, Italy. It is a dense fruitcake of nuts, spices, and dried fruits, bound together by a sugar syrup spiked with honey. In contrast to American fruitcakes it is less cakey, more like candy, with the intense taste of the fruit and nuts. You'll enjoy it with grappa, espresso, or even freshly brewed tea. Special thanks to my friend Corby Kummer, senior editor of *The Atlantic Monthly* magazine, whose expert knowledge of and passion for Italian cuisine guided me to this recipe.

1. Adjust rack to lower third of oven and preheat oven to 325 degrees F. Press a sheet of heavy-duty aluminum foil to fit inside a 9-inch square baking pan. Generously grease and flour the foil.

2. Batter: Using a chef's knife, chop the candied citron and orange peel, dried figs, and golden raisins until finely minced (to yield 2 cups). In a large bowl, combine with the nuts.

3. In a small bowl, stir the flour, cocoa powder, and spices to blend.

4. In a 1½-quart heavy-bottomed saucepan, combine the water, honey, and granulated sugar over medium-low heat. Stir occasionally, washing down any sugar crystals clinging to the sides of the pan with a brush dipped in cold water, until the sugar is dissolved. Increase the heat and simmer, without stirring, until the mixture reaches 238 degrees F, the soft-ball stage, on a candy thermometer.

5. Immediately pour the syrup over the fruit and nuts. Pour the dry ingredients on top and stir until well combined. Without delay, spoon into baking pan, spreading evenly with a rubber spatula.

CONTINUED ➤

## BATTER

4 ounces (½ cup packed) candied citron

4 ounces (½ cup) candied orange peel

3 ounces (⅓ cup) dried figs

1½ ounces (¼ cup) golden raisins

4 ounces (¾ cup) unblanched almonds, toasted

4 ounces (¾ cup) hazelnuts, toasted

2 ounces (½ cup) walnut halves

6 tablespoons unsifted all-purpose flour

2 teaspoons unsifted cocoa powder

1 teaspoon ground cinnamon

½ teaspoon ground coriander

¼ teaspoon ground nutmeg

1 tablespoon water

½ cup honey

⅔ cup (130 grams) granulated sugar

## DECORATION

¼ cup (25 grams) unsifted powdered sugar

½ teaspoon ground cinnamon

¼ teaspoon ground coriander

6. Bake for 25 to 30 minutes, or until set. Remove pan to a wire rack to cool completely. Lift foil and remove from pan.

7. Decoration: Sift the powdered sugar, cinnamon, and coriander into a small bowl. Sprinkle half the mixture over the panforte. Invert on a cutting board, peel off the foil, and sprinkle with the remaining spicy mixture. Using a sharp knife, cut into 1½-inch square pieces. To make cutting easier and less sticky, wipe the knife after each cut with a paper towel saturated with unflavored vegetable oil.

8. Store the panforte in an airtight sturdy plastic or metal container for several months.

## BAKING NOTE

It is best to use edible rice paper to line the baking pan. If it is not available to you, you can peel away the greased and floured foil from the confection after it is completely cool, even though it is slightly sticky.

# macaroon trios

➤ **Makes 4 dozen 1½-inch macaroons**

. . . . . . . . . . . . . . . . . . . . . . . . . . . . . . . .

These cookies, easy to make quickly when time is limited, begin as clusters of three small dots of batter, which form the macaroon trios' interesting shape after baking. Laden with a generous amount of almonds and pine nuts, these macaroons are reminiscent of Italian specialty macaroons. It's better to underbake than to overbake them, to preserve a moist, chewy center and a nutty flavor.

1.  Adjust rack to lower third of oven and preheat oven to 325 degrees F. Line two large cool baking sheets with parchment paper.

2.  In a medium bowl, blend the sugar and ground almonds briefly with a wire whisk. Pour the egg whites, flavorings, and salt over the dry ingredients, then stir just to blend together. Using a 14-inch pastry bag fitted with a ½-inch plain decorating tip (such as Ateco #6), pipe clusters of three small dots of batter, each dot about ½ inch in diameter. Space clusters about 1 inch apart. Sprinkle the pine nuts over the macaroons. Gently tap macaroons with a damp pastry brush to flatten the points left from piping and to secure the pine nuts in the batter.

3.  Bake, one sheet at a time, for 13 to 15 minutes, or until macaroons are blond and the pine nuts are golden.

4.  Remove baking sheet from oven. Lift parchment paper with macaroons to a wire rack to cool completely. The macaroons stick to parchment while warm but when completely cool, they lift off parchment easily.

    CONTINUED ➤

---

¾ cup (150 grams) granulated sugar

8 ounces (1⅓ cups) unblanched almonds, toasted and finely ground (see Baking Note)

⅓ cup (about 3 large) egg whites

1 teaspoon pure vanilla extract

¼ teaspoon almond extract

⅛ teaspoon salt

2½ ounces (½ cup) pine nuts

5. Macaroons are best eaten the same day baked. Stack in airtight sturdy plastic containers and store at room temperature up to 2 days; or freeze, up to 10 days.

## BAKING NOTE

The important factor in this recipe is to begin with 2 cups finely ground almonds in order for the cookies to bake full in shape with a chewy texture. The food processor yields 2 cups finely ground almonds from 8 ounces (1 ⅓ cups) unblanched almonds, while other nut grinders, such as electric ones, produce 2 cups finely ground almonds from 6 ounces (1 cup) unblanched almonds.

# glazed almond weave

➤ **Makes 4 dozen 1-x-2½-inch sticks**

Toasted whole almonds, coated in a light honey glaze, weave into a close-fitting pattern over a buttery crust during baking. Any time you serve these stunning cookies, I guarantee you're showing off one of the best pastries you can make.

1. Adjust rack to lower third of oven and preheat oven to 375 degrees F.

2. Dough: Put the flour, sugar, and salt in a food processor bowl. Process just to blend the ingredients. Add the butter slices all at once, and process with on/off bursts until the mixture has the consistency of cornmeal.

3. Whisk the egg and vanilla together in a small bowl. With the motor on, pour the egg mixture down the feed tube. Process just until the ingredients form a ball.

4. Divide the dough into eight pieces and scatter them over an ungreased 10-x-15-x-1-inch cool baking pan. With floured finger-tips, pat the dough to extend the portions to cover the pan as evenly as possible.

5. Bake for 12 to 13 minutes, or until crust appears set and is ivory-colored. After 5 minutes, check the dough for any lifting; if so, prick the spot(s) with a skewer to release the trapped air. When crust is set, remove it from the oven. Reduce oven temperature to 350 degrees F.

CONTINUED ➤

## DOUGH

2 cups (280 grams) unsifted all-purpose flour

½ cup (100 grams) granulated sugar

⅛ teaspoon salt

6 ounces (1½ sticks) unsalted butter, room temperature, cut into ½-inch slices

1 large egg

1 teaspoon pure vanilla extract

## TOPPING

½ cup (4 ounces) heavy cream

2 ounces (½ stick) unsalted butter

¼ cup honey

1 cup (200 grams) granulated sugar

1 pound (scant 3 cups) blanched almonds

6. Topping: Combine the cream, butter, honey, and sugar in a heavy-bottomed 1½-quart saucepan. Heat over medium-low heat, stirring occasionally, until the sugar is dissolved and the butter is melted. Raise the heat to medium-high, and boil the mixture until it registers 235 degrees F, the soft-ball stage, on a candy thermometer, about 6 minutes. Turn off heat, stir in the almonds. Pour over crust; return crust to oven. Bake for 15 to 17 minutes, or just until the nuts are golden.

7. Place baking pan on a wire rack to cool and allow the topping to firm. With a ruler and a sharp paring knife, cut into 1-x-2½-inch sticks.

8. After cutting, cover baking pan with aluminum foil and store up to 4 days at room temperature. Seal the foil around the rim of the pan without letting the foil touch the topping's shiny surface.

## BAKING NOTE

The dough is best made in the food processor. Besides making the dough quickly, the processor distributes the fat throughout the mixture without aerating the dough too much.

# viennese triangles

➤ **Makes 6 dozen 1-inch triangles**

These Old World bar cookies, rich with almonds and a hint of spice and jam, tantalize even the most sophisticated palates. No one would guess that another appealing feature of these cookies is that this is an ideal recipe for using leftover egg whites.

1. Adjust rack to lower third of oven and preheat oven to 350 degrees F.

2. Dough: Put the flour, sugar, and salt in a food processor bowl. Process just to blend the ingredients. Add the butter slices all at once, and process with on/off bursts until the mixture has the consistency of cornmeal.

3. Whisk the egg and vanilla together in a small bowl. With the motor on, pour the egg mixture down the feed tube. Process just until the ingredients form a ball.

4. Divide the dough into eight pieces and scatter them over an ungreased 10-x-15-x-1-inch cool baking pan. With floured finger-tips, pat the dough to extend the portions to cover the pan as evenly as possible.

5. Topping: Spread a thin layer of raspberry jam over the unbaked dough. In a 2½-quart heavy-bottomed saucepan, combine the remaining filling ingredients except the almond extract and baking powder. Stirring constantly over very low heat, bring the mixture to a boil. Still stirring, allow mixture to cook for 3 to 4 minutes, or until it registers 180 to 190 degrees F on a candy thermometer. Stir constantly to prevent any scorching. Remove from heat and stir in the extract and baking powder.

CONTINUED ➤

## DOUGH

2 cups (280 grams)
   unsifted all-purpose flour

½ cup (100 grams)
   granulated sugar

⅛ teaspoon salt

6 ounces (1½ sticks) unsalted
   butter, room temperature,
   cut into ½-inch slices

1 large egg

1 teaspoon pure vanilla extract

## TOPPING

⅓ cup seedless raspberry jam

¾ cup (about 6 large) egg whites

6½ ounces (2½ cups)
   sliced almonds, toasted

1½ cups (300 grams)
   granulated sugar

3 tablespoons all-purpose flour

1 teaspoon ground cinnamon

1 tablespoon light corn syrup

½ teaspoon almond extract

¼ teaspoon baking powder

6. Without delay, pour over unbaked crust, spreading it evenly. Bake for 20 minutes or until golden brown. Place on a wire rack to cool completely before cutting.

7. Using a ruler as a guide and a small sharp paring knife, cut into 2-inch-wide strips. Then cut across each strip diagonally in alternate directions to form 2-inch triangular-shaped bars. Cut these triangles in half to form 1-inch bite-sized triangles.

8. Dark Chocolate Satin Glaze: Combine the shortening and chocolate in a 3-quart bowl. Place it over a saucepan filled with enough hot tap water (120 to 130 degrees F) to reach the bottom of the bowl. Stir the mixture occasionally until the glaze is liquid and smooth and registers close to 110 degrees F on a candy thermometer. If water cools while melting the chocolate, maintain the water's 120-degree-F temperature over very low heat.

9. Dip just the edges of each triangle in the chocolate glaze. Put the coated cookies on a strip of aluminum foil in a cool room until the chocolate sets.

10. Store in a covered foil-lined cardboard box, such as a cake box, at room temperature up to 4 days.

## DECORATING NOTE

Dipping the edges into chocolate is decorative, adds flavor, and holds any crumbs from the cookie base in place.

### DARK CHOCOLATE SATIN GLAZE

¼ cup (1½ ounces) vegetable shortening

1 pound semisweet chocolate, chopped

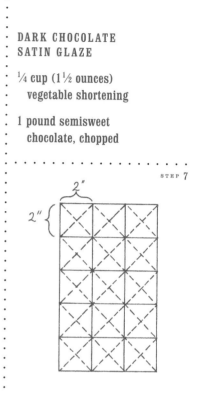

STEP 7

# pecan diamonds

➤ Makes 4 dozen 1½-inch diamonds

. . . . . . . . . . . . . . . . . . . . . . . . . . . .

Treat yourself to mouth-watering bar cookies of crunchy pecans covered with creamy, honey-flavored brown sugar caramel on a butter crust. This luscious topping is an adaptation of a recipe given to me by Myrtle Singer of Manalapan, Florida.

1. Adjust rack to lower third of oven and preheat oven to 375 degrees F.

2. Dough: Put the flour, sugar, and salt in a food processor bowl. Process just to blend the ingredients. Add the butter pieces all at once, and process with on/off bursts until the mixture has the consistency of cornmeal.

3. Whisk the egg and vanilla together in a small bowl. With the motor on, pour the egg mixture down the feed tube. Process just until the ingredients form a ball.

4. Divide the dough into eight pieces and scatter them over an ungreased 10-x-15-x-1-inch cool baking pan. With floured finger-tips, pat the dough to extend the portions to cover the pan as evenly as possible.

5. Bake for 10 minutes. Don't allow the dough to color. Remove from oven. Reduce oven temperature to 350 degrees F.

6. Topping: Combine the butter, honey, and sugars in a heavy-bottomed 1½-quart saucepan. Heat over medium-low heat until butter melts; then raise heat to medium and bring the mixture to a boil. Without stirring, allow mixture to boil only 1 minute. Turn off heat, stir in the cream, nuts, and zest. Pour over bottom crust; return crust to oven. Bake for 30 to 35 minutes, or until the topping is an amber color. Topping will bubble toward the end of baking.

CONTINUED ➤

## DOUGH

2 cups (280 grams) unsifted all-purpose flour

½ cup (100 grams) granulated sugar

⅛ teaspoon salt

6 ounces (1½ sticks) unsalted butter, room temperature, cut into ½-inch slices

1 large egg

1 teaspoon pure vanilla extract

## TOPPING

8 ounces (2 sticks) unsalted butter

½ cup honey

¼ cup (50 grams) granulated sugar

1¼ cups (250 grams) packed light brown sugar

¼ cup heavy cream

8 ounces (2 cups) whole pecans

8 ounces (2 cups) whole pecans, coarsely chopped

1 teaspoon finely grated orange zest

7. Place on a wire rack to cool to allow the topping to firm before cutting. Using a ruler as a guide and a small paring knife, make marks at 2-inch intervals on the long sides and 1½-inch intervals on the short sides. Cut along the diagonals as shown in the illustration to form diamond-shaped bars.

8. After cutting, cover baking pan with aluminum foil and store up to 4 days at room temperature. Seal the foil around the rim of the pan without letting the foil touch and disrupt the topping's glossy surface.

## BAKING NOTE

Mild-tasting clover and light, delicate, citrus-tasting orange blossom honeys are best suited for baking, since their flavors will enhance rather than overpower the baked items. But if you're partial to another variety of honey, feel free to use it in this recipe.

STEP 7

# swiss japonais

➤ **Makes 2 to 3 dozen 1¾-inch Japonais**

Swiss Japonais (pronounced zhah-po-nay), two almond meringue disks filled and frosted with a praline buttercream, then coated with meringue dust, makes an incredibly delicious two bites.

1. Adjust one rack to lower third of oven and second rack to upper third; preheat oven to 225 degrees F. Line two large cool baking sheets with parchment paper to fit. Trace 1½-inch-diameter circles on the parchment with a pencil, using a cutter as a guide; cover both sheets with circles, spacing circles about ¼ inch apart. Fit a 16-inch pastry bag with a ½-inch plain decorating tip (such as Ateco #6).

2. Japonais Meringue: In a small bowl, blend the ground nuts and the ¼ cup sugar briefly with a wire whisk; set aside. Using an electric mixer, preferably with a whisk attachment, whip the egg whites in a large mixing bowl on low speed for 30 seconds or until the surface is frothy. Increase speed to medium, pour in the 2 tablespoons sugar, and continue whipping until soft peaks form, about 45 seconds.

3. Maintaining medium speed, add the ⅔ cup sugar in a steady stream. Continue whipping until a small amount rubbed between your thumb and forefinger feels smooth, not granular, about 2 minutes. Tap whisk against the side of the bowl. Sprinkle the almond-sugar mixture over the meringue, and, using a rubber spatula, fold the two together.

CONTINUED ➤

## JAPONAIS MERINGUE

2 ounces (⅓ cup) unblanched almonds, finely ground

¼ cup (50 grams) granulated sugar

⅔ cup (5 large) egg whites, room temperature

2 tablespoons granulated sugar

⅔ cup (130 grams) granulated sugar

4. Scoop all the mixture into the pastry bag. Pipe spirals to fit the traced circles on the parchment. Bake for 60 to 75 minutes, or until spiral disks are flat, lightly colored, and dry. As they cool, they will crisp. Remove one meringue from oven as a sample to test if drying time in oven is enough. Place baking sheet on a wire rack to cool. Gently lift meringues from parchment when cool.

5. Praline: Lightly grease a baking sheet with vegetable oil. Place the sugar in a 1½-quart heavy-bottomed saucepan or 10-inch skillet. Place over low heat until sugar dissolves; swirl to distribute the heat evenly. When sugar has dissolved, raise the heat to medium-high and cook until the melted sugar reaches an amber color, about 8 to 10 minutes. Pour in the nuts, remove from heat, and swirl; then pour out onto the baking sheet. Set aside to cool and firm for about 1 hour.

6. Crumble enough of the meringue disks to make 1½ cups of fine crumbs. You can grind them through a nut mill or chop with a chef's knife on a cutting board. Put the crumbs on a plate.

7. Match the remaining disks to make pairs: The base of the bottom disk is the flat baked surface, while the disk on top has its flat baked side up. Gently rub the curved sides of each pair together to ensure a more even, level fit. Place each matched pair on a baking sheet.

8. Praline Buttercream: In the large bowl of an electric mixer, whip the egg yolks until light and fluffy, about 4 minutes. Remove bowl from mixer stand. Combine the water and sugar in a 1-quart saucepan over low heat. Stir occasionally, washing down any crystals clinging to the sides of the pan with a brush dipped in cold water, until the sugar is dissolved. Increase heat and cook the syrup, without stirring, until it reaches 238 degrees F on a candy thermometer. Pour into the center of the yolks and quickly whisk vigorously to combine. Return bowl to mixer, and whip at medium

## DECORATION

### Praline

½ cup (100 grams) granulated sugar

1 ounce (2 tablespoons) whole blanched almonds, roasted

1 ounce (2 tablespoons) whole hazelnuts, roasted and most skins removed

### Praline Buttercream

4 egg yolks

¼ cup water

½ cup (100 grams) granulated sugar

8 ounces (2 sticks) unsalted butter, room temperature

1 recipe Praline Powder

speed until the egg yolk mixture thickens and cools to body temperature, about 5 minutes. Maintaining speed, add the butter to the cooled mixture, 2 tablespoons at a time. Continue mixing until all the butter has been incorporated and the buttercream is smooth and homogeneous.

9. Praline Powder: Break the cool, firm praline into small pieces, and place them in a food processor bowl. Process until the praline has the consistency of fine crumbs. Pour the crumbs through a sieve to strain out any larger lumps. Stir ½ cup praline powder into the buttercream and store the remaining powder in an airtight container at room temperature for another use.

10. Using a pastry bag fitted with a ¼-inch plain decorating tip (such as Ateco #2), pipe a scant teaspoon of the buttercream, spiral fashion, on top of each bottom disk. Fit the top disk on the buttercream, and press it gently to level. Then refrigerate the sandwiched disks for about 30 to 60 minutes, just to firm the buttercream to facilitate handling when you frost them. Set the filled pastry bag aside at room temperature.

11. To frost the Japonais, stack one on top of another, and pipe about three or four rows of buttercream around the outside of the two sandwiched pastries. Using a small flexible metal icing spatula, smooth the buttercream around them in a thin layer. Then roll them in the meringue crumbs, wheel fashion, as illustrated. Put them back on the baking sheet, separating the two.

12. Any excess buttercream left on the spatula after smoothing the sides of the Japonais may be used to refill the pastry bag as necessary. After frosting and coating the pastries, return the baking sheet to refrigerator to firm the buttercream around the Japonais, about 30 minutes.

CONTINUED ➤

13. Pipe a spiral of buttercream on top of each Japonais; sprinkle it with meringue crumbs, and press lightly so they adhere. Finish each pastry by piping a small dot of buttercream on top for decoration. Return the baking sheet with the Japonais to the refrigerator to firm the buttercream, then cover the sheet with plastic wrap.

14. Stack undecorated disks in an airtight metal container and store at room temperature up to 3 days. The decorated Japonais are best served the next day; or freeze, well wrapped, in an airtight plastic container up to 1 week.

## TECHNIQUE NOTE

This recipe illustrates several time-saving techniques of assembling, filling, frosting, and coating round petits fours, whether meringue disks, short dough, or cake. See step 11 in the recipe.

## STORING NOTE

During overnight storage in the refrigerator, the crisp Japonais meringue disks absorb moisture from the buttercream, thereby softening the disks to a pleasant chewy consistency.

# crispy miniatures

tuiles . . . . . . . . . . . . . . . . . . . . . . . . . . . . . . . . . . 113

florentine squares . . . . . . . . . . . . . . . . . . . . . . . 114

black walnut genoise wafers . . . . . . . . . . . . . . 116

ladies' wafers . . . . . . . . . . . . . . . . . . . . . . . . . . 118

cognac wafers . . . . . . . . . . . . . . . . . . . . . . . . . . 120

cigarettes . . . . . . . . . . . . . . . . . . . . . . . . . . . . . 122

nougatine cones . . . . . . . . . . . . . . . . . . . . . . . . 124

miniature krumkake . . . . . . . . . . . . . . . . . . . . . 126

crispy corkscrews . . . . . . . . . . . . . . . . . . . . . . . 128

champagne biscuits . . . . . . . . . . . . . . . . . . . . . 130

chocolate fringe cups . . . . . . . . . . . . . . . . . . . . 132

chantilly fans . . . . . . . . . . . . . . . . . . . . . . . . . . 134

# tuiles

➤ **Makes 4 dozen 1½-inch disks**

What I like best about these crispy thin cookies is that their delicate texture and subtle nutty flavor do not overpower but instead complement any fruit, fresh or poached.

1. Adjust rack to lower third of oven and preheat oven to 325 degrees F. Unwrap an end of a chilled stick of unsalted butter and rub it over two large cool Teflon-coated baking sheets to apply a very thin film of fat.

2. In a large mixing bowl, whisk the whites with the sugar just until foamy, about 30 seconds. Whisk in the flour, and then the butter and vanilla until well blended.

3. Drop teaspoonsful of batter 1½ inches apart on a baking sheet. Rap the baking sheet on the work surface to spread the batter slightly. Sprinkle a few sliced almonds on each disk.

4. Bake, one sheet at a time, for 8 minutes, or just until the edges are golden with ivory-colored centers. Place baking sheet on a wire rack to cool for only 15 seconds. With a metal spatula, lift the cookies one at a time, and lay over a rolling pin to curve each cookie while it is still pliable. Cookies crisp as they cool.

5. Repeat the baking and shaping process with the remaining batter.

6. Stack in an airtight metal container and store at room temperature up to 1 week. Keep tuiles in container until serving, since they are very susceptible to any moisture in the air. See Storage Containers in the equipment section (page 22).

⅓ cup (about 3 large) egg whites

½ cup (100 grams) granulated sugar

⅓ cup (45 grams) unsifted all-purpose flour

2½ ounces (5 tablespoons) unsalted butter, melted and cooled to lukewarm

1 teaspoon pure vanilla extract

2 ounces (⅔ cup) sliced almonds, preferably blanched

# florentine squares

➤ **Makes 5½ dozen 1½-inch squares**

. . . . . . . . . . . . . . . . . . . . . . . . . . . . . . . . .

I love these crunchy, candy-like cookies so much that often I don't even coat them with chocolate, though it really is an important feature. Without sacrificing any of their rich flavor, it's easier to decorate them with just a few zigzags of chocolate than to coat them completely. If you want to follow tradition, add finely grated zest or small pieces of candied orange peel to the mixture before baking. You can even use this recipe to form whimsical lollipop sticks for the Truffle Lollipops, page 324.

1.  Adjust rack to lower third of oven and preheat oven to 400 degrees F. Line a 12-x-15½-x-½-inch baking sheet with aluminum foil, leaving a 2-inch overhang at each short end.

2.  Batter: Pour the cream, corn syrup, and sugar into a 1½-quart heavy-bottomed saucepan. Stir to combine, then add the butter. Stir over medium-low heat until the butter melts. Then raise the heat to medium, and stir constantly with a wooden spoon—especially toward the end of cooking—to prevent scorching. Cook until the mixture reaches 238 degrees F, the soft-ball stage, on a candy thermometer, about 10 minutes; the mixture will appear between ivory- and straw-colored. Remove from heat, and stir in almonds.

3.  Pour the mixture onto the center of the foil-lined baking sheet, and spread it in as thin a layer as possible. A pool about 8 inches in diameter is fine. Bake for 3 minutes; then spread the more liquid mixture evenly over the baking sheet. If the mixture still does not completely cover the baking sheet, bake another minute, then tilt the baking sheet to allow the mixture to spread evenly. Bake for about 5 to 6 minutes total, or until golden but not dark brown. Though the mixture bubbles while baking, the bubbles form more slowly toward the end of the baking time than at the beginning.

## BATTER

⅓ cup heavy cream

2½ tablespoons light corn syrup

¾ cup (150 grams) granulated sugar

3 ounces (6 tablespoons) unsalted butter

5 ounces (1½ cups) sliced almonds

## DECORATION

4 ounces semisweet or bittersweet chocolate, finely chopped

4. Place baking sheet on a wire rack and cool for 2 to 3 minutes. While the mixture is still warm but no longer liquid, cut 1½-inch squares using a ruler and pastry wheel. If the mixture is too warm, it will not cut cleanly. If it is too cool, it will splinter or not cut; in that case return it to the oven for a few seconds to soften it a bit.

5. Decoration: When the squares are completely cool, place the chocolate in a bowl over water at about 120 degrees F. When about two-thirds of the chocolate has melted, remove the bowl from the water. With a dry rubber spatula, stir until the liquid chocolate melts the soft or unmelted chocolate that remains. Fill a small handmade paper cone with the chocolate and snip off the tip. Pipe thin lines of chocolate back and forth over the squares' surface. Refrigerate the squares briefly, just to set the chocolate. Remove from the refrigerator and set aside in a cool, dry place.

6. To store, remove squares from the foil and place them in layers, separated by strips of aluminum foil, in an airtight metal or plastic container in a cool place up to 1 week.

## VARIATION NOTE

Using a food processor, whirl the baked Florentine Squares (without any chocolate decoration) to make coarse or fine crumbs. Then sprinkle these crumbs over unbaked cookies, or even fill cutouts in cookies with them before baking. These bits and pieces can also be incorporated in cookie doughs before slicing and baking.

# black walnut genoise wafers

➤ **Makes 3 dozen 1¾-inch sandwiches**

. . . . . . . . . . . . . . . . . . . . . . . . . . . . . . . .

The batter for these thin nutty cookies, crispy outside, soft and chewy inside, reminds me of a genoise that you bake in cookie form. Black walnuts have a distinctive taste, more dominant and pungent than the English walnut.

1. Adjust rack to lower third of oven and preheat oven to 375 degrees F. Grease and flour two large baking sheets, tapping out excess flour.

2. Batter: Blend the flour and salt briefly in a small bowl with a wire whisk; set aside. In the large bowl of an electric mixer, preferably with a whisk attachment, whip the eggs and sugar at medium speed until mixture is thick and taupe-colored, about 3 minutes. Batter should still flow freely when the beaters are lifted. Avoid whipping the mixture too thick or stiff, or the baked result will be a crisp rather than a chewy texture. Now, with a rubber spatula, fold in the salted flour, then the nuts.

3. Spoon or pipe, using a 16-inch pastry bag fitted with a ⅝-inch plain decorating tip (such as Ateco #8), rounded ½ teaspoonsful of batter on baking sheets, placing them 1½ inches apart to leave space for spreading while baking.

4. Bake, one sheet at a time, for about 4 minutes or until lightly browned around the edges. Cookies puff at the beginning of baking but deflate toward the end. Do not overbake. Place baking sheet on a wire rack to cool for 2 minutes only. With a metal spatula, transfer the cookies to another wire rack to cool completely.

**BATTER**

⅓ cup (45 grams) unsifted all-purpose flour

⅛ teaspoon salt

2 large eggs

1 cup (200 grams) packed light brown sugar

4 ounces (1 scant cup) black walnuts, finely chopped (see Baking Note)

**FILLING**

3 ounces white chocolate, finely chopped

5. Filling: Turn half the cooled cookies baked-bottom side up on a clean baking sheet. In a small bowl, melt the chocolate over water at about 110 degrees F. Using a small handmade paper cone, its tip snipped off, pipe a dot of chocolate similar in size to a chocolate chip in the center of each disk. Place the remaining cookie disks on top, baked-bottom side down, to form pairs.

6. With a rubber spatula, spread the remaining melted chocolate over a sheet of aluminum foil into a layer about ⅛ inch deep. Roll each sandwiched cookie in the chocolate, wheel fashion, just to coat the edge. Place on a clear baking sheet as each cookie is decorated. Refrigerate on the baking sheet just long enough to set the chocolate, about 10 minutes.

7. These are best when eaten the same day baked; or freeze, stacked in an airtight sturdy plastic container, up to 1 week.

STEP 6

## BAKING NOTE

Because the nuts provide structure as well as flavor in this recipe, it is important to measure the chopped nut pieces as accurately as possible. With a food processor, through variations of brand, speed, blade, timing, and force, you can grind a given weight of whole or even coarsely chopped nuts into widely varying volumes of chopped nuts. A nut mill grinds nuts into the same volume every time, so for this recipe use a nut mill to chop the nuts to yield 1 cup. See How to Measure Nuts (page 16).

# ladies' wafers

➤ Makes 7 dozen 1½-inch cookies

. . . . . . . . . . . . . . . . . . . . . . . . . . . . . . . . . . . .

Flavored with cognac and tiny currants, these classic coin-sized French cookies, known as *Palets de Dames,* sparkle after a light brushing with a sugar glaze.

1. Adjust rack to lower third of oven and preheat oven to 375 degrees F. Unwrap an end of a chilled stick of unsalted butter and rub it over three large cool baking sheets, preferably Teflon-coated, to apply a very thin film of fat.

2. Batter: Toss the currants with the cognac in a small bowl; set aside. Briefly blend the flour and the salt in another bowl; set aside.

3. In a large bowl of an electric mixer, cream the butter at medium-low speed until creamy, about 1 minute. Increase to medium speed and beat in the sugar until the mixture is light and fluffy. Add the eggs, one at a time, scraping down the sides of the bowl. Add the vanilla and continue mixing until the mixture is smooth. Reduce to low speed, and add all the flour mixture at once, blending just until smooth. With a rubber spatula, stir in the macerated currants.

4. Using a 16-inch pastry bag fitted with a ½-inch plain decorating tip (such as Ateco #6), pipe small mounds about 1 inch in diameter and 1½ inches apart on baking sheets.

5. Bake, one sheet at a time, just until the edges are golden brown with ivory-colored centers, about 10 minutes. Place baking sheet on a wire rack and decorate while warm. Reduce oven temperature to 200 degrees F.

## BATTER

1¾ ounces (⅓ cup) dried currants

1 tablespoon cognac

1 cup (140 grams) unsifted all-purpose flour

⅛ teaspoon salt

4 ounces (1 stick) unsalted butter, room temperature

⅔ cup (130 grams) granulated sugar

3 large eggs, room temperature

1 teaspoon pure vanilla extract

## COGNAC SUGAR GLAZE

½ cup (50 grams) unsifted powdered sugar

4 teaspoons cognac

6. Cognac Sugar Glaze: Mix the sugar and cognac together until smooth. With a pastry brush, apply a thin coating of glaze to each cookie. Return the cookies, one baking sheet at a time, to the oven for about 3 to 4 minutes, or until the glaze is set. Using a metal spatula, remove cookies to a wire rack to cool.

7. Stack in an airtight metal container and store at room temperature up to 1 week.

### VARIATION NOTE

For a contemporary touch, substitute dried cherries or dried cranberries for the currants and kirsch for the cognac in the sugar glaze. Using a chef's knife, chop them coarsely on a cutting board before adding them to the batter.

# cognac wafers

➤ **Makes 2 ½ dozen 1-inch cookie sticks**

. . . . . . . . . . . . . . . . . . . . . . . . . . . . . . . . . . . . . .

These simple but sophisticated cookies are perfect at the end of the meal, either alone with a cup of coffee or served three on a plate with fresh blackberries and ollalie berries. Light, crisp wafers are layered with tiny dots of cognac buttercream to create a glamorous miniature.

1.  Adjust rack to lower third of oven and preheat oven to 325 degrees F. Unwrap an end of a chilled stick of unsalted butter and rub it over two large cool Teflon-coated baking sheets to apply a very thin film of fat.

2.  Batter: In a large mixing bowl, using an electric mixer on medium speed, whisk the egg whites with the sugar just until foamy, about 1 minute. Maintaining the same speed, whisk in the flour, scraping the mixture down the sides of the bowl. Add the butter and vanilla and whisk until well blended.

3.  Drop about twelve ½ teaspoonsful of batter 1 ½ inches apart on the baking sheet. Rap the baking sheet on the work surface to spread the batter slightly.

4.  Bake, one sheet at a time, for about 8 minutes, or just until the edges are golden with ivory-colored centers. Place baking sheet on a wire rack and cool for just 5 seconds. With a metal spatula, remove wafers to a rack to cool. If wafers are too crisp to remove from the baking sheet, return to oven for a few seconds to soften again.

5.  Repeat the baking and shaping process with the remaining batter.

## BATTER

⅓ cup (about 3 large) egg whites

½ cup (100 grams) granulated sugar

⅓ cup (45 grams) unsifted all-purpose flour

2 ½ ounces (5 tablespoons) unsalted butter, melted and cooled to lukewarm

1 teaspoon pure vanilla extract

## COGNAC BUTTERCREAM FILLING

2 egg yolks

2 tablespoons water

¼ cup (50 grams) granulated sugar

4 ounces (1 stick) unsalted butter, room temperature

1 tablespoon cognac

## DECORATION

¼ cup (25 grams) unsifted powdered sugar

6. Cognac Buttercream Filling: Using an electric mixer, whip the yolks in a medium bowl until light and fluffy, about 4 minutes. Combine the water and sugar in a 1-quart heavy saucepan over low heat. Stir occasionally, washing down any sugar crystals clinging to the sides of the pan with a brush dipped in cold water, until the sugar is dissolved. Increase the heat and cook the syrup, without stirring, until it reaches 238 degrees F on a candy thermometer. Pour into the center of the egg yolks and quickly whisk vigorously to combine. Continue mixing at medium speed until the egg yolk mixture thickens and cools to body temperature, about 5 minutes. At same speed, add the butter, 2 tablespoons at a time. Continue mixing until all the butter has been incorporated and the buttercream is smooth and homogeneous. Whip in the cognac until smooth.

7. Set two-thirds of the cookies, baked-bottom side up, on a large clean baking sheet. Using a handmade paper cone, its tip snipped off, pipe tiny dots of cognac buttercream similar in size to a chocolate chip in the center of each disk. Put one cookie on top of another, then place a plain cookie on top; press each stack gently to spread the buttercream evenly between the cookie layers. Decorate the cookies with a light dusting of the powdered sugar.

8. Stack undecorated cookies in an airtight metal container and store at room temperature up to 3 days. Store decorated cookies in one layer in a covered foil-lined cardboard container, such as a cake box, at room temperature up to 1 day.

# cigarettes

➤ **Makes 6 dozen 1½-inch rolls**

- 7 tablespoons (100 grams) unsalted butter, room temperature
- 1¼ cups (125 grams) unsifted powdered sugar
- ½ cup (about 4 large) egg whites, room temperature
- 1 teaspoon pure vanilla extract
- 12 tablespoons (100 grams) unsifted all-purpose flour

What I especially like about this batter is that you can bake it in any shape and size you wish: cones, cups, cigars, cylinders, cigarettes, or cornucopias. When I wanted to mark a milestone birthday for my husband, I fashioned cigar-shaped cookies from this classic batter as one of the grand finale desserts. Stacked on a large silver tray, the faux cigars had slender cellophane strips tucked into one end to simulate smoke. Similar to a fortune cookie, each rolled cookie had a narrow strip of paper with a humorous quote about aging from such notables as Miss Piggy and Bernard Baruch inside it.

1. Adjust rack to lower third of oven and preheat oven to 350 degrees F. Unwrap an end of a chilled stick of unsalted butter and rub it over two large cool Teflon-coated baking sheets to apply a very thin film of fat.

2. In the large bowl of an electric mixer, cream the butter at medium speed until it has the consistency of mayonnaise. Add the powdered sugar, 2 tablespoons at a time, and beat until each addition of sugar is absorbed by the butter before you add more. Whip until light and fluffy.

3. Maintaining the same speed, gradually add the egg whites. Wait for each portion of whites to be incorporated before adding the next. Add the vanilla. Don't worry if the mixture appears curdled at this point. Lower speed and add the flour, combining thoroughly.

4.  Drop 3 or 4 teaspoonsful of batter on each baking sheet. Using a small offset metal spatula, spread each mound into paper-thin squares approximately 1½ x 1½ inches. Bake for 2 to 3 minutes, or until pale gold. Remove baking sheet from oven to a wire rack. Turn each cookie over with a spatula, and quickly roll, baked-bottom side in, around a chopstick or wooden dowel 6 inches long and ⅜ inch in diameter. Remove from the wooden form to another wire rack until cool. If the cookies become too brittle to shape, return them to the oven just until they soften, a few seconds.

5.  Repeat the baking and shaping process with the remaining batter.

6.  Stack in an airtight metal container and store at room temperature up to 1 week.

### SHAPING NOTE

Here's a way to make a reusable template for easily shaping the batter uniformly, quickly, and efficiently: With a pencil or felt pen, trace a form such as a circle, triangle, or butterfly on the surface of a thin plastic lid from a storage container similar to those used to cover nuts and cheese. Use a utility knife to cut out the shape you traced. Trim the outside edge from the lid.

To use the stencil, drop a teaspoon of batter inside it and using a small offset metal spatula, spread the batter across it. Lift the stencil and continue shaping cookies on baking sheet as recipe specifies. When you've finished shaping a batch of cookies, simply wash and dry the stencil.

# nougatine cones

➤ **Makes 4 dozen 1 ½-inch-long cones**

. . . . . . . . . . . . . . . . . . . . . . . . . . . . . . . . . .

These thin lacy wafers, rolled into tiny cones while hot from the oven, make perfect receptacles for chocolate ganache or coffee buttercream. When I want a simpler, less rich cookie, I dip just the edges of the cone's wide end in melted chocolate.

1. Adjust rack to lower third of oven and preheat oven to 350 degrees F. Unwrap an end of a chilled stick of unsalted butter and rub it over two large cool Teflon-coated baking sheets to apply a very thin film of fat.

2. Put the butter, corn syrup, and sugar in a 1-quart heavy-bottomed saucepan. Stir over low heat until the butter is melted. Remove from heat, and stir in the nuts and flour.

3. Drop five or six ½ teaspoonsful of batter 1 ½ inches apart on each baking sheet. A quick and easy method is to pipe the soft dough from a 14-inch pastry bag fitted with a ½-inch plain decorating tip (such as Ateco #6). Bake, one sheet at a time, for 6 to 7 minutes, or until golden brown. While baking, the cookies bubble; a clue that they are finished baking is when the bubbling subsides.

4. Place baking sheet on a wire rack to cool for just 15 seconds. With a metal spatula, lift one wafer at a time and roll it around a wooden cornet to shape the cookie while it is still flexible. Remove cone from the form, and place it on a wire rack to cool; continue rolling the remaining cookies.

2 ounces (4 tablespoons) unsalted butter

¼ cup light corn syrup

¼ cup (50 grams) granulated sugar

4 ounces (¾ cup) hazelnuts, chopped medium fine to yield ¾ cup (see Baking Notes)

¼ cup (35 grams) unsifted all-purpose flour

5. Repeat the baking and shaping process with the remaining batter.

6. When the cookies are cool and firm, stack them in an airtight metal container and store at room temperature up to 1 week.

## BAKING NOTES

Hazelnuts or almonds, blanched or unblanched, are fine for this cookie. If you prefer the flavor of toasted nuts, put them on a baking sheet in a 325-degree-F preheated oven for about 10 minutes or until pale gold.

See How to Measure Nuts (page 16).

## SERVING NOTE

For entertaining, I bake tiny 1-inch wafers without rolling them. Before serving, pipe a dramatic rosette of whipped cream in the center of each dessert plate; then, stick several wafers in the cream, rose petal–fashion.

# miniature krumkake

➤ **Makes 3 dozen 2-inch-long cones**

. . . . . . . . . . . . . . . . . . . . . . . . . . .

These crunchy cone-shaped cookies, with their embossed pattern, bake one at a time in cookie irons. These irons, traditional in Italy, Norway, and France, have a variety of names—*cialde, pizelle, krumkake,* and *gaufrette.* No matter which iron you use, making these cookies is a festive event.

1. In a 3-quart bowl, blend the flour, powdered sugar, and sesame seeds briefly with a wire whisk. Mix in the sour cream and vanilla until thoroughly combined.

2. Open iron and spray nonstick cooking spray lightly on both sides of it. Place over medium heat. Alternating sides of the iron, heat until water dripped inside iron sizzles. Open iron and spoon 1 level measuring teaspoonful batter into the center. Close it and bake over heat, first on one side, then on the other, turning every 10 to 15 seconds until the cookie is light golden brown. It's fine to open iron occasionally to check doneness.

3. With a small metal spatula, lift cookie while warm and, while still pliable, wrap around a wooden cornet to form a cone shape or roll into a cylinder around a wooden dowel ½ inch in diameter. Slip cookie off the wooden form to cool.

4. Return iron to heat; repeat the baking and shaping process with the remaining batter. If at any time the cookies brown too quickly or burn, adjust the heat.

5. When cookies are cool and firm, store them in an airtight metal container at room temperature up to 1 week.

½ cup (70 grams) unsifted all-purpose flour

½ cup (50 grams) unsifted powdered sugar

1 tablespoon sesame seeds

½ cup (5 ounces) sour cream

1 teaspoon pure vanilla extract

## BAKING NOTE

Cookie irons without nonstick surfaces work best. You need to season them when new. To season, place over medium heat until a drop of water dripped inside sizzles. Open iron and brush amply with vegetable oil. Close and return to heat just until oil smokes. Remove from heat and let iron cool in open position. Wipe clean with a paper towel.

## SERVING NOTE

After shaping, these krumkake look like tiny ice cream cones. When the weather is sunny and warm, stage an ice cream festival: With a tiny ice cream scoop, fill several krumkake cones with a variety of ice creams and sorbets, such as vanilla, orange, chocolate, strawberry, and coffee. Arrange three or five cones fan-fashion on each dessert plate.

# crispy corkscrews

➤ **Makes 3 dozen 2-inch-long spirals**

The corkscrew spiral shape is what gives these cookies their name. Forming them takes some patience, but the payoff is evident when you see the delicate spirals on a tray of assorted cookies. The cookies' simple flavors of butter and sugar balance perfectly with a glass of dry champagne.

1. Adjust rack to lower third of oven and preheat oven to 375 degrees F. Unwrap an end of a chilled stick of unsalted butter and rub it over two large cool Teflon-coated baking sheets to apply a very thin film of fat.

2. In the large bowl of an electric mixer, cream the butter at medium speed until smooth, about 45 seconds. Beat in the sugar until fluffy. Add the egg whites, a tablespoon at a time, blending well after each addition. With a rubber spatula, scrape down the sides of the bowl. Add the flour, combining thoroughly.

3. Using a 14-inch pastry bag fitted with a ¼-inch plain decorating tip (such as Ateco #2), pipe only three strings about ¼ inch wide, 3 inches long, and at least 1½ inches apart on each baking sheet. Bake cookies, one sheet at a time, for about 4 minutes, or just until edges are light golden brown.

4. Place baking sheet on a wire rack. Without delay, lift the end of one string at a time with a metal spatula, and wrap the cookie spiral-fashion around a 6-inch wooden dowel or wooden spoon handle about ⅜ inch in diameter. After shaping a cookie, gently slip it off the dowel to a wire rack until cool. Repeat the baking and shaping process with the remaining batter.

3 ounces (6 tablespoons) unsalted butter, softened

½ cup granulated sugar

⅓ cup (about 3 large) egg whites, room temperature

¾ cup plus 1 tablespoon (114 grams) unsifted all-purpose flour

5. When firm, store in an airtight metal container at room temperature up to 1 week.

## BAKING NOTE

For maximum results with a minimum amount of effort, I bake these cookies relay-fashion. When I remove one baking sheet from the oven, I replace it with another, then I shape the just-baked cookies into spirals while they are warm, then I prepare another baking sheet to exchange with the one in the oven when the time is right. In this way, you can make a batch very quickly.

STEP 3

STEP 4

# champagne biscuits

➤ **Makes 6 dozen 3-inch-long cookies**

. . . . . . . . . . . . . . . . . . . . . . . . . . . . . . .

These crispy, finger-length cookies are ideal with fresh fruit, ice cream, and sorbet. I think they are even more delicious with a decorative zigzag of white chocolate drizzled over half the cookie.

1.  Adjust rack to lower third of oven and preheat oven to 375 degrees F. Unwrap one end of a chilled stick of unsalted butter and rub it over two large cool Teflon-coated baking sheets to apply a very thin film of fat.

2.  Batter: In the large bowl of an electric mixer, cream the butter on medium speed until smooth, about 45 seconds. Beat in the sugar until fluffy. Beat in the whole egg, blending thoroughly, then add the egg white. With a rubber spatula, scrape down the sides of the bowl. Lower speed and add the flavorings, then the flour, combining thoroughly.

3.  Using a 16-inch pastry bag fitted with a ¼-inch plain decorating tip (such as Ateco #2), pipe strings about ¼ inch wide, 3 inches long, and at least 1½ inches apart. Bake, one sheet at a time, for about 5 to 6 minutes, or just until edges and bottoms are light golden brown.

4.  Place the baking sheet on a wire rack and lift the cookies with a metal spatula to another wire rack to cool. If cookies become difficult to remove, return baking sheet to the oven for a few seconds until they soften.

## BATTER

4 ounces (1 stick)
   unsalted butter, softened

½ cup (100 grams)
   granulated sugar

1 large egg, room temperature

2 tablespoons (about 1 large)
   egg white, room temperature

1 teaspoon pure vanilla extract

¼ teaspoon almond extract

¾ cup (105 grams)
   unsifted all-purpose flour

## DECORATION

2 ounces white chocolate,
   finely chopped

5. Decoration: When firm, put cookies on a baking sheet lined with waxed paper. Melt the chocolate in a bowl set over water at about 105 degrees F. Using a small paper cone, its tip snipped off, pipe thin lines of chocolate zigzag-fashion across half of each cookie. Set aside in a cool place or refrigerate just until the chocolate firms, about 10 minutes.

6. Stack undecorated cookies in an airtight metal container and store at room temperature up to 1 week. Store decorated cookies in a single layer in a covered foil-lined cardboard container, such as a cake box, at room temperature up to 2 days.

# chocolate fringe cups

➤ **Makes 4 dozen 1¾-inch cookie cups**

Circles of thinly spread batter are piped with chocolate around the edge, baked, and shaped while warm from the oven. They come out looking like wavy swatches of fabric, making a delightful and unusual cup for fresh raspberries or other fruits.

1. Adjust rack to lower third of oven and preheat oven to 375 degrees F. Unwrap an end of a chilled stick of unsalted butter and rub it over two large cool Teflon-coated baking sheets to apply a very thin film of fat.

2. To streamline shaping these cookies, make a reusable 3-inch round plastic template. With a pencil or felt pen, trace a 3-inch circle on a thin plastic lid (as thin as a playing card) from a storage container. Use a utility knife to cut out the traced shape from the template.

3. Batter: In the large bowl of an electric mixer, cream the butter at medium speed until it has the consistency of mayonnaise. Add the sugar and beat until mixture is well combined. Scrape down the sides of the bowl.

4. Maintaining the same speed, gradually add the egg whites. Wait for each portion of whites to be incorporated before adding the next. Add the vanilla. Lower mixer speed and add the flour, combining thoroughly.

5. Decoration: Melt the chocolate in a small bowl that fits snugly over a pan of water at about 120 degrees F; set aside.

6. Set the reusable template on the baking sheet and drop a small amount of batter inside it. With a small offset metal spatula, spread the batter very thinly and evenly within the template.

## BATTER

2 ounces (4 tablespoons) unsalted butter, room temperature

⅔ cup (130 grams) granulated sugar

⅓ cup (about 3 large) egg whites, room temperature

1 teaspoon pure vanilla extract

½ cup (70 grams) unsifted all-purpose flour

## DECORATION

2 ounces semisweet chocolate

7. Carefully lift the template. Repeat this procedure until four round cookies are formed on each baking sheet.

8. Fill a small handmade paper cone with the chocolate. Snip its tip off and pipe a thin string of chocolate ¼ inch in from the edges of the unbaked rounds of batter.

9. Bake, one sheet at a time, for 3 to 5 minutes, or until pale golden. Place baking sheet on a wire rack and, without delay, lift one cookie at a time with a metal spatula and drape each cookie, baked-bottom side up, over the top of a spice jar or vinegar bottle (see Baking Notes). Using a ⅓-cup measuring cup as a mold, place it over each cookie just long enough to shape it into a cup. Remove cookies from jar or bottle tops and set them in empty egg carton cups until cool and set. If any cookies become brittle before molding, return to oven for a few seconds until pliable again.

10. Repeat this procedure with the remaining batter.

11. Stack in an airtight metal container and store at room temperature up to 1 week. Fill with fresh fruit or a favorite cream filling close to serving time.

## BAKING NOTES

Shaping the pliable cookies into cups begins over 1-inch-diameter vinegar or 1¾-inch-diameter spice bottle caps. To set their shape, the cookies are put in egg carton cups while cooling. Later, the egg carton becomes handy again. It cradles these fragile cookies with just enough support to prevent their breaking when filling them with small pieces of fresh seasonal fruit.

I recommend a low oven temperature here so these very thin cookies won't bake too dark and crisp too soon.

STEP 6

STEP 8

STEP 9

# chantilly fans

➤ **Makes 5 dozen 1½-inch wedges**

The name of this cookie comes from its interesting shape. A creamy bat-ter, flecked with ground hazelnuts, is thinly spread over a circular mold. While warm from the oven, it is folded into quarters, creating a fan. This technique produces four thin, crispy layers with a delicate texture that crumbles with each bite, releasing a sweet, nutty flavor. If the first cookie you fold isn't perfect, don't worry. The next one is easier and the third time, you'll feel like a pro.

1. Adjust rack to lower third of oven and preheat oven to 350 degrees F. Unwrap an end of a chilled stick of unsalted butter and rub it over two large cool Teflon-coated baking sheets to apply a very thin film of fat.

2. For a reusable template, use the removable rubber ring (⅛ inch thick, 2½ inches in diameter) from a canning or old-fashioned-type storage jar. Its proportions make it easy to form uniformly shaped cookies quickly.

3. In a deep 1½-quart mixing bowl, whip the heavy cream until soft peaks form. Refrigerate it. In another small bowl, blend the ground nuts and the potato starch briefly with a wire whisk. Using an electric mixer at medium speed, preferably with the whisk attach-ment, whip the egg whites in a large bowl until small bubbles appear, about 30 seconds. Gradually add the sugar, about ½ table-spoon at a time, and continue whipping until thick, stiff, glossy peaks form, about 3 minutes. With a rubber spatula, fold in the dry ingredients alternately with the whipped cream, beginning and ending with the dry ingredients.

⅓ cup heavy cream

1¾ ounces (scant ⅓ cup) hazelnuts, toasted and finely ground

2 tablespoons potato starch

¼ cup (about 2 large) egg whites

⅓ cup (65 grams) granulated sugar

4. Put the reusable template on the baking sheet and drop a small amount of batter, about 1 mounded teaspoon, inside it. Using a small offset metal spatula, spread the batter evenly across the ring.

5. Carefully lift the template. Repeat this procedure until five wafers are formed on each baking sheet. Bake, one sheet at a time, for 5 minutes only, or just until edges are golden brown, the centers are ivory-colored, and cookies no longer appear shiny or wet on top. Don't overbake. Place baking sheet on a wire rack. While cookies are warm, using a small metal spatula, lift one wafer at a time and flip it over (baked-bottom side up) back onto the hot baking sheet. Fold it in half, then in half again to form a quarter-circle wedge. Set the wedges on another wire rack until cool.

6. Repeat the baking and shaping process with the remaining batter.

7. Gently stack these delicate cookies in an airtight metal container and store at room temperature up to 3 days.

STEP 4

STEP 5

### BAKING NOTES

After toasting the hazelnuts, remove just the dark brown skins that come off easily after rubbing them together in the palms of your hands. (Too many skins can cause a bitter taste.)

If cookies crisp before you can fold them, return for a few seconds to the oven until pliable, and don't bake the next batch as long.

**PART II**

# spicy miniatures

spicy twin thins . . . . . . . . . . . . . . . . . . . . . . . . . . . . 139

bittersweet gingersnaps . . . . . . . . . . . . . . . . . . . 141

pains d'amande . . . . . . . . . . . . . . . . . . . . . . . . . . 143

sesame spice chips . . . . . . . . . . . . . . . . . . . . . . . 145

hahnpfeffernüsse . . . . . . . . . . . . . . . . . . . . . . . . 147

springerle . . . . . . . . . . . . . . . . . . . . . . . . . . . . . . 149

chrabeli . . . . . . . . . . . . . . . . . . . . . . . . . . . . . . . . . 151

speculaas . . . . . . . . . . . . . . . . . . . . . . . . . . . . . . . 152

lemon-laced gingersnaps . . . . . . . . . . . . . . . . . . 154

lebkuchen circles . . . . . . . . . . . . . . . . . . . . . . . . 156

biberli . . . . . . . . . . . . . . . . . . . . . . . . . . . . . . . . . . 158

# spicy twin thins

➤ Makes 3 dozen 1½-inch sandwiches

Here's another intriguing spicy shortbread-like dough with a twist—literally. This cookie is formed by putting two five-point-star-shaped cookies together to create a ten-point star. The technique is simple, but the results are stunning. While the cookies are still warm from baking, sprinkle finely chopped white chocolate over the tops. Place one cookie on top of the other and rotate to form the ten-point star. Then accent each of the star sandwiches with chopped pistachio nuts.

1. Dough: Put the flour, sugar, spices, and salt in a food processor bowl. Process just to blend ingredients. Add the butter pieces all at once, and process with on/off bursts until the mixture has the consistency of cornmeal.

2. Whisk the egg yolk with the vanilla and zest in a small bowl. With the motor running, pour the egg mixture down the feed tube and process just until ingredients form a ball.

3. Divide the dough in half and roll out each portion between two sheets of waxed paper to form ⅛-inch-thick rounds about 11 inches in diameter. Leaving the dough circles between the waxed paper sheets, stack them on a baking sheet, and refrigerate until firm, for at least 2 hours or up to 3 days; or freeze, well wrapped, up to 1 month.

4. Adjust rack to lower third of oven and preheat oven to 325 degrees F. Line two cool baking sheets with parchment paper.

5. Remove one dough circle package at a time from refrigerator. Peel off top sheet of waxed paper, replace it loosely on top, and flip the entire package over. Peel off and discard the second sheet of waxed paper.

CONTINUED ➤

## DOUGH

2 cups (280 grams)
  unsifted all-purpose flour

⅔ cup (130 grams)
  granulated sugar

½ teaspoon each ground
  ginger and freshly ground
  black pepper

¼ teaspoon each ground
  cinnamon and allspice

⅛ teaspoon salt

8 ounces (2 sticks) unsalted
  butter, room temperature,
  cut into ½-inch slices

1 egg yolk

1 teaspoon pure vanilla extract

2 teaspoons finely grated
  lemon zest

## DECORATION

4 ounces white chocolate,
  finely chopped

1 ounce (3 tablespoons) pistachio
  nuts, blanched, roasted, and
  finely chopped

6. Using a 1½-inch star cutter, cut out shapes in the dough and set them ½ inch apart on the baking sheets.

7. Bake, one sheet at a time, for 8 to 10 minutes, or until the cookies are no longer shiny and feel slightly firm when lightly touched. Place baking sheet on a wire rack.

8. Decoration: While cookies are still hot, sprinkle the finely chopped chocolate on them. Sprinkle the pistachio nuts over only half of the chocolate-coated cookies.

9. The heat from the cooling cookies melts the chocolate and makes it easy to sandwich two cookies together. Using a small metal spatula, center a pistachio–chocolate-topped cookie on top of a chocolate-topped cookie. Twist the cookie on top so the star points are between the bottom cookie's star points. Now gently press the pair together to form a ten-point star. Repeat with the remaining cookies while the chocolate is soft.

10. Transfer cookies to a clean baking sheet and put in a cool room to allow the chocolate to set, about 1 hour.

11. Stack cookies in an airtight metal container, separating the layers with strips of aluminum foil, and store at room temperature up to 1 week.

# bittersweet gingersnaps

➤ **Makes 5 dozen cutouts, depending on size**

One bite and you'll know these are cookies with a snap. Crunchy, spicy rectangles are dipped diagonally into bittersweet chocolate for an eye-catching, boldly flavored combination. A small amount of vegetable shortening makes the Faux-Tempered Chocolate easier to handle and gives a shine similar to that of tempered chocolate once it sets. You save time without sacrificing flavor.

1. Dough: In a bowl, whisk or stir with a rubber spatula the flour, cinnamon, ginger, cloves, allspice, and salt to combine; set aside.

2. Using an electric mixer, beat the butter and sugar just until creamy and smooth. Lower speed and mix in the egg. Add the dry ingredients, mixing just until completely blended.

3. Divide the dough into thirds, and roll one portion at a time between two sheets of waxed paper to form a 13½-x-10½-inch rectangle ⅛ inch thick. Leaving the dough rectangles between the sheets of waxed paper, transfer them to a baking sheet and refrigerate until firm, for at least 2 hours or up to 3 days; or freeze, well wrapped, up to 1 month.

4. Adjust rack to lower third of oven and preheat to 350 degrees F. Line two large cool baking sheets with parchment paper.

5. Remove one dough package at a time from refrigerator. Peel off top sheet of waxed paper, replace it loosely on top, and flip the entire package over. Peel off and discard the second sheet of waxed paper.

CONTINUED ➤

## DOUGH

2¾ cups (385 grams) unsifted all-purpose flour

1 teaspoon ground cinnamon

1½ teaspoons ground ginger

½ teaspoon ground cloves

¼ teaspoon ground allspice

¼ teaspoon salt

8 ounces (2 sticks) unsalted butter, softened

1¼ cups packed dark brown sugar

1 large egg

## FAUX-TEMPERED CHOCOLATE

2 tablespoons solid vegetable shortening

1 pound semisweet chocolate, finely chopped

6. Using a fluted pastry wheel and a ruler as a guide, trim the ragged edges; then measure and cut the dough into six 1½-inch strips. Cut the strips at 2-inch intervals, creating 1½-x-2-inch rectangular shapes. Place the cookie rectangles on the baking sheets about 1 inch apart. If dough softens, return it to refrigerator just until it firms enough to handle.

7. Bake, one sheet at a time, 8 to 10 minutes or until pale brown on top and brown on bottom. Place baking sheet on a wire rack to cool for 5 minutes. Then lift cookies from parchment with a spatula to a rack to cool. Cookies crisp as they cool. (Cookies may be stored at this point in airtight metal containers at room temperature for up to 10 days.)

8. Faux-Tempered Chocolate: Place the solid vegetable shortening and chocolate in a 1-quart bowl that fits snugly over a saucepan half filled with 120- to 130-degree-F water, to melt ingredients. Stir occasionally until smooth. If necessary, maintain the water's temperature over very low heat.

9. Dip the cookies, one at a time, diagonally into the liquid chocolate to glaze, shaking off excess glaze, and then set each cookie on aluminum foil or parchment-lined baking sheets. Allow the chocolate on the cookies to set up at room temperature, about 1 hour before storing.

10. Store cookies in one layer in a covered foil-lined cardboard container, such as a cake box, at room temperature up to 2 days.

# pains d'amande

➤ **Makes 7 dozen 1 ½-inch squares**

This traditional Belgian cookie, known as almond bread, is another favorite from my catering baking business in the early 1970s. The raw sugar's light golden color and distinctly old-fashioned flavor, similar to that of turbinado-style sugar, gives this cookie its unique taste, texture, and appearance. A slow baking develops a crispy texture and toasty flavor. Though the dough is pale in color, it becomes honey-colored and delicious when baked.

1. Sift the flour and baking soda onto a sheet of waxed paper; set aside.

2. In a 1 ½-quart saucepan over low heat, combine the butter, sugar, cinnamon, and water. Stir occasionally just until the butter melts. Do not allow the mixture to boil. Don't be concerned if some of the sugar has not dissolved by the time the butter has melted. Remove from heat and stir in the almonds. Pour this mixture into a 3-quart mixing bowl; set aside for about 30 minutes at room temperature until lukewarm, about 90 degrees F.

3. Add the dry ingredients all at once; stir until thoroughly blended.

4. Press the soft dough into an 8 ½-x-4 ½-inch straight-sided pan (such as a 1 ½-quart Pyrex loaf pan) lined with plastic wrap. Cover surface with plastic wrap and refrigerate until firm, for at least 4 hours or up to 3 days; or freeze, well wrapped, up to 1 month.

5. Adjust rack to lower third of oven and preheat oven to 325 degrees F. Line two large cool baking sheets with parchment paper.

CONTINUED ➤

2 ⅓ cups (325 grams) unsifted all-purpose flour

¼ teaspoon baking soda

4 ounces (1 stick) unsalted butter, chilled and cut into quarters

1 ⅓ cups (280 grams) Hawaiian washed raw sugar

½ teaspoon ground cinnamon

⅓ cup water

3 ounces (1 cup) sliced almonds

6.  Lift out the firm dough from the pan, on its plastic, to a cutting board. Using a sharp chef's knife, cut it in half crosswise and then cut the halves lengthwise into thirds. Using a sharp knife, cut each bar into ⅛-inch or thinner slices, and space them, cut sides down, ¼ inch apart on the baking sheets. (The dough slices as though it were fudge.) You can use a sawing action with a serrated knife in order to cut through the nuts to make very thin slices.

7.  Bake, one sheet at a time, for 8 to 10 minutes, or until the undersides are light golden; then turn cookies over and bake for an additional 8 to 10 minutes, or until crisp and honey-colored. Place baking sheet on a wire rack to cool. Lift cookies from parchment when cool.

8.  Stack cookies in an airtight metal container and store at room temperature up to 10 days.

## BAKING NOTE

Hawaiian washed raw sugar is available in supermarkets in 2-pound plastic bags. If you cannot locate it, you can substitute turbinado sugar.

## VARIATION NOTE

For a more intense almond flavor, use 4 ounces (⅔ cup) whole blanched almonds instead of the sliced almonds. Cutting the dough into thin slices is trickier, though, since the larger almond pieces can cause the dough to fall apart.

# sesame spice chips

➤ **Makes 8 dozen 1½-inch cookies**

I fondly remember these molasses-cinnamon cookies from my childhood. However, I've made them even better by adding sesame seeds. These round, cinnamon-brown cookies are great served with baked apples. I've even concluded a formal dinner party by arranging them on a silver plate and passing them when coffee was served. Substitute these cookies for graham crackers in your next pie for the best crumb crust ever.

1. Adjust rack to lower third of oven and preheat oven to 350 degrees F. Line two large cool baking sheets with parchment paper.

2. Dough: Sift the flour, baking soda, spices, and salt on a sheet of waxed paper; set aside. In the large bowl of an electric mixer, cream the butter at medium-low speed until smooth, about 1 minute. Beat in the sugar at medium speed until creamy. Add the egg and beat just until fluffy, then gradually add the molasses until incorporated, scraping down the sides of the bowl. Lower speed, gradually blend in the dry ingredients, and mix just until thoroughly combined.

3. Using a 16-inch pastry bag fitted with a ½-inch plain decorating tip (such as Ateco #6), pipe half teaspoons of dough 1 inch apart on cool baking sheets.

4. Decoration: Using a damp pastry brush, flatten the cookies slightly to remove the tip left from piping. Generously sprinkle the sesame seeds over cookies. With another baking sheet, press down evenly on cookies to flatten them all at once.

CONTINUED ➤

## DOUGH

2 cups (240 grams) unsifted all-purpose flour

2 teaspoons baking soda

1 teaspoon ground cinnamon

¼ teaspoon each ground ginger, allspice, and salt

6 ounces (1½ sticks) unsalted butter, room temperature

1 cup (200 grams) granulated sugar

1 large egg

¼ cup light molasses

## DECORATION

5 ounces (⅔ cup) sesame seeds

5. Bake, one sheet at a time, for 8 minutes, or until cookies are flat, feel slightly firm to the touch, and are cinnamon brown. Place baking sheet on a wire rack to cool. Lift cookies from parchment when cool.

6. Stack in an airtight metal container at room temperature and store up to 1 week.

## BAKING NOTES

If you want more sesame seed flavor, shape teaspoons of soft dough, 1 teaspoon at a time, into balls, then roll in sesame seeds to coat before flattening and baking them.

You'll enjoy serving these cookies with baked apples, poached pears, or simply homemade applesauce. For a special hostess gift, package these along with a pound of toasted unsalted macadamia nuts—perfect partners.

# hahnpfeffernüsse

➤ **Makes 8 dozen 1-inch balls**

Just as you wouldn't think of eating the crust of an apple pie without the apples, you must not eat these cookies without the sugar glaze. The glaze works together with the cookie, enclosing its spiciness and adding good taste.

*Pfeffernüsse* means "peppernut" in German, suggesting the cookies' healthy dose of spices and resemblance to unshelled walnuts. Their small thick shapes and abundant assortment of spices are two characteristics most recipes share in common. However, Hahnpfeffernüsse, with no fat and lots of flour, bake hard with a spirited peppery, pungent flavor. The texture softens and the fragrant flavor heightens and improves after the cookies have been stored in an airtight metal container at least 1 week.

Baking powder, a modern addition to the recipe, produces a softer texture. Anise flavoring is customary in pfeffernüsse glazes. Use anise oil rather than anise extract for a richer, more authentic, intense flavor. Anise oil is available at well-stocked pharmacies, baking supply and specialty equipment shops, and supermarkets. Citron and nuts provide additional texture and flavor.

1. Adjust rack to lower third of oven and preheat oven to 350 degrees F. Line two large cool baking sheets with parchment paper.

2. Dough: Sift the flour, baking powder, spices, and salt on a sheet of waxed paper; set aside. In the large bowl of an electric mixer, preferably with a whisk attachment, whip the eggs and yolk with the sugar at medium speed until thick and taupe-colored, about 2 minutes. Lower speed and mix in the coffee. By hand, using a rubber spatula, gradually blend in the zest, the dry ingredients, and then the nuts and citron. Mix just until thoroughly combined.

CONTINUED ➤

## DOUGH

3 cups (420 grams)
  unsifted all-purpose flour

1 teaspoon baking powder

2 teaspoons ground cinnamon

½ teaspoon allspice

¼ teaspoon each freshly ground
  black pepper, mace, and nutmeg

⅛ teaspoon each ground
  cardamom and cloves

¼ teaspoon salt

2 large eggs, room temperature

1 egg yolk, room temperature

1 cup (200 grams) packed
  dark brown sugar

1½ tablespoons cold
  brewed black coffee

1 teaspoon finely
  grated lemon zest

1½ ounces (¼ cup) blanched
  almonds, finely ground

1½ ounces (¼ cup)
  finely chopped citron

## PFEFFERNÜSSE ICING

1 cup water

3 cups granulated sugar

⅛ teaspoon anise oil

3. For each cookie, pinch off a piece of dough measuring 1 teaspoon in size, and drop 1 inch apart on cool baking sheets. Then, shape into balls with your palms.

4. Bake, one sheet at a time, for 10 to 12 minutes, or until firm to the touch and lightly browned on the bottom. Place baking sheet on a wire rack until the cookies are cool. Repeat the shaping and baking process with the remaining dough.

5. Adjust rack to lower third of oven and preheat oven to 200 degrees F. Line two large baking sheets with aluminum foil.

6. Pfeffernüsse Icing: In a 1½-quart heavy-bottomed saucepan, combine the water and sugar over low heat. Stir occasionally, washing down any sugar crystals clinging to the sides of the pan with a brush dipped in cold water, until the sugar is dissolved. Increase heat and, without stirring, gently boil to 230 degrees F, the thread stage, on a candy thermometer. Remove from heat, pour in the anise oil, and swirl the pan to blend.

7. While syrup is hot, drop about 20 cookies at a time in the icing and completely cover with the syrup. Lift one at a time from icing with a fork. Tap the fork on the pan to remove excess. Place cookies ½ inch apart on foil-lined baking sheets. Put the baking sheets in oven for about 7 minutes to dry the glaze. Place baking sheets on wire racks, and lift cookies to another wire rack to cool and dry the cookies' undersides.

8. When icing is dry and set, stack cookies in an airtight sturdy plastic container and store at room temperature for at least 1 week or up to 2 months before serving. During this time, the cookies soften while the flavors mellow. If cookies remain hard, add some apple wedges to the container and cover tightly for 1 day or until cookies are soft; then discard the apple pieces.

# springerle

➤ **Makes about 3 dozen, depending on size of molds**

$\frac{1}{3}$ cup anise seeds

3 $\frac{1}{2}$ cups (490 grams)
unsifted all-purpose flour

$\frac{1}{8}$ teaspoon salt

4 large eggs

3 $\frac{3}{4}$ cups (1 pound)
unsifted powdered sugar

1 ounce (2 tablespoons)
unsalted butter, softened

2 teaspoons finely
grated lemon zest

These ivory-colored cookies, crunchy and chewy in texture and embossed with designs from a special mold, remind me of the holidays in Indiana when I was a child. Though the anise flavor was too sophisticated for me then, I savor its powerful flavor now.

Springerle are especially appealing with any tangy fruit, such as fresh currants or raspberries, or even with lemon curd. As simple as it may seem, a cup of coffee and a springerle perk up anyone's workday.

If you don't like the crunch of anise seeds on the surface of the cookies, roll a rolling pin over seeds to crush them. Use $\frac{1}{4}$ teaspoon anise oil in the dough if you prefer to eliminate using them altogether.

1. Unwrap one end of a stick of unsalted butter and rub it over two large cool baking sheets to apply a film of fat. Sprinkle the anise seeds evenly over them; set aside.

2. Sift the flour and salt onto waxed paper; set aside. In the large bowl of an electric mixer, preferably with a whisk attachment, whip the eggs at medium speed until fluffy, thick, and ivory in color, about 2 minutes. Gradually add the sugar and whip until the mixture is thick enough that when the whisk is lifted, the batter flows back into the bowl in ribbons, about 10 minutes. Whisk in the soft butter.

3. Lower the speed and gradually whisk in the flour mixture and zest. Scoop the mixture out onto a floured surface and knead just until the dough is smooth and cohesive. Cover dough's surface with waxed paper and let rest at room temperature for 1 hour.

CONTINUED ➤

4.  To imprint designs in the dough, roll out half of the dough at a
    time on a lightly floured surface into a 10½-inch square about ¼
    inch thick. Dust a wooden springerle board with flour, and tap it to
    remove the excess. Press the springerle board firmly into dough to
    imprint the designs as deeply and clearly as possible. Remove board
    and, using a pastry wheel, cut the designs apart and place them
    an inch apart on top of the anise seeds on the baking sheets. Brush
    any excess flour from the cookies with a clean dry pastry brush.
    Reflour mold before imprinting again. Set cookies aside, uncovered,
    at room temperature for at least 8 hours or up to 24 hours to sur-
    face dry and set the embossed impressions before baking.

5.  Adjust rack to lower third of oven and preheat oven to 250 degrees
    F. Bake for 27 to 30 minutes, or until barely straw-colored and
    firm (lightly touch a few). Do not allow cookies to color. Transfer
    cookies to a wire rack to cool.

6.  Stack in sturdy airtight plastic containers and store at room tem-
    perature up to 1 month. If cookies get too hard, add some apple
    wedges to the container, and cover tightly for 1 day or until cookies
    are softer; then discard the apple pieces.

# chrabeli

➤ **Makes 12 dozen 1½-inch cookies**

1 recipe Springerle dough
(page 149)

⅓ cup anise seeds

STEP 2

If you don't have wooden molds or a wooden rolling pin to imprint designs in the Springerle dough, it's easy to make these leaf-shaped cookies with the same dough.

1. Adjust rack to lower third of oven and preheat oven to 250 degrees F. Unwrap an end of a stick of unsalted butter and rub it over two large cool baking sheets to apply a film of fat. Sprinkle the anise seeds evenly over them; set aside.

2. Divide the dough equally into 8 portions, about ¼ cup each. With fingertips, roll each portion of dough back and forth on a lightly floured surface into a 15-inch-long rope about ⅜ inch in diameter. Cut each rope into 2-inch lengths to yield uniformly shaped pieces. With fingertips, bend each shape on the anise-seed-coated baking sheet into a crescent; space crescents ½ inch apart. With the pointed tip of scissors, snip three short slashes in the upper side of each crescent along the curve.

3. Bake for 15 minutes, or until the cookies feel firm (lightly touch a few). Do not allow them to color. Transfer the cookies to a wire rack to cool.

4. Stack in sturdy airtight plastic containers and store at room temperature up to 1 month. If cookies get too hard, add some apple wedges to the container, and cover tightly for 1 day or until cookies are softer; then discard the apple pieces.

# speculaas

➤ **Makes 3 to 4 dozen, depending on size of cutter or molds**

These thin, mildly spicy, crunchy cookies with a dusting of nuts on top are traditionally presented as shaped figures printed from decorative wooden molds. Though I include instructions for making impressions from any decorative mold, I prefer cutting out round shapes from chilled dough circles. This allows you to make Speculaas at your convenience. A low oven temperature ensures even baking and at the same time imparts a toasty flavor.

1. Sift the flour, baking soda, spices, and salt into a large mixing bowl. Add the sugars and, using an electric mixer on low speed, beat just until combined. Increase mixer speed to medium-low, add the butter, and blend until mixture is crumbly and resembles a streusel. Maintaining same speed, blend in the water, 1 tablespoon at a time. Mix just until ingredients come together in a cohesive ball.

2. Divide the dough in half, and roll each portion between two sheets of waxed paper to form a circle 12 inches in diameter and ⅛ inch thick. Leaving the dough circles between the waxed paper, transfer to a baking sheet and refrigerate until firm, at least 2 hours or up to 3 days; or freeze, well wrapped, up to 1 month.

3. Adjust rack to lower third of oven and preheat oven to 300 degrees F. Line two large cool baking sheets with parchment paper; sprinkle just enough sliced almonds to cover each sheet.

4. Remove one dough package at a time from refrigerator. Remove the top waxed paper sheet, and lay it loosely back on the dough. Turn the dough over, peel off the second waxed paper sheet, and discard the waxed paper.

2 cups (280 grams) unsifted all-purpose flour

½ teaspoon baking soda

1 ½ teaspoons ground cinnamon

¼ teaspoon freshly ground black pepper

⅛ teaspoon each ground cloves and nutmeg

1 dash cayenne pepper

⅛ teaspoon salt

½ cup (100 grams) granulated sugar

½ cup (100 grams) packed light brown sugar

5 ounces (1 ¼ sticks) unsalted butter, softened

3 tablespoons cold water

1 ½ ounces (½ cup) sliced almonds

5. Using a 1½-inch round cutter, cut out shapes in the dough. Place cutouts about ½ inch apart on nut-covered baking sheets, lightly pressing cookies into nuts. Bake, one sheet at a time, for about 20 minutes, or until golden brown on the bottom. With a metal spatula, remove the cookies to a wire rack to firm as they cool.

6. Stack cookies in an airtight metal container and store at room temperature up to 10 days. Serve cookies nutty side up.

## SHAPING NOTES

If you're using wooden molds, dust them well with flour, then tap out excess before making an imprint. Press pieces of dough into molds, and roll a rolling pin over dough to ensure filling the crevices. With the tip of a small knife, trim excess dough to shape it neatly. Tap the mold on the work surface to release the forms. If necessary, ease the dough's release with tip of knife. Put each cookie, imprinted side up, on nut-covered cool baking sheets. With a clean dry pastry brush, brush off excess flour and lightly press cookies into almonds without disturbing the imprint.

Before baking, set aside the cookies, uncovered, at room temperature for at least 8 hours or up to 24 hours to surface dry and set the embossed impressions.

# lemon-laced gingersnaps

➤ **Makes 8 dozen 1½-inch cookies**

. . . . . . . . . . . . . . . . . . . . . . . . .

These gingersnaps are given an additional depth of flavor with dark molasses and a few tablespoons of cold coffee. The cookies are even better drizzled with lemon icing.

1. Dough: Sift the flour, baking soda, and salt on a sheet of waxed paper; set aside. In a small bowl, combine the molasses and coffee; set aside.

2. In the large bowl of an electric mixer, cream the butter at medium-low speed until smooth, about 1 minute. Increase speed to medium, add the sugar, and mix until well combined and slightly fluffy. Blend in the spices. Maintaining the same speed, add the flour mixture in three additions, alternating with the liquid, until thoroughly combined.

3. Cover the dough's surface with plastic wrap and refrigerate until the soft dough is firmer, about 1 hour. Then divide dough into four equal parts; roll each portion on a lightly floured surface into a cylinder about 7 inches long and 1¼ inches in diameter. Wrap each log in plastic wrap and refrigerate until the dough is firm, at least 4 hours or up to 1 week; or freeze, well wrapped, up to 1 month.

4. Adjust rack to lower third of oven and preheat oven to 350 degrees F. Line two large cool baking sheets with parchment paper.

5. Remove one dough cylinder at a time from refrigerator. With a sharp knife, cut the dough into thin slices less than ⅛ inch thick. Place the slices about ½ inch apart on the cool baking sheets. Bake, one sheet at a time, until the cookies are no longer shiny and appear set, about 8 to 10 minutes. With a metal spatula, remove cookies to a wire rack to cool.

## DOUGH

2½ cups (350 grams)
    unsifted all-purpose flour

1 teaspoon baking soda

¼ teaspoon salt

⅓ cup dark molasses

2 tablespoons cold
    brewed black coffee

7 ounces (1¾ sticks)
    unsalted butter, softened

¾ cup (150 grams)
    granulated sugar

1 tablespoon ground ginger

1 teaspoon ground cinnamon

½ teaspoon ground cloves

## LEMON ICING

1 ounce (2 tablespoons)
    unsalted butter, softened

2 tablespoons lemon juice

1 cup (100 grams)
    unsifted powdered sugar

6. Lemon Icing: Beat ingredients in a small bowl until smooth. Using a small handmade paper cone, its tip snipped off, pipe thin lines of icing over the cookies in one direction. Then pipe lines perpendicular to the original lines, making a crisscross pattern. Set aside to allow icing to dry.

7. Stack undecorated cookies in an airtight metal container and store at room temperature up to 10 days. Store decorated cookies in one layer in an airtight container at room temperature up to 3 days.

# lebkuchen circles

➤ **Makes 6 dozen 1-inch cookies**

Lebkuchen, a spicy cake-like honey-flavored dough, soft and chewy to eat, is Europe's gingerbread. I bake these in late November before the holiday season becomes frantic. While the cookies are stored in airtight containers, the honey draws in moisture and improves the flavor and texture. For Valentine's Day, you can cut out heart shapes and decorate them along the edges with royal-icing scribbling to resemble lace.

1.  Dough: In a 1½-quart saucepan over low heat, heat the honey, sugar, and butter just until butter is melted and sugar is almost dissolved. Do not boil. Add the lemon juice, zest, and spices, blending completely. Transfer the mixture to a large bowl and set aside at room temperature to cool, about 30 minutes.

2.  Sift the flour, baking powder, baking soda, and salt on a sheet of waxed paper. Add the ground nuts, egg, and citron to the cooled honey mixture, blending well. Stir in the flour mixture in three additions, blending thoroughly into a soft dough. Cover surface of dough with plastic wrap, and refrigerate until it is firmer, at least 4 hours or up to 3 days. A cold, firm dough is less sticky than a soft one, so less flour is needed for rolling.

3.  Adjust rack to lower third of oven and preheat oven to 350 degrees F. Line two large cool baking sheets with parchment paper.

4.  Work with a third of the dough at a time; keep unused portion covered in refrigerator. On a floured work surface, roll out dough ⅜ inch thick. Using a 1-inch round cutter, cut out circles and space 1 inch apart on baking sheets. Press a split almond on top of each cookie.

## DOUGH

⅔ cup honey

1 cup granulated sugar

2 ounces (½ stick) unsalted butter

1 tablespoon fresh lemon juice

2 teaspoons finely grated lemon zest

1 tablespoon ground cinnamon

¼ teaspoon each ground cardamom, cloves, ginger, and nutmeg

3 cups (420 grams) unsifted all-purpose flour

½ teaspoon baking powder

½ teaspoon baking soda

¼ teaspoon salt

1½ ounces (¼ cup) blanched almonds, finely ground

1 large egg

3 ounces (½ cup) finely chopped citron

40 blanched almonds, split (see Technique Notes)

## COGNAC SUGAR GLAZE

½ cup (50 grams) unsifted powdered sugar

4 teaspoons cognac

5. Bake, one sheet at a time, for 10 to 12 minutes, or until golden brown. Place baking sheet on a wire rack and glaze cookies while warm.

6. Cognac Sugar Glaze: Mix the sugar and cognac together until smooth. Using a pastry brush, coat the cookies lightly. With a metal spatula, transfer cookies to wire racks to cool completely. To seal in as much moisture as possible for a lengthy storage, apply the glaze over bottoms as soon as top coating dries.

7. Store in an airtight sturdy plastic container at room temperature for at least 2 weeks or up to several months before serving. If cookies get too hard, add some apple wedges to the container and cover tightly for 1 day or until cookies are soft again; then, discard the apple pieces.

### TECHNIQUE NOTES

Put the almonds and water to cover in a small saucepan, and bring to a boil. Remove from heat; let stand for 1 minute to soften. Using a slotted spoon, remove nuts, one at a time, and using the tip of a small paring knife, split almonds in half along their natural seams.

You roll this dough in flour rather than between two sheets of waxed paper because this honey-rich dough is sticky and would only adhere to the waxed paper.

### BAKING NOTES

Using fat in the recipe, in this instance butter, adds flavor and makes the cookies softer and less brittle than those made from a recipe without fat.

Besides using it to make cookies for festive Christmas decorations, you can also roll this dough less than ¼ inch thick and cut out assorted shapes for friends as housewarming, engagement, or birthday presents. You can even personalize them with Royal Icing (page 175).

# biberli

➤ **Makes 6 dozen 1½-inch cookies**

. . . . . . . . . . . . . . . . . . . . . . . . . . . . . .

A thin layer of Lebkuchen dough without the ground nuts and citron is wrapped around a lemon-scented almond paste filling to showcase this versatile dough at its best. It's a good idea to plan ahead when baking Biberli, since aging develops their proper flavor and texture.

1. Dough: In a 1½-quart saucepan over low heat, heat the honey, sugar, and butter just until butter is melted and sugar is almost dissolved. Do not boil. Add the lemon juice, zest, and spices, blending completely. Transfer the mixture to a large bowl and set aside at room temperature to cool, about 30 minutes.

2. Sift the flour, baking powder, baking soda, and salt on a sheet of waxed paper. Add the egg. Stir the flour mixture into the cooled honey mixture in three additions, blending thoroughly into a soft dough.

3. Cover surface of dough with plastic wrap and refrigerate until it is partially chilled, about 2 hours. If longer storage is necessary, refrigerate up to 3 days.

4. Filling: In food processor bowl, process all the ingredients just until blended smoothly; set aside.

5. Adjust rack to center of oven and preheat oven to 350 degrees F. Line two large cool baking sheets with parchment paper.

6. On a floured work surface, roll dough to form a 12-inch square, ¼ inch thick. Using a ruler and pastry wheel, cut into six strips, each 2 inches wide.

## DOUGH

⅔ cup honey

1 cup (200 grams) granulated sugar

2 ounces (½ stick) unsalted butter

1 tablespoon fresh lemon juice

2 teaspoons finely grated lemon zest

1 tablespoon ground cinnamon

¼ teaspoon each ground cardamom, cloves, ginger, and nutmeg

3 cups (420 grams) unsifted all-purpose flour

½ teaspoon baking powder

½ teaspoon baking soda

¼ teaspoon salt

1 large egg

7. Using a 14-inch pastry bag fitted with a ½-inch plain decorating tip (such as Ateco #6), pipe a rope of filling down the center of each strip. (The filling will be about ½ inch thick.) Bring the two edges of dough together to wrap around the filling. Pinch the edges together to seal the seam. Then, roll each rope back and forth to smooth its surface and even out its thickness to ¾ inch. Cut each roll into ¾-inch-wide slices. As you lift each cookie between your thumb and index finger to set seam side down on a baking sheet, reshape its round top, since slicing the cookies flattens and distorts their shape. Space ½ inch apart.

8. Bake, one sheet at a time, for about 10 minutes, or until the cookies are no longer shiny and feel slightly firm (lightly touch a few). Place baking sheet on a wire rack to cool. Lift cookies from parchment when cool.

9. Lemon Sugar Glaze: Mix the sugar, lemon juice, and water until smooth. Using a pastry brush, coat cookies lightly with glaze. Set aside to dry.

10. Store in an airtight container at room temperature up to 1 month. For best flavor and texture, store at least one day before serving.

FILLING

8 ounces (1 scant cup) almond paste, room temperature

¼ cup (50 grams) granulated sugar

Zest of 1 lemon

1 egg white

LEMON SUGAR GLAZE

½ cup (50 grams) unsifted powdered sugar

2 teaspoons fresh lemon juice, strained

2 teaspoons water

PART II

# chocolate miniatures

chocolate macaroons . . . . . . . . . . . . . . . . . . . . . . . .163

double kisses . . . . . . . . . . . . . . . . . . . . . . . .166

chocolate thimbles . . . . . . . . . . . . . . . . . . . . .168

neapolitan wedges . . . . . . . . . . . . . . . . . . . . . .171

hedgehogs . . . . . . . . . . . . . . . . . . . . . . . . . .174

chocolate tulips . . . . . . . . . . . . . . . . . . . . . . .178

tiffany rings . . . . . . . . . . . . . . . . . . . . . . . . .180

chocolate coins . . . . . . . . . . . . . . . . . . . . . . . .183

chocolate starlets . . . . . . . . . . . . . . . . . . . . . . .186

white blossom circles . . . . . . . . . . . . . . . . . . . . .188

cocoa cavaliers . . . . . . . . . . . . . . . . . . . . . . . .190

chocolate pistachio cigarettes . . . . . . . . . . . . . . .192

chocolate shadows . . . . . . . . . . . . . . . . . . . . . .194

chocolate candy-cane cookies . . . . . . . . . . . . . . .196

dutch chocolate minicakes . . . . . . . . . . . . . . . . .198

# chocolate macaroons

➤ **Makes 5 dozen 1½-inch sandwiches**

. . . . . . . . . . . . . . . . . . . . . . . . . . . . . . . . . .

Years ago while touring in France, I discovered a cookie unlike any other I had ever tasted. One bite filled my mouth with more chocolate flavor than a double chocolate sundae. The French call these delicately textured, intensely flavored cookies Chocolate Macaroons, but they do not resemble the American version at all. The French version sandwiches two chocolate cookies with a creamy dark chocolate filling. A heart full of thanks to the Christophe Patisserie in Roanne, France, for this recipe.

1. Adjust rack to *upper* third of oven and preheat oven to 475 degrees F. Line two large cool baking sheets, each measuring 14 x 17 x ½ inches, with parchment paper. Place two additional pieces of parchment paper, identical in size to the ones on the baking sheets, on the work surface near the baking sheets. Fit a 16-inch pastry bag with a ⁵⁄₁₆-inch plain decorating tip (such as Ateco #5).

2. Batter: Pour ½ pound of powdered sugar and half the ground nuts and cocoa into a large medium-mesh sieve. Shake over a sheet of waxed paper to blend the ingredients. Sieve the remaining ½ pound powdered sugar and the remaining nuts and cocoa over the waxed paper. Add to the sifted mixture any nut particles that remain in the sieve.

3. In the large bowl of an electric mixer, preferably with a whisk attachment, whip the egg whites at medium-low speed until the whites form soft frothy peaks, about 2 minutes. Increase to medium speed, add the ½ cup powdered sugar and the honey, and whip just until billowy, thick, but not dry, peaks form, about 3 minutes.

CONTINUED ➤

## BATTER

3¾ cups (1-pound box) unsifted powdered sugar

9 ounces (1⅔ cups) unblanched almonds, finely ground (see Baking Note)

½ cup (50 grams) unsifted cocoa powder

1 cup (about 7 to 8 large) egg whites, room temperature

½ cup (50 grams) unsifted powdered sugar

1 teaspoon honey

## DARK CHOCOLATE GANACHE

6 ounces semisweet chocolate, finely chopped

¾ cup (6 ounces) heavy cream

4. Using a rubber spatula, fold in all the dry ingredients. As you fold, the mixture will deflate somewhat to resemble a brownie batter. Without delay, scoop all of the mixture into the pastry bag. Piping the batter may be easier if you anchor the parchment by smearing some batter on each corner under the paper. Pipe candy "kiss" shapes, ¾ to 1 inch in diameter, on the cool baking sheets. The kiss pattern will dissolve before baking, leaving a smooth surface. Pipe the remaining batter on the additional sheets of parchment paper.

5. Allow to dry at room temperature for 30 minutes to prevent the cookies' surface from cracking during baking.

6. Just before baking each batch, double-pan the cookies: Place the baking sheet on a second sheet of the same size. This will diffuse the flow of heat on the baking sheet. Place one baking sheet of cookies in the oven, and immediately reduce the temperature to 425 degrees F. Reduce the temperature 25 degrees F every 2 minutes. Bake, one sheet of cookies at a time, for *8 minutes only,* finishing at 350 degrees F. Lowering the temperature in this way maintains a constant flow of heat but prevents the cookies from overbaking, inflating, and cracking.

7. Place baking sheet on a wire rack until cookies are completely cool. With a metal spatula, carefully lift cookies from the paper.

8. Continue to bake the other batches in the same manner. Each time be certain to preheat oven to 475 degrees F. To bake the cookies piped on the two sheets of parchment, merely slide the paper onto a cool baking sheet.

9. Dark Chocolate Ganache: Put the chocolate in a medium bowl. In a small saucepan, heat the heavy cream just to the boil. Remove from heat. Pour over chocolate; whisk until chocolate melts and mixture is smooth and shiny. Set aside to cool until it develops enough body to pipe.

10. Turn half the macaroons baked-bottom side up. Using a 14-inch pastry bag fitted with a ¼-inch plain decorating tip (such as Ateco #2), pipe a bulb of filling equivalent to ½ teaspoon. Place plain macaroons, dome side up, on top of the filled ones; press gently to fit the pair together.

11. These are best eaten the same day; or freeze, separating the layers with strips of waxed paper, in airtight sturdy plastic containers up to 1 month.

## BAKING NOTE

Because the nuts provide structure as well as flavor in this recipe, it is important to grind them to yield 2⅓ cups. The food processor does this with no problem.

## TECHNIQUE NOTE

It's easier to fill the pastry bag with all the mixture at once when you set the bag, fitted with its decorative tip, into a deep 1½-quart bowl for support. To hold the bag open for filling, fold a portion of the bag's top edges over the bowl.

# double kisses

➤ **Makes 3 ½ dozen 1 ½-inch cookies**

These cookies aim to surprise. A delicious, simple chocolate–peanut butter shortbread wraps around a chocolate candy. The balance of ingredients makes it possible for the cookies to hold their candy "kiss" shape after baking. Individual foil wrapping makes these cookies all the more fun and special, and perfect for handing out to your friends or packing in a decorated box to give to your special someone.

1. Adjust rack to lower third of oven and preheat oven to 350 degrees F. Line a large cool baking sheet with parchment paper.

2. In a small bowl, blend the flour and cocoa powder briefly with a wire whisk; set aside. In the large bowl of an electric mixer on medium-low speed, cream the butter until smooth, about 1 minute. Increase speed to medium, add the peanut butter, then the sugar, and mix until well combined and slightly fluffy. Lower speed, add the egg white, then the flour mixture in two additions, scraping down the sides of the bowl, and combine ingredients thoroughly.

3. Using 2 level teaspoons of dough, form a flat disk in the palm of your hand. Center a candy kiss on dough and bring the dough up to cover completely, keeping the kiss upright. Pinch dough on top to resemble kiss shape. Space cookies an inch apart on baking sheet.

4. Bake for 8 to 10 minutes, or until the cookies are no longer shiny and the bottoms are brown. Don't overbake. Place baking sheet on a wire rack to cool. Lift cookies from parchment when completely cool. The cookies' structure remains fragile only while warm.

1 ½ cups (210 grams) unsifted all-purpose flour

¼ cup (25 grams) unsifted cocoa powder

4 ounces (1 stick) unsalted butter, room temperature

¼ cup creamy peanut butter

⅔ cup (130 grams) granulated sugar

2 tablespoons (1 large) egg white

42 milk chocolate candy kisses, foil removed

5. To make individual kisses, center each cookie on a 5-inch square of aluminum foil, bring up edges, and twist them to enclose cookie completely. If desired, before twisting the foil, insert a name or personal message on a narrow paper strip.

6. Store in an airtight metal container at room temperature up to 10 days.

# chocolate thimbles

➤ **Makes 2 dozen 1½-inch cases**

1½ pounds semisweet or
bittersweet chocolate,
for tempering

Here's the ultimate chocolate miniature, since chocolate is the only ingredient used to mold these tiny cases that resemble the shape of a thimble.
You can fill them with my Punsch Cakelets (page 305) or my Five-Spice
Marshmallows (page 332), a favorite creamy vanilla mousse, or a rich
chocolate bavarian cream—or simply tiny fresh stemmed strawberries.

For this recipe, you need to bring the melted chocolate to the temperature at which it is stable and will set properly, since the chocolate must
be firm and shiny after molding. This process is known as tempering.
There are many ways to temper chocolate (see Express Method, page 315).
This one that is based on a traditional method is precise—it relies on occasional temperature checks for both the water bath and the chocolate. The
following approach, the Traditional Method, will guide you successfully
through the process.

1. Cut twenty-four 4-inch squares of waxed paper. Press one paper
   square at a time over the base of a glass spice jar that measures
   about 1½ inches in diameter or any other cylindrical object with a
   smaller diameter. Set these molded paper forms near the stove.

2. Chop the chocolate into ⅛-inch matchstick pieces, reserving one
   chunk of chocolate that weighs approximately 2 ounces.

3. Fill the bottom vessel of a double boiler with enough 125-degree-F
   water to just touch the bottom and sides of the top container without floating it. Maintain this temperature throughout the melting
   process by reheating the water from time to time over *very* low
   heat. An instant-read thermometer is the quickest way to check the
   water's temperature. Fill the top of the double boiler with half the
   chopped chocolate.

4. Stir the chocolate occasionally and, as it melts, gradually add the remaining chopped chocolate. When the melted chocolate reaches 115 to 120 degrees F, replace the 125-degree-F water with 95-degree-F water. Let the melted chocolate sit over the cooler water and stir chocolate frequently until the chocolate reaches 98 to 100 degrees F. Be sure to wipe the stem of the thermometer after each measurement.

STEP 1

STEP 7

STEP 9

5. Remove the top half of the double boiler. Add the reserved chunk of chocolate to the melted chocolate. Stir the chocolate slowly and evenly with a dry rubber spatula. The chunk of chocolate helps lower the temperature gradually and evenly as it melts into the melted chocolate. It also "seeds" the melted chocolate with stable cocoa butter crystals, which help keep it in good temper as the chocolate hardens. Dark chocolate must be cooled to 86 to 90 degrees F. If the melted chocolate cools too much and loses its fluidity, simply replace the top vessel of the double boiler over hot tap water to reheat the chocolate. Never let the chocolate's temperature exceed 90 degrees F, or the stable cocoa butter crystals will start to melt and the temper will be lost.

6. When the chocolate has cooled to the correct temperature (86 to 90 degrees F), remove what is left of the chunk of chocolate and set it aside. Replace the water with 86- to 90-degree-F water to maintain the chocolate's correct temperature.

7. Hold the molded paper cups by the edges and dip them, one by one, into the chocolate, coating the outside. Place them on a foil-lined tray, right side up.

8. Repeat the dipping process. Another coat of chocolate strengthens the cup and makes it less fragile. Place in a cool room or refrigerate briefly until chocolate sets.

CONTINUED ➤

9. Grasping the edges of the waxed paper, gingerly twist it until it releases from the chocolate cup. Don't fret if the chocolate chips a bit around the edges—it gives each cup individual charm. After all, they are handmade, not machine made.

10. Store in one layer in an airtight metal or plastic container in a cool room up to 1 week.

# neapolitan wedges

➤ **Makes 6 dozen 1-inch wedges**

The glazing and cutting techniques transform simple cookies into dazzling petits fours. The instructions given here are detailed but not time-consuming. Following them will reward you with a generous amount of trapezoid-shaped wedges with layers of short dough and red currant jelly buttercream, topped with a modernistic marble effect in the thin chocolate glaze.

1. Dough: Divide the dough in half. Roll out each portion between two sheets of waxed paper to form a rectangle 8 x 14 inches and ⅛ inch thick. Leaving the dough between the waxed paper, transfer the rectangles to a baking sheet and refrigerate until firm, at least 2 hours or up to 3 days; or freeze, well wrapped, up to 1 month.

2. Adjust rack to lower third of oven and preheat oven to 325 degrees F. Line two large cool baking sheets with parchment paper.

3. Remove one dough package at a time from refrigerator. Peel off top waxed paper sheet, replace it loosely on top, and flip the entire package over. Peel off and discard the second sheet of waxed paper.

4. Using a ruler and pastry wheel, trim the edges of the dough. Measure and cut three 2-inch-wide strips, each about 13½ inches long. While the dough is still cool and firm, lift the strips onto one of the baking sheets, spacing them ½ inch apart.

5. Bake, one sheet at a time, for 13 to 16 minutes, or until the strips are pale blond, are no longer shiny, and feel slightly firm when lightly touched. Place baking sheet on a wire rack to cool the cookie strips completely. While warm, they're more fragile than when cool.

CONTINUED ➤

## DOUGH

1 recipe Miniature Tartlet Pastry (page 205)

## BUTTERCREAM

4 ounces (1 stick) unsalted butter, softened

2 tablespoons red currant jelly

## ROYAL ICING

1 cup (100 grams) unsifted powdered sugar

2 tablespoons (1 large) egg white

⅛ teaspoon cream of tartar

Red food coloring

## GLOSSY CHOCOLATE GANACHE GLAZE

¼ cup heavy cream

1 tablespoon light corn syrup

4 ounces semisweet chocolate, finely chopped

6. Buttercream: Using a rubber spatula, stir the butter in a 1½-quart mixing bowl until it looks like mayonnaise. Stir in the jelly until smooth.

7. Place three of the strips close together, baked-bottom side up, preferably on a portable plastic or polyethylene cutting board. With a flexible metal icing spatula, spread a total of 3 tablespoons of the buttercream in a very thin, even coating over two of the cookie layers.

STEP 7

STEP 14

8. With a long metal icing spatula, lift the layers one at a time, and stack them to form one strip. If a layer should break when being lifted, just fit it in place as though it were a jigsaw puzzle piece. When the strip is sliced into individual wedges, there will be no evidence of the break.

9. Assemble the other strip in the same manner. Refrigerate until the filling is firm, for at least 2 hours or, well covered, up to 2 days. The advantage of a longer chilling time is that it firms the buttercream and allows moisture from the buttercream to soften the cookie strips and make slicing into wedges easier.

10. Remove the two cookie strips from the refrigerator.

11. Royal Icing: Mix the sugar, egg white, and cream of tartar together in a 1½-quart mixing bowl. With a hand mixer on medium speed, whip until the mixture is thick and has a marshmallow-like consistency, about 5 minutes. Add 1 drop red food coloring to tint the icing a pastel pink. Fill a small handmade paper cone with 3 tablespoons of the icing; set it aside. Cover the remaining icing's surface with plastic wrap to prevent drying.

12. Glossy Chocolate Ganache Glaze: Combine the heavy cream and corn syrup in a 1-quart heavy-bottomed saucepan. Heat just to boiling. Turn off heat, stir in the chocolate just until melted and smooth.

13. While the glaze is warm and liquid, spoon about 2 tablespoons of it over the top of one of the pastry strips. With a long flexible metal icing spatula spread a thin, even layer over its surface. Try to contain the glaze on top of the strip, guiding it with the spatula and preventing it from flowing down the sides. Repeat the procedure to glaze the second strip.

14. Without delay, cut a small tip from the paper cone, and pipe four evenly spaced lengthwise lines over the glazed surface of one strip. Repeat on the other strip. Then draw the tip of a small paring knife back and forth across the lines, pulling the chocolate slightly to create a marbling effect. Wipe the knife tip clean between strokes. Allow the glaze to dry at room temperature, about 1 hour.

15. With a sharp knife, slice each strip diagonally in alternate directions to form wedges, about 1 inch wide at the base and 1¼ inches wide at the top. Use a two-handed chopping motion, cutting straight down, rather than a sawing motion.

16. Store wedges in one layer in a covered foil-lined cardboard container, such as a cake box, at room temperature up to 2 days.

# hedgehogs

➤ **Makes 4 dozen 1½-inch edible pets**

These charming chocolate and rum buttercream creatures, each with its own personality, are known as *Igels* in Austria. They captured my heart in Belgium and Germany, and I know you'll love them too. Include them on an assorted miniature tray for a touch of delicious whimsy.

1. Dough: In a medium bowl, briefly blend the flour, cocoa powder, and rice flour with a wire whisk; set aside. In the large bowl of an electric mixer, cream the butter at medium-low speed until smooth, about 1 minute. Beat in the sugar at medium speed until fluffy, scraping down the sides of the bowl. Lower speed and gradually add the flour mixture, combining thoroughly.

2. Divide the dough in half; roll one portion at a time between two sheets of waxed paper to form a circle 10 inches in diameter and ⅛ inch thick. Leaving the dough between the waxed paper, transfer the circles to a baking sheet and refrigerate until firm, for at least 2 hours or up to 3 days; or freeze, well wrapped, up to 1 month.

3. Adjust rack to lower third of oven and preheat oven to 350 degrees F. Line two large cool baking sheets with parchment paper.

4. Remove one dough circle at a time from the refrigerator. Peel off top waxed paper sheet, replace it loosely on top, and flip the entire package over. Peel off and discard the second sheet of waxed paper.

## DOUGH

1¾ cup (245 grams) unsifted all-purpose flour

⅓ cup (35 grams) unsifted cocoa powder

¼ cup (45 grams) rice flour

7 ounces (1¾ sticks) unsalted butter, room temperature

⅔ cup (130 grams) granulated sugar

## FILLING

Rum Silk Buttercream

4 egg yolks

¼ cup water

½ cup (100 grams) granulated sugar

8 ounces (2 sticks) unsalted butter, room temperature

1 tablespoon dark rum

2½ ounces (½ cup) pine nuts

5. Pinch the wide end of a ½-inch plain decorating tip (such as Ateco #6) into an oval to make an oval cutter. Using the cutter, cut out oval shapes in the dough, and space them ½ inch apart on baking sheets. Bake, one sheet at a time, for 10 to 13 minutes, or until cookies appear dull brown and feel slightly firm (lightly touch a few). Place baking sheet on a wire rack until the cookies are completely cool. To store, stack in an airtight metal container at room temperature up to 1 week.

6. Rum Silk Buttercream: In the large bowl of an electric mixer, whip the egg yolks until light and fluffy, about 4 minutes. Remove bowl from mixer stand. In a 1-quart heavy-bottomed saucepan, combine the water and sugar over low heat. Stir occasionally, washing down any sugar crystals clinging to the sides of the pan with a brush dipped in cold water, until sugar is dissolved. Increase the heat and cook, without stirring, until the syrup reaches 238 degrees F on a candy thermometer. Pour into the center of the yolks and quickly whisk vigorously to combine. Return bowl to mixer, and whip at medium speed until the egg yolk mixture thickens and cools to body temperature, about 5 minutes. Maintaining medium speed, gradually add the butter to the cooled egg yolk mixture, a tablespoon at a time. Continue mixing until all the butter has been incorporated and the buttercream is smooth and homogeneous. Add the rum, whipping until thoroughly combined.

7. Set the cookies close together on one large clean baking sheet. Using a 14-inch pastry bag fitted with a ½-inch plain decorating tip (such as Ateco #6), pipe an oval bulb of buttercream on each cookie. Hold a cookie in one hand as you pipe with the other. Then stick eight pine nuts into each buttercream oval as illustrated. Refrigerate to firm the buttercream, at least 2 hours.

CONTINUED ➤

### DECORATION

Dark Chocolate Satin Glaze

¼ cup (1½ ounces) solid vegetable shortening

1 pound semisweet chocolate, chopped

### ROYAL ICING

1 cup (100 grams) unsifted powdered sugar

2 tablespoons (1 large) egg white

⅛ teaspoon cream of tartar

8. Dark Chocolate Satin Glaze: Combine the shortening and chocolate in a 3-quart mixing bowl. Place it over a saucepan filled with enough hot tap water (120 to 130 degrees F) to reach the bottom of the bowl. Stir the mixture occasionally until the glaze is liquid and smooth and registers close to 110 degrees F on a candy thermometer. If water begins to cool while melting the chocolate, maintain the 120-degree-F temperature over very low heat.

9. Place the chilled Hedgehogs an inch apart on two wire racks set over shallow baking pans to catch drips. Ladle about 2 tablespoons glaze over each Hedgehog, to cover completely. After masking the pastries, gently move each one slightly on the rack with a small metal spatula while the glaze is liquid, to remove chocolate drippings from its underside. This neat finish also keeps the pastries from sticking to the rack.

10. Pour the glaze from the baking pans back into the saucepan, and reheat. Pour through a sieve in case any cookie crumbs have fallen into it.

11. The warm glaze sets up quickly after touching the cold, firm buttercream, leaving a gorgeous sheen. Do not refrigerate the pastries after they have been glazed.

12. Royal Icing: When the glaze has set, mix the royal icing ingredients together in a 1½-quart mixing bowl. With a hand mixer on medium speed, whip until the mixture is thick and has a marshmallow-like consistency, about 5 minutes. Fill a small handmade paper cone with 2 tablespoons icing and pipe three tiny dots on each Hedgehog. Then, dip a toothpick into some of the remaining liquid chocolate glaze, and place a dot of it on two of the icing dots, forming the Hedgehog's eyes. Now their true personalities will be evident.

STEP 7

STEP 9

**NEAPOLITAN WEDGES** PG 171

PISTACHIO PETITS FOURS PG 283    LEMON MERINGUE TARTLETS PG 219

. . . . . . . . . . . . . . . . . . . . . . . . . . .

LEFT CHOCOLATE STARLETS PG 186

DREI AUGEN PG 56    PINEAPPLE POCKETS PG 60

MIMOSA ROSETTES PG 82

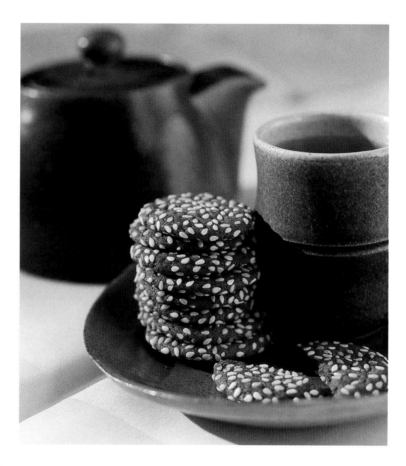

SESAME SPICE CHIPS PG 145

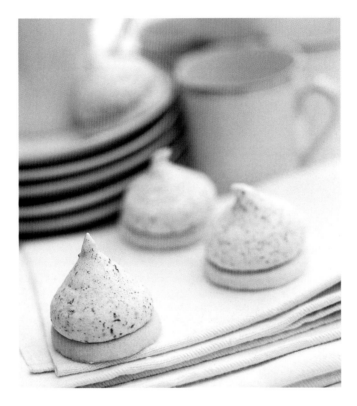

MERINGUE BUBBLES PG 95

. . . . . . . . . . . . . . . . . . . . . . . . . . . . . . . . . . .

RIGHT **S'MORE SQUARES** PG 298    **POLKA DOT MINICAKES** PG 300

**SCHEHERAZADE TARTLETS** PG 222    **POIRETTES** PG 226

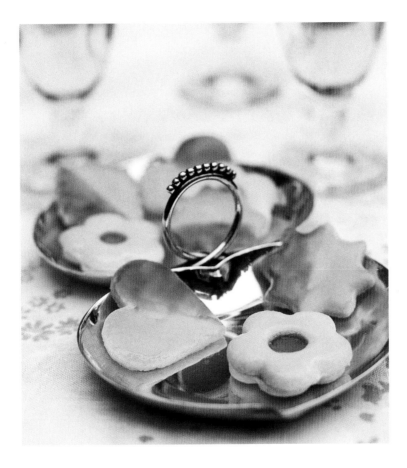

HARLEQUINS PG 51    APRICOT MEDALS PG 58

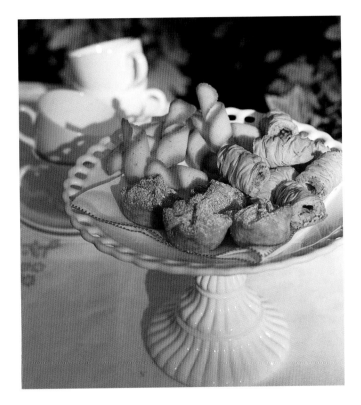

**SWEET CHEESE PUFFS** PG 236    **CRISPY CORKSCREWS** PG 128

**PHYLLO ACCORDIONS** PG 273

. . . . . . . . . . . . . . . . . . . . . . . . . . . . . . . . . . . . .

LEFT **GOLDEN CARAMELS** PG 326

TIFFANY RINGS ᴘɢ 180    CHOCOLATE-PISTACHIO TIGRÉS ᴘɢ 303

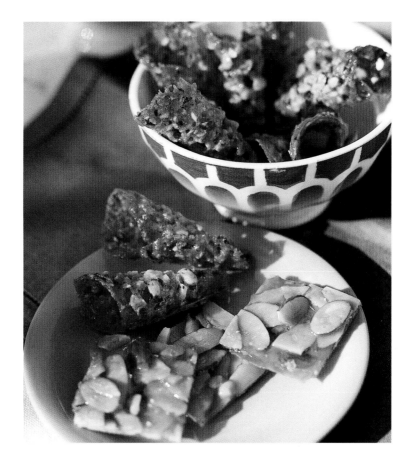

NOUGATINE CONES ᴘɢ 124    FLORENTINE SQUARES ᴘɢ 114

CANDIED LADY APPLES PG 328

· · · · · · · · · · · · · · · · · · · · · · · · · · · · · · · · · · · · ·

RIGHT MINIATURE CARAMEL CREAM VOL-AU-VENTS PG 262

SPICY TWIN THINS PG 139    LEMON-LACED GINGERSNAPS PG 154

**HEDGEHOGS** PG 174   **HONEY BEE MINICAKES** PG 286

13. Gently lift each pastry with a small metal spatula, and arrange in a single layer in a foil-lined cardboard container, such as a cake box. Cover and store at room temperature up to 2 days.

## DECORATING NOTE

An easier way to decorate these Hedgehogs is to omit the pine nuts. Coat them with the chocolate glaze and, before it sets up, apply chocolate sprinkles over two-thirds of each pastry. Pipe "eyes" on the uncovered portion with the royal icing.

# chocolate tulips

➤ **Makes 4 dozen 1½-inch cookies**

Dough is pressed into fluted tins and filled with an almond paste mixture to create these delicacies. Creamy chocolate ganache tops them to make delicious multilayered sweets. Their spectacular appearance is the result of a simple trick that transforms each dollop of ganache into a Chocolate Tulip.

1.  Adjust rack to lower third of oven and preheat oven to 350 degrees F. Arrange four dozen ungreased fluted tartlet tins, 1½ inches in diameter, close together on a baking sheet that measures at least 12 x 15½ x ½ inches.

2.  Dough: Pinch off the dough, 1 teaspoon at a time, and drop into fluted tins. One by one, roll the dough pieces into balls in the palms of your hands. With index finger, press center of each dough ball into a tin, and then press dough up the sides while rotating tin to distribute it evenly.

3.  Almond Paste Frangipane Filling: Process all the filling ingredients in a food processor bowl until the mixture is smooth. Fill each tartlet with about 1 teaspoon filling.

4.  Bake tartlets on the baking sheet for 15 to 20 minutes, or until the filling is golden and the crust is pale golden. Place baking sheet on a wire rack until tins are cool enough to touch, about 10 minutes. Squeeze each tin gently with your thumb and forefinger, turn it upside down, and let the tartlet drop into the palm of your hand. If it's difficult to release the tartlets, they could be either underbaked or left to cool too long in the tins. In that case, return to the oven for a few minutes more.

## DOUGH

½ recipe Miniature Tartlet Pastry (page 205)

## ALMOND PASTE FRANGIPANE FILLING

4 ounces (½ cup) almond paste

⅓ cup (65 grams) granulated sugar

1 teaspoon dark rum

1 teaspoon pure vanilla extract

1 ounce (2 tablespoons) unsalted butter, room temperature

## DECORATION

Chocolate Ganache Cream

12 ounces semisweet chocolate, chopped

1 cup (8 ounces) heavy cream

3 ounces (6 tablespoons) unsalted butter, room temperature

½ cup (50 grams) unsifted cocoa powder (optional)

5. Chocolate Ganache Cream: When the tartlets are completely cool, place the chocolate in a 3-quart mixing bowl. In a small saucepan, heat the cream until it boils. Pour over the chocolate pieces and whisk together until chocolate melts and mixture is shiny. Add the butter, whisking it in 1 tablespoon at a time, until completely blended. Set aside at room temperature about 30 minutes, or until it develops enough body to stay in place without falling off a rubber spatula.

6. Scoop about 1 to 2 teaspoons of the ganache on a small metal spatula, and apply it on top of a tartlet as illustrated. Manipulate the ganache with the spatula to a point in the center. Remove excess ganache from the spatula, and begin with another portion for the next tartlet. Repeat until all the tartlets are covered, placing them on a clean baking sheet as each is finished. Refrigerate not more than 30 minutes, or just long enough to partially firm the ganache.

STEP 6

STEP 7

7. Remove the tartlets from the refrigerator, and, if desired, gently tap cocoa through a sieve over each tartlet. Make three separate diagonal slices in each chilled ganache dome with the end of a small, flexible metal icing spatula as illustrated. Dip the spatula's blade into very hot water before each diagonal slice, and wipe the blade clean for the next cut. As you cut, press each portion of chocolate slightly outward, forming a petal effect; a small pyramid is formed in the center after you have completed the three slices.

8. Stack undecorated cookies in airtight sturdy plastic containers, separating the layers with waxed paper, and freeze up to 1 month. Store decorated cookies in one layer in covered, foil-lined cardboard containers, such as cake boxes, at room temperature up to 3 days.

## VARIATION NOTE

Pipe out mounds of the ganache cream on top of each tartlet in the shape of a candy "kiss." (Pipe the ganache when you can manipulate it as the instructions direct in the recipe above.)

# tiffany rings

➤ **Makes 3½ dozen 1½-inch cookies**

Maple and milk chocolate make a dynamic duo in these cookies which get their name from the hole that's cut from the middle of each small round of thinly rolled dough. These tender cookies, sweetened with both maple sugar and maple syrup, are decorated with a shiny two-tone chocolate glaze.

1. Dough: In a medium bowl, blend the flour and salt briefly with a wire whisk; set aside. In the large bowl of an electric mixer, cream the butter at medium-low speed until smooth, about 1 minute. Beat in the sugars at medium speed until the mixture is well combined and slightly fluffy. With a rubber spatula, scrape down the sides of the bowl. Beat in the maple syrup and vanilla until smooth and blended. Lower mixer speed, and gradually blend in the flour mixture until the mixture is thoroughly combined.

2. Divide the dough in half; roll out each portion of dough between two sheets of waxed paper to form a circle 11 inches in diameter and ⅛ inch thick. Leaving the dough between the sheets of waxed paper, transfer the circles to a baking sheet and refrigerate until firm, for at least 2 hours or up to 3 days; or freeze, well wrapped, up to 1 month.

3. Adjust rack to lower third of oven and preheat oven to 325 degrees F. Line two cool baking sheets with parchment paper.

4. Remove one dough circle package at a time from the refrigerator. Peel off top waxed paper sheet, replace it loosely on top, and flip the entire package over. Peel off and discard the second sheet of waxed paper.

## DOUGH

2⅓ cups (325 grams) unsifted all-purpose flour

⅛ teaspoon salt

8 ounces (2 sticks) unsalted butter, room temperature

¼ cup (50 grams) granulated sugar

¼ cup (40 grams) granulated pure maple sugar

2 tablespoons pure maple syrup

1 teaspoon pure vanilla extract

## DECORATION

Milk Chocolate Suede Glaze

¼ cup (1½ ounces) solid vegetable shortening

1 pound milk chocolate, finely chopped

2 ounces semisweet chocolate, melted

5. Using a 1½-inch round cutter, cut out circles in the dough. Put the circles ½ inch apart on baking sheets. Using a ½-inch plain decorating tip (such as Ateco #6) as a cutter, cut out a hole in the center of each cookie. (Dough from the centers is reusable.)

6. Bake, one sheet at a time, for 8 to 10 minutes, or until the cookies are no longer shiny, are light beige, and feel slightly firm (lightly touch a few). Place baking sheet on a wire rack to cool cookies completely.

7. Milk Chocolate Suede Glaze: Combine the shortening and milk chocolate in a 3-quart mixing bowl. Place it over a saucepan filled with enough hot tap water (120 degrees F) to reach the bottom of the bowl. Stir the mixture occasionally until the glaze is liquid, smooth, and close to 110 degrees F. If water begins to cool while melting the chocolate, maintain the 120-degree-F temperature over very low heat.

8. Set the cookies, spacing them 1 inch apart, on wire racks set over shallow baking pans to catch drips. Ladle about 2 tablespoons glaze over each cookie, masking it completely. After masking pastries, gently move each one slightly on the rack with a small metal spatula while the glaze is liquid, to remove chocolate drippings from its underside. This neat finish also keeps the pastries from sticking to the rack.

9. Using a small handmade paper cone with its tip snipped off, pipe thin lines of the liquid semisweet chocolate, zigzag fashion, back and forth over each glazed cookie.

10. Stack undecorated cookies in an airtight metal container and store up to 1 week. Store decorated cookies in one layer in a covered foil-lined cardboard container, such as a cake box, at room temperature up to 2 days.

CONTINUED ➤

## BAKING NOTES

You can find pure granulated maple sugar in specialty food stores and specialty food sections in supermarkets.

It's tricky to incorporate milk chocolate into a cookie dough and achieve a tasty result. The solution is to use it as an ingredient in a glaze, as I do in these cookies.

# chocolate coins

➤ Makes 5 dozen 1¼-inch cookies

Chocolate, cocoa powder, and almond paste collaborate to create a delicate balance of flavors in these luxurious cookies. Dough is formed into a roll and sliced into coins. After baking, thinly rolled chocolate marzipan, the same diameter as the cookie, is used to top each one before a shiny chocolate glaze is applied. A small scalloped piece of marzipan and a jewel-like dot of jelly crown each cookie to give it a touch of drama.

1. Dough: In a bowl, whisk the flour and salt briefly with a wire whisk; set aside. In the large bowl of an electric mixer, break up the almond paste at low speed. Add the sugar and continue to mix until incorporated. Increase speed to medium and beat in the butter until the mixture is smooth, scraping down the sides of the bowl. Add the egg yolk, then the vanilla, and beat until mixture is fluffy. Lower speed, and gradually blend in the dry ingredients, combining thoroughly.

2. Divide the dough in half, and roll each portion into one 9-inch-long cylinder about 1¼ inches in diameter. Wrap in plastic and refrigerate until firm, at least 4 hours or up to 3 days, or freeze, well wrapped, up to 1 month.

3. Adjust rack to lower third of oven and preheat oven to 325 degrees F. Line two large cool baking sheets with parchment paper.

4. Remove one cylinder of dough at a time from refrigerator. Using a sharp knife, slice the dough into rounds ⅛ inch thick, and set them about ½ inch apart on baking sheets.

5. Bake, one sheet at a time, for 8 to 10 minutes, or until the cookies are no longer shiny and feel firm (lightly touch a few). Place baking sheet on a wire rack until cookies are completely cool.

CONTINUED ➤

## DOUGH

1 cup (140 grams) unsifted all-purpose flour

⅛ teaspoon salt

2½ ounces (¼ cup) almond paste, room temperature

⅓ cup (65 grams) packed light brown sugar

3 ounces (6 tablespoons) unsalted butter, room temperature

1 egg yolk

¼ teaspoon pure vanilla extract

## CHOCOLATE MARZIPAN FILLING

2 cups (200 grams) unsifted powdered sugar

¼ cup (25 grams) unsifted cocoa powder

½ teaspoon coffee powder

8 ounces (scant 1 cup) almond paste, room temperature

2 ounces (4 tablespoons) unsalted butter

2 tablespoons light corn syrup

⅛ teaspoon each pure vanilla and almond extract

6. Chocolate Marzipan Filling: In a medium bowl, blend the powdered sugar, cocoa powder, and coffee powder briefly with a wire whisk; set aside. In the large bowl of an electric mixer, break up the almond paste at low speed. Add the butter, then the corn syrup and the vanilla and almond extracts, and mix until smooth and incorporated, scraping down the sides of the bowl. Blend in the dry ingredients just until mixture is thoroughly combined.

7. Roll out the marzipan less than ⅛ inch thick on a surface lightly dusted with powdered sugar. Using a round cookie cutter the same dimension as cookies, cut out circles and set one on top of each cookie.

8. European Chocolate Glaze: In a 1-quart heavy-bottomed saucepan, heat the water with the sugar, stirring occasionally to dissolve the sugar. Bring just to a boil. Turn off heat, and stir in the chocolates and oil until smooth. If necessary, stir in additional hot tap water to adjust glaze's viscosity for coating cookies.

9. Set the cookies 1 inch apart on wire racks set over shallow baking pans to catch drips. Then, ladle about 2 tablespoons warm and liquid glaze over each cookie, to cover completely. After masking pastries, gently move each one slightly on the rack with a small metal spatula while the glaze is liquid, to remove chocolate drippings from its underside. This neat finish also keeps the pastries from sticking to the rack.

10. When glaze has set, after about 1 hour, roll out the marzipan 1/16 inch thick on a surface lightly dusted with powdered sugar. Using a ½-inch round scalloped cutter, cut out shapes and place one in the center of each glazed cookie. Using a small paper cone with its tip snipped off, pipe a tiny dot of jelly in the center of each scalloped circle.

## DECORATION

European Chocolate Glaze

⅔ cup water

1 cup plus 2 tablespoons (225 grams) granulated sugar

8 ounces semisweet chocolate, finely chopped

4 ounces unsweetened chocolate, finely chopped

2 teaspoons vegetable oil

3 ounces (⅓ cup) marzipan (See Decorating Note)

2 tablespoons red currant jelly

11. Stack undecorated cookies in an airtight metal container and store up to 1 week. Store decorated cookies in one layer in a covered, foil-lined cardboard container, such as a cake box, at room temperature up to 1 day.

## DECORATING NOTE

I make the chocolate marzipan for the filling from scratch to achieve the best flavor. However, when I need unflavored marzipan, as for the Chocolate Coins decoration, I save time and buy Odense-brand marzipan.

# chocolate starlets

➤ Makes 4 dozen 1½-inch tartlets

These are rich with the flavor of walnuts, a hint of spice, and, of course, chocolate. Decorating them couldn't be easier, after you turn the fluted tartlets over to show off their star-like shape.

1. Adjust rack to lower third of oven and preheat oven to 350 degrees F. Arrange four dozen ungreased fluted tins, 1½ inches in diameter, close on a large baking sheet that measures at least 12 x 15½ x ½ inches.

2. Dough: Pinch off the dough, 1 teaspoon at a time, and drop into fluted tins. One by one, roll dough pieces into balls in the palms of your hands. With index finger, press center of each dough ball into a tin; then press dough up the sides of the tin while rotating the tin to distribute the dough evenly.

3. Filling: In a medium bowl, whisk the flour, ground nuts, and cinnamon to blend; set aside. In the large bowl of an electric mixer at medium-low speed, cream the butter in a 1½-quart mixing bowl until soft, creamy, and smooth, about 30 seconds. Beat in the sugar until the mixture is lighter in texture and the sugar has been absorbed. Add the yolks and continue mixing until incorporated and smooth. Lower speed, and gradually add the dry ingredients until the mixture is smooth and thoroughly combined.

4. Using a 16-inch pastry bag fitted with a ⅜-inch plain decorating tip (such as Ateco #3), pipe the equivalent of ½ teaspoon of filling into each pastry-lined tin. Lift the tip slightly as each tin is filled in order to cut off the flow of filling. (Piping filling from a pastry bag is easier, more uniform, and less fattening than using a spoon since it reduces the temptation of licking your finger clean after scooping filling from the spoon.)

## DOUGH

½ recipe Chocolate Miniature Tartlet Pastry (page 214)

## FILLING

½ cup (70 grams) unsifted all-purpose flour

5 ounces (1½ cups) walnuts, finely ground

½ teaspoon ground cinnamon

4 ounces (1 stick) unsalted butter, room temperature

½ cup plus 2 tablespoons (125 grams) granulated sugar

3 egg yolks

## DECORATION

½ cup (50 grams) unsifted powdered sugar

### CHOCOLATE HONEY GANACHE GLAZE

2 tablespoons heavy cream

2 teaspoons honey

2 ounces semisweet chocolate, finely chopped

5. Bake for about 15 minutes, or until the top of the filling is light golden and the chocolate crust is no longer shiny but dull and feels slightly firm to the touch. Cool the tartlets, on the baking sheet, on a rack for 10 minutes, or until cool enough to touch. Remove each tartlet by pinching the tin with thumb and forefinger and turning it upside down, so that the pastry falls into your hand.

6. Decoration: Place tartlets upside down on a rack so each tartlet displays its star shape. Tap the powdered sugar from a sieve to sprinkle sugar over the top of each tartlet.

7. Chocolate Honey Ganache Glaze: Combine the heavy cream and honey in a small heavy-bottomed saucepan. Heat just to boiling. Turn off heat, stir in the chocolate just until melted and smooth. Set aside just until it thickens to the consistency of honey, about 30 minutes. Fill a small handmade paper cone half full of the glaze, snip off the cone's tip, and pipe a small dot in the center of each tartlet.

8. Stack undecorated tartlets in an airtight metal container and store at room temperature up to 10 days, or freeze up to 1 month. Store decorated tartlets in a single layer in a covered, foil-lined cardboard container, such as a cake box, at room temperature up to 2 days.

# white blossom circles

➤ **Makes 8 dozen 1½-inch cookies**

Making these chocolate shortbread cookies is a cinch. To dress them up, all you do is top each circle with a swirl of white chocolate ganache.

1. Dough: In a medium bowl, blend the flour, cocoa powder, and rice flour briefly with a wire whisk; set aside. In the large bowl of an electric mixer, cream the butter at medium-low speed until smooth, about 1 minute. Beat in the sugar at medium speed until well combined and slightly fluffy, scraping down the sides of the bowl. Lower speed, and gradually add the flour mixture, combining thoroughly.

2. Divide the dough in quarters. Form into four cylinders 6 inches long and 1¼ inches in diameter. Roll each cylinder in the additional granulated sugar to coat. Wrap in plastic and refrigerate until firm, for at least 4 hours or up to 3 days; or freeze, well wrapped, up to 1 month.

3. Adjust rack to lower third of oven and preheat oven to 300 degrees F. Line two large cool baking sheets with parchment paper.

4. Remove one cylinder of dough at a time from refrigerator. Using a sharp knife, cut ³⁄₁₆-inch-thick slices from dough and place ¾ inch apart on baking sheets.

5. Bake, one sheet at a time, for 12 to 14 minutes, or until the cookies are no longer shiny and feel slightly firm and set (lightly touch a few). Do not overbake, since chocolate scorches easily. Place baking sheet on a wire rack to cool. Lift cookies from parchment when cool.

**DOUGH**

1¾ cups (245 grams) unsifted all-purpose flour

⅓ cup (35 grams) unsifted cocoa powder

¼ cup (45 grams) rice flour

7 ounces (1¾ sticks) unsalted butter, room temperature

⅔ cup (130 grams) granulated sugar

Additional granulated sugar for coating

**WHITE CHOCOLATE GANACHE**

⅓ cup (2½ ounces) heavy cream

5 ounces white chocolate, finely chopped

6. White Chocolate Ganache: Combine the cream and white chocolate in a 3-quart bowl. Place it over a saucepan filled with enough hot tap water (120 degrees F) to reach the bottom of the container. Stir the mixture occasionally until it is smooth. If water begins to cool while melting the chocolate, maintain the 120-degree-F temperature over very low heat. Set the ganache aside at room temperature for about 30 minutes or until it develops enough body that when a small amount is lifted on a rubber spatula, it stays in place without falling off.

7. With a 14-inch pastry bag fitted with a swirl-shaped decorating tip (such as Ateco #5-A), pipe a flower-like form on each cookie.

8. Stack undecorated cookies in an airtight metal container and store at room temperature up to 1 week; or freeze up to 1 month. Store decorated cookies in a single layer in a covered foil-lined cardboard container, such as a cake box, at room temperature up to 2 days.

### DECORATING NOTE

An alternate decoration is to place five small white chocolate petals on each cookie to form a flower. To make the petals, place a strip of aluminum foil on a flat work surface. Melt 2 ounces finely chopped white chocolate in a small bowl set over a pan of water at 110 degrees F, stirring occasionally until smooth. Remove bowl from water and, with a rubber spatula, stir chocolate occasionally to cool it a bit, about 5 minutes. While it is still smooth and liquid, dip the back side of a small spoon into the chocolate, and smear it gently onto the foil, moving the spoon toward you. Repeat the procedure using about ⅛ teaspoon chocolate for each petal. Place in a cool room and allow the petals to set until firm. Slip the blade of a small metal spatula under each one to release it from the foil.

# cocoa cavaliers

➤ **Makes 5 dozen 1½-inch cookies**

. . . . . . . . . . . . . . . . . . . . . . . . . . .

Here's an easy technique for converting thick cylinders of dough into triangular shapes. In this case, a chocolate triangle-shaped cookie is topped with an almond paste streusel.

1. Dough: In a medium bowl, blend the flour and cocoa powder briefly with a wire whisk; set aside. In the large bowl of an electric mixer, cream the butter at medium-low speed until smooth, about 1 minute. Beat in the sugar at medium speed until well combined and slightly fluffy, scraping down the sides of the bowl. Lower speed, and gradually add the flour mixture, combining thoroughly.

2. Divide the dough in thirds and roll each portion of dough into a cylinder about 8 inches long. Wrap each cylinder in plastic wrap. Working with one cylinder at a time, place a 1½-inch-wide and at least 12-inch-long ruler along *each* long side of the dough cylinder, so that both rulers are perpendicular to the work surface. Apply enough pressure to both rulers to slant them so that they meet at the top, thereby shaping the dough cylinder into a triangular log. This procedure extends the dough to about 9 inches. Twist the plastic wrap at each end to close. Refrigerate the logs until firm, for at least 4 hours or up to 3 days; or freeze, well wrapped, up to 1 month.

3. Almond Paste Streusel: In a 3-quart bowl, mix the almond paste and sugar with your fingertips to remove any lumps in the almond paste. Add the butter until blended. Mix in the flour and, with fingertips, separate the mixture into tiny crumbly pieces. Cover and set aside at room temperature.

## DOUGH

1½ cups (210 grams) unsifted all-purpose flour

½ cup (50 grams) unsifted cocoa powder

6 ounces (1½ sticks) unsalted butter, room temperature

⅔ cup (130 grams) granulated sugar

## ALMOND PASTE STREUSEL

3 ounces (⅓ cup) almond paste, room temperature

2 tablespoons packed light brown sugar

1½ ounces (3 tablespoons) unsalted butter, room temperature

⅔ cup (90 grams) unsifted all-purpose flour

4. Adjust rack to lower third of oven and preheat oven to 325 degrees F. Line two large cool baking sheets with parchment paper.

5. Remove one triangular dough log from the refrigerator at a time. Using a sharp knife, cut ³⁄₁₆-inch-thick slices and space ½ inch apart on baking sheet. Using a small pastry brush, lightly brush each cookie with water, and then carefully sprinkle streusel over top (any streusel on baking sheet will burn as cookies bake). Repeat the procedure for the remaining logs of dough.

6. Bake, one sheet at a time, for 10 to 12 minutes, or until the cookies are no longer shiny but appear dull and feel slightly firm (lightly touch a few). Do not overbake and do not let the streusel color more than pale blond. Place baking sheet on a wire rack to cool. Lift cookies from parchment when cool.

7. Stack in an airtight metal container and store at room temperature up to 1 week; or freeze up to 1 month.

### BAKING NOTES

If the dough is not cohesive after mixing it, add 1 tablespoon water and continue to mix until thoroughly combined.

In this recipe, use water instead of an egg wash. Water helps the streusel adhere to the cookies and becomes invisible during baking through evaporation. An egg wash would leave a film on the chocolate dough and could burn during baking.

STEP 2

# chocolate pistachio cigarettes

➤ **Makes 3½ dozen 1½-inch-long cigarettes**

. . . . . . . . . . . . . . . . . . . . . . . . . .

To decorate these intensely flavored chocolate cookies, dip both ends in melted chocolate, then in blanched, roasted finely ground pistachio nuts.

1.  Adjust rack to lower third of oven and preheat oven to 375 degrees F. Unwrap an end of a chilled stick of unsalted butter and rub it over two large cool Teflon-coated baking sheets to apply a very thin film of fat.

2.  Batter: In a small bowl, briefly blend the flour and the cocoa powder with a wire whisk or rubber spatula; set aside. In the large bowl of an electric mixer, cream the butter at medium speed until smooth, about 2 minutes. Beat in the sugar until mixture is light and fluffy. Gradually add the egg whites, then the vanilla. Don't worry if the mixture appears curdled at this point. Lower mixer speed and blend in dry ingredients until mixture is smooth and thoroughly combined.

3.  Drop four ½ teaspoonsful batter on each baking sheet. Using a small offset metal spatula, spread into paper-thin squares about 1½ x 1½ inches.

4.  Bake, one sheet at a time, for 5 to 7 minutes, or until the wafers no longer appear glossy, but are dull. Do not overbake or cookies will scorch. Place baking sheet on a wire rack.

5.  While cookies are warm and pliable, roll one at a time, baked-bottom side in, around a wooden dowel ⅜ inch in diameter and 6 inches long. After shaping a cookie, gently slip it off the dowel to a wire rack until cool. Repeat baking and rolling procedure with the remaining batter.

## BATTER

⅓ cup (45 grams) unsifted all-purpose flour

2 tablespoons unsifted cocoa powder

2 ounces (½ stick) unsalted butter, room temperature

½ cup (100 grams) granulated sugar

¼ cup (about 2 large) egg whites, room temperature

1 teaspoon pure vanilla extract

## DECORATION

2 ounces semisweet chocolate, finely chopped

2 ounces pistachios, blanched, roasted, and finely ground

6. Decoration: Melt the chocolate in a small bowl set over a saucepan of hot water at 120 degrees F. Dip just the tips of the cigarette cookies in the chocolate, then in the ground pistachio nuts. Set cookies on aluminum foil until chocolate sets.

7. Stack cigarettes in an airtight metal container and store at room temperature up to 3 days. (See the information on nontoxic blue crystals on page 22.)

### BAKING NOTE

When baking these cookies, it won't take too long to complete the batch if you set up a system similar to a production line. When I remove one baking sheet from the oven, I replace it with another, then I shape the just-baked cigarettes while they are still warm, then I form batter into squares on another sheet to exchange with the one that is baking. This keeps a constant flow of baking and shaping.

# chocolate shadows

➤ **Makes 6 dozen 1½-inch cookies**

When I want a simple but elegant cookie for entertaining, I bake these butter cookies topped with a swirl of chocolate dough. Orange sorbet and orange sections served in stem glasses with these fine-textured Chocolate Shadows make a grand dessert.

1. Butter Dough: In the large bowl of an electric mixer, cream the butter at medium-low speed until smooth, about 1 minute. Beat in the sugars at medium speed until creamy. Add the egg yolk, and then the vanilla, beating just until fluffy, and scraping down the sides of the bowl. Lower mixer speed, gradually add the flour, and mix just until thoroughly combined.

2. Divide the dough in half; roll one portion at a time between two sheets of waxed paper to form a circle about 11 inches in diameter and ⅛ inch thick. Leaving the dough between the sheets of waxed paper, transfer the circles to a baking sheet and refrigerate until firm, at least 2 hours or up to 3 days; or freeze, well wrapped, up to 1 month.

3. Chocolate Dough: In a mixing bowl, blend the flour and salt briefly with a wire whisk; set aside. In the large bowl of an electric mixer, cream the butter at medium-low speed until fluffy. Add the sugar and continue to mix until well combined and fluffy, scraping down the sides of the bowl. Add the cocoa powder, beating until incorporated. Then beat in the eggs, one at a time, until the mixture is fluffy. Add the orange zest. Lower speed, and gradually blend in the flour mixture, combining thoroughly; set aside.

4. Adjust rack to lower third of oven and preheat oven to 325 degrees F. Line two large cool baking sheets with parchment paper.

## BUTTER DOUGH

6 ounces (1½ sticks) unsalted butter, room temperature

¼ cup (50 grams) granulated sugar

½ cup (50 grams) unsifted powdered sugar

1 egg yolk

1 teaspoon pure vanilla extract

1½ cups (210 grams) unsifted all-purpose flour

## CHOCOLATE DOUGH

2 cups (280 grams) unsifted all-purpose flour

⅛ teaspoon salt

8 ounces (2 sticks) unsalted butter, room temperature

¾ cup (150 grams) granulated sugar

½ cup (50 grams) unsifted cocoa powder

3 large eggs, room temperature

2 teaspoons finely grated orange zest

5. Remove one butter dough package at a time from the refrigerator. Peel off top waxed paper sheet, replace it loosely on top, and flip the entire package over. Peel off and discard the second sheet of waxed paper.

6. Using a 1½-inch round scalloped cookie cutter, cut out shapes in the dough. Place the cutouts about ½ inch apart on baking sheets.

7. Fill a 16-inch pastry bag fitted with an open star decorating tip (such as Ateco #2) with half the chocolate dough. Pipe a rosette of chocolate dough the equivalent of 1 teaspoon on top of each unbaked butter cookie. Refill bag with the remaining dough when needed.

8. Bake, one sheet at a time, for 10 minutes, or until the cookies' scalloped edges and bottoms are faintly colored. Do not overbake. Place baking sheet on a wire rack for 10 minutes. Lift cookies from parchment to a rack to cool completely.

9. Decoration: Heat the jam just to warm and liquefy it. Using a small pastry brush, coat the chocolate rosettes with the jam.

10. Chocolate Butter: Melt the butter and chocolate in a small bowl set over a saucepan of water at 120 degrees F. Using a small handmade paper cone with its tip snipped off, pipe a small dot of chocolate on top of each cookie.

11. Stack undecorated cookies in an airtight metal container, using strips of aluminum foil between layers to pad the cookies and prevent abrasions that might disturb the cookies' shapes, and store at room temperature up to 1 week; or freeze, well wrapped, up to 1 month. (Aluminum foil does not absorb the butter from the cookies.) Store decorated cookies in one layer in covered foil-lined cardboard containers, such as cake boxes, at room temperature up to 3 days.

## TECHNIQUE NOTE

Use only half the chocolate dough in the pastry bag at a time. Filling it too full makes the pastry bag difficult to manipulate.

### DECORATION

½ cup strained apricot or cherry jam

### CHOCOLATE BUTTER

1 ounce (2 tablespoons) unsalted butter

3 ounces semisweet chocolate, finely chopped

# chocolate
# candy-cane cookies

➤ **Makes about 30 sandwiched cookies**

. . . . . . . . . . . . . . . . . . . . . . . . . . . . . . . . . .

Like a cup of rich cocoa stirred with a peppermint stick, these brownie-like cookies have a swirled candy-cane center.

1. Sift the flour, cocoa powder, and baking powder onto a sheet of waxed paper; set aside. In a small saucepan, melt the butter and chocolate over very low heat. Remove from heat; stir in the sugar. Pour into a large bowl; set aside to cool slightly, about 10 minutes. Add the eggs and vanilla, stirring just until blended. Stir in the flour mixture.

2. Divide the dough mixture in half and roll each portion between two sheets of waxed paper to form a circle 11½ inches in diameter and ³⁄₁₆ inch thick. Remove the waxed paper from one of the circles. Using a 1½-inch round cutter, cut out circles in the dough. Using the narrow end of a ¾-inch plain pastry tip (such as Ateco #9) as a cutter, cut out a hole in the center of each circle. Don't remove any of the cutouts from dough; keep rounds intact on waxed paper. Replace waxed paper on top of dough. Leaving the dough circles between the waxed paper, stack them on a baking sheet and refrigerate until firm, for at least 4 hours or up to 3 days.

3. Adjust rack to lower third of oven and preheat oven to 350 degrees F. Line two large baking sheets with parchment paper.

1½ cups (210 grams) unsifted all-purpose flour

2 tablespoons unsifted cocoa powder

⅛ teaspoon baking powder

4 ounces (1 stick) unsalted butter

6 ounces unsweetened chocolate, chopped

1 cup (200 grams) granulated sugar

2 large eggs

1 teaspoon pure vanilla extract

6 small (2 ounces) candy canes, finely chopped

4. Remove the dough packages from the refrigerator. Peel off top sheet of waxed paper, replace it loosely on top, and flip the entire package over. Peel off and discard the second sheet of waxed paper. Using the 1½-inch round cutter, cut out circles in the uncut dough. Space the cookies ½ inch apart on a baking sheet. Center a dough ring with a hole on top of a solid round, and gently press just to sandwich the two cookies together. Spoon about ¼ teaspoon chopped candy cane in the center of each cookie. Repeat with the remaining cookies. Bake for 8 minutes only, or just until the candy begins to melt (not liquefy). Transfer cookies to a rack to cool.

5. Stack in an airtight plastic container at room temperature up to 3 days; or freeze up to 10 days.

# dutch chocolate minicakes

➤ Makes 2½ dozen 1½-inch minicakes

· · · · · · · · · · · · · · · · · · · · · · · · · · · · · · · · · · · ·

With the taste and texture of rich, chewy brownies, these bite-sized baby cakes were a signature pastry when I owned my baking business. Baked in miniature muffin cups, the batter is given added zing by hazelnuts, cocoa powder, and semisweet chocolate.

1. Adjust rack to lower third of oven and preheat oven to 350 degrees F. Line 2½ dozen miniature muffin cups that measure 1⅞ x ¾ inches with miniature cupcake liners.

2. Batter: Sift the flour, cocoa powder, and baking powder on a sheet of waxed paper; set aside. In a small saucepan, melt the butter and chocolate over very low heat. Remove from heat; stir in the granulated sugar. Pour into a 3-quart mixing bowl; set aside to cool slightly, about 5 minutes. Add the eggs and vanilla, stirring just until blended. Stir in the flour mixture, then the nuts.

3. Fill each paper-lined muffin cup three-quarters full. Bake in preheated oven for 10 minutes only. Don't overbake. Remove pans to wire racks to cool for 5 minutes to allow cakes to firm a bit. Carefully remove cakes to other racks to cool.

4. Decoration: Sprinkle with the powdered sugar before serving.

5. These are best eaten the same day they are baked; or freeze, in airtight sturdy plastic containers, up to 1 month.

## BATTER

⅓ cup (46 grams) unsifted all-purpose flour

1 tablespoon unsifted cocoa powder

½ teaspoon baking powder

3 ounces (6 tablespoons) unsalted butter

6 ounces semisweet chocolate, chopped

½ cup (100 grams) granulated sugar

2 large eggs

1 teaspoon pure vanilla extract

4 ounces (1 scant cup) toasted hazelnuts, coarsely chopped to yield 1 cup

## DECORATION

¼ cup (25 grams) unsifted powdered sugar

# miniature pastries

The key to making miniature
pastries successfully is the
proper blending of fat and flour

**Miniature pastry doughs can be flaky**, tender, crisp, and/or short according to how you blend the butter with the flour.

### MIXING MINIATURE PASTRY DOUGHS

The ratio of butter to flour, the butter's temperature, and the type of liquid added, such as sour cream, egg, or water, all contribute to the texture of miniature pastries. However, the key to making miniature pastries successfully is the proper blending of fat and flour.

In Sour Cream Pastry (page 235), it's the incomplete blending of chilled butter into the flour that gives it a flaky texture. In Cream Cheese Pastry (page 251), the chilled butter is blended more intimately into the flour to make it tender, rather than flaky or crisp. And in Miniature Tartlet Pastry (page 205), it's the complete blending of the butter into the sugar and flour that yields a short, crisp, and tender crust.

In Heavy Cream Flaky Pastry (page 257), chilled butter is blended into the flour until the particles are the size of small peas before the dough is rolled and folded to produce a flaky and tender pastry that lifts slightly during baking. Blitz Puff Pastry (page 266) has a crisp, flaky texture similar to that of traditional puff pastry. Though the Blitz may not rise as high, it's quicker and easier to make.

Though each recipe specifies proper blending procedures for successful results, you may choose to make the pastry either by hand or machine.

Pastries, especially small quantities, made by hand are flakier, since there's less chance of overmanipulating. Hands, even using a metal pastry blender, move more slowly than a machine, giving you more control when blending the butter into the flour.

But that is not to say that very fine pastries cannot be made in a heavy-duty mixer or a food processor. When using a mixer, use the paddle attachment and blend the butter into the flour on low speed.

## ROLLING MINIATURE PASTRY DOUGHS

A cool, smooth-surfaced work area at about hip level provides the best leverage for rolling the dough.

To roll a rectangular or square shape, begin with an oblong or square piece of chilled dough. Set it on a lightly floured work surface. Flatten the dough lightly. Roll from the center away from you, then lift the rolling pin and return it to the center and roll toward you, each time stopping short of the edges. For uniform thickness, use even strokes. Lift dough often to make sure it does not stick. Redust the work surface with just enough flour to keep the dough sliding as it extends without sticking. If the rolling pin sticks to the dough, lightly dust it with flour.

To lift a large piece of dough without tearing or stretching it, roll the pastry loosely onto the rolling pin, and transfer it to a baking sheet or wherever the recipe specifies.

Never turn the dough over and roll on the other side. If dough sticks to the work surface, carefully slide a metal spatula under the stuck portion, and then lift dough and dust surface with a little flour. Rub off any pieces of dough adhering to the rolling pin; they could puncture the dough.

To roll a circular shape, begin with a round disk of chilled dough. Beginning in the center of the disk, push the rolling pin outward in one stroke, using enough pressure to extend the dough gradually. Avoid rolling over the edges; this helps avoid cracking or creating too thin an edge. Lift and rotate the dough a one-eighth turn clockwise (one-eighth turns keep the dough circular, one-quarter turns make it square). Follow procedures described for the rectangular or square shape, except always roll dough from the center outward.

# tartlet miniatures

miniature tartlet pastry .......................205

caramel carmenitas ...........................207

garnet tartlets .................................210

rose tartlets ...................................212

double chocolate tartlets .....................214

chocolate cherry chaps .......................216

mazarine tartlets ..............................217

lemon meringue tartlets .....................219

raspberry lemon tartlets .....................221

scheherazade tartlets ........................222

jade buttercups ...............................224

poirettes .......................................226

lemon drops ...................................228

swiss bettinas .................................230

midas cups ....................................231

# miniature tartlet pastry

➤ **Makes 8 dozen round fluted miniature tartlet shells, 1½ inches in diameter**

This favorite not-too-sweet cookie recipe is my first choice for miniature tartlet shells. The butter-rich, not overly sweet, egg-enriched dough with fat intimately mixed into the sugar and flour yields a short, crisp, and tender crust after baking and a well-balanced taste to complement any filling.

These characteristics make it perfect for lining tartlet tins and pans for bar cookies. Therefore, I think it's more appropriate to classify it as a sweetened short pastry than as a cookie. This dough is a joy to handle because the sugar curtails gluten development, reducing the risk of shrinkage or toughness. You can press it into tartlet tins, roll it, or even reroll it.

1. Put the flour, salt, and sugar in a food processor bowl. Process just to blend the ingredients. Scatter all the butter slices over the flour mixture, and process with on/off bursts until the mixture has the consistency of cornmeal.

2. Whisk the egg and vanilla together in a small bowl. With the motor on, pour the egg mixture down the feed tube. Process until the ingredients form a ball. Remove the dough to the work surface, and with the heel of your hand press dough together until it is smooth and cohesive.

3. Adjust rack to lower third of oven and preheat oven to 350 degrees F. Arrange four dozen ungreased 1½-inch fluted tartlet tins close together on a 12-x-15½-x-½-inch baking sheet.

CONTINUED ➤

2½ cups (350 grams) unsifted all-purpose flour

⅛ teaspoon salt

⅓ cup (65 grams) granulated sugar

8 ounces (2 sticks) unsalted butter, chilled and cut into ¼-inch slices

1 large egg

1 teaspoon pure vanilla extract

4. Pinch off 1 teaspoon of the dough and drop it into a tin. Repeat until all the tins contain dough. One by one, roll each piece of dough into a ball in the palm of your hands. This step aids in shaping the tartlet shells more evenly. To press dough into tins, with index finger, press center of dough ball into the tin, then press dough up the sides while rotating the tin to distribute the dough evenly. The object is to use just enough dough to line the tartlet tin without creating a thick shell. (Notice that I recommend completing one task before beginning another: Fill baking sheet with tins, pinch off a teaspoon of dough for each tin, roll dough between your palms to form a smooth ball, and last press the balls evenly into the tins. Handling one movement at a time is easier and faster. You discover your own rhythm from the repetition.)

STEP 4

STEP 5

5. Bake tartlet shells in oven for 12 to 15 minutes, or until light golden. Remove baking sheet from oven to rack to cool. When the tins are cool enough to touch, squeeze each tin gently with your thumb and forefinger, turn it upside down, and let the miniature tartlet shell drop into the palm of your hand.

6. Repeat the filling and baking procedure with the remaining dough.

7. Stack cooled unfilled shells in an airtight metal container and store at room temperature up to 1 week.

## STORING NOTE

Refrigerate the dough, well wrapped, up to 1 week; or freeze up to 1 month. Bring dough to room temperature before working with it.

## VARIATION NOTE

To make whole-wheat tartlets, substitute unbleached whole-wheat flour for half the all-purpose flour.

# caramel carmenitas

➤ Makes 3 dozen 2½-inch-long barquettes

. . . . . . . . . . . . . . . . . . . . . . . . . . . . . .

The genuine taste of the popular pecan is a treasure when added to a silky smooth creamy caramel filling.

1. Dough: To make these tartlets, you may form individual balls of dough and press them into 1½-inch fluted tins as the Miniature Tartlet Pastry recipe specifies. For variety, however, this recipe uses barquette (boat-shaped) tartlet tins, 2½ inches long, 1 inch wide on top, with ½-inch-deep sloping sides. I've discovered that rolling a thinly rolled portion of room-temperature dough up on a rolling pin and unrolling it over a quantity of tins is the quickest, easiest, and most efficient way to fill a lot of them all at once.

2. Adjust rack to lower third of oven and preheat oven to 350 degrees F. Lay moist towels on work surface, and group barquette molds on top of the towels to ready them for filling with rolled-out dough.

3. Set the room-temperature dough on the work surface. Then, with the heel of your hand, smear a small amount of the dough, about the size of an egg, on your work surface by pushing it away from you. Repeat with small amounts of the remaining dough. When you've worked all the dough in this manner, give it a few more strokes to bring it together. This kneading action is called *fraisage* and aids in developing just enough structure to make rolling and working with the dough more manageable. It reduces the dough's tendency to tear or crack while being rolled and lifted.

CONTINUED ➤

## DOUGH

1 recipe Miniature Tartlet Pastry (page 205)

## CARAMEL PECAN BUTTERCREAM

½ cup (100 grams) granulated sugar

1 ounce (2 tablespoons) unsalted butter

⅓ cup heavy cream, room temperature

4 ounces (1 stick) unsalted butter, room temperature

2 ounces (½ cup) pecans, toasted and finely ground

## DECORATION

4 ounces (1 cup) pecans, finely chopped

4.  Divide the dough in fourths. Roll out one portion at a time on a lightly floured surface until it is no more than ⅛ inch thick. Rearrange the tins, close together, in the approximate shape of the dough. Roll up dough on rolling pin and unroll over barquettes. Dust dough lightly with flour and, with a small ball of dough, ease the dough into the molds. Roll rolling pin over molds to trim edges and remove excess dough.

5.  Arrange the dough-filled tins on a baking sheet. Bake for 12 to 15 minutes, or until light golden. Remove baking sheet with the tins to a wire rack to cool. When tins are cool enough to handle, turn each one upside down and let the tartlet fall into the palm of your other hand. Repeat the rolling and baking process with the remaining dough.

6.  Caramel Pecan Buttercream: Heat the sugar in a 1½-quart heavy-bottomed saucepan or an unlined copper sugar pot over low heat. Stir occasionally with a small wooden spoon until sugar dissolves. Increase the heat to medium-high and cook until the melted sugar becomes amber in color, about 7 minutes. Turn off heat, add the 2 tablespoons butter, then the cream. Be careful—the mixture bubbles madly. With the spoon, stir until the ingredients blend together smoothly. Pour into a bowl and refrigerate until cold. Using an electric mixer at medium speed, whip the 4 ounces butter in a medium mixing bowl until light and fluffy, about 2 minutes. Gradually add the caramel cream, a couple of tablespoons at a time. When the mixture is airy and the ingredients are fully incorporated, stir in the ground pecans.

STEP 2

STEP 4

7. Scoop the equivalent of 1 to 2 teaspoons of the buttercream onto a small metal spatula, and put it in a shell. With the spatula, manipulate the buttercream into a mound in the center. Slope the sides with the spatula to crest at the top. Remove excess buttercream from the spatula, and begin with another portion for the next barquette.

8. Decoration: Dip each tartlet into the pecans, tipping it so that only one side of the buttercream is coated.

9. Stack unfilled tartlet shells in an airtight metal container and store at room temperature up to 1 week. Store filled tartlets in one layer in a covered foil-lined cardboard container, such as a cake box, at room temperature up to 1 day.

## TECHNIQUE NOTE

Filling a quantity of tins all at once works well with any shape tin—round, square, rectangle, or even barquette. The only requirement is that the tins have sharp edges in order to enable you to cut off excess dough neatly after lining.

# garnet tartlets

➤ **Makes 4 dozen 1½-inch round tartlets**

The combination of cream cheese and hazelnuts, glazed with currant jelly, produces a tart reminiscent of a nutty cheesecake.

1. Dough: To make these tartlets, you may form individual balls of dough and press them into 1½-inch fluted tins as the Miniature Tartlet Pastry recipe specifies. For variety, however, this recipe uses tins that measure 1½ inches in diameter with ¾-inch-deep sloping sides or 1¾ inches in diameter with ½-inch-deep sloping sides. I've discovered that filling these tins when the dough is chilled and firm is the quickest, easiest, and most efficient way.

2. Divide the dough in half. Roll out each portion between two sheets of waxed paper to a circle slightly less than ⅛ inch thick and 10 inches in diameter. Leaving the dough between the sheets of waxed paper, transfer to a baking sheet and refrigerate until firm, at least 2 hours or up to 3 days; or freeze, well wrapped, up to 1 month.

3. Adjust rack to lower third of oven and preheat oven to 350 degrees F. Arrange four dozen ungreased tins, 1½ inches in diameter with ¾-inch-deep sloping sides or 1¾ inches in diameter with ½-inch-deep sloping sides, close together on a large baking sheet.

4. Remove one dough circle at a time from refrigerator, peel off top waxed paper sheet, replace it loosely on top, and flip the entire package over. Peel off and discard the second sheet of waxed paper.

5. Using a 2¼-inch round cutter, cut out circles in the dough. Place a dough circle on each tin. Using your index finger or a tin the same shape, press the dough into tins.

## DOUGH

½ recipe Miniature Tartlet Pastry (page 205)

## CREAMY HAZELNUT FILLING

8 ounces cream cheese

1½ ounces (scant ⅓ cup) hazelnuts, toasted and finely ground

½ cup (100 grams) granulated sugar

1 large egg

1 tablespoon sour cream

1 teaspoon finely grated lemon zest

## DECORATION

1 cup red currant jelly

3 tablespoons cassis liqueur

6. Creamy Hazelnut Filling: Process all the ingredients in a food processor bowl until mixture is smooth, about 30 seconds. Spoon or pipe, with a 14-inch pastry bag fitted with a ¼-inch plain decorating tip (such as Ateco #2), about 1 teaspoon filling into each tartlet.

7. Bake for 12 to 15 minutes, or until the crust is light golden. Place baking sheet on a wire rack for 10 minutes, or until tins are cool enough to touch. Squeeze each tin between your thumb and forefinger, turn upside down, and let the miniature tartlet fall into the palm of your other hand. Place on a rack to cool completely.

8. Decoration: Heat the jelly just to warm and liquefy it. Turn off heat, stir in the cassis. With a pastry brush, coat each tartlet.

9. Stack undecorated tartlets in an airtight sturdy plastic container, separating layers with waxed paper, and freeze up to 1 month. Store decorated tartlets in one layer in a covered foil-lined cardboard container, such as a cake box, at room temperature up to 1 day.

# rose tartlets

➤ **Makes 3 dozen 2-x-1¼-inch oval tartlets**

. . . . . . . . . . . . . . . . . . . . . . . . . . . . . . . . . . . .

These rich dark chocolate–glazed tartlets, filled with whipped cream delicately scented with almond liqueur and thin strips of red rose petals, capture the essence of romance in taste, presentation, and aroma.

1. Dough: To make these tartlets, you may form individual balls of dough and press them into the 1½-inch fluted tins as the Miniature Tartlet Pastry recipe specifies. For variety, however, this recipe uses oval-shaped tartlet tins, 2 inches long, 1¼ inches wide, with slightly sloping sides. I've discovered that when I use an unusual-shaped tin, the quickest, easiest, and most efficient way to fill the tins is to trace a stencil of the dough shape needed, since a standard cutter is not available in a similar form.

2. To make a stencil of the tartlet's dimensions, press a small piece of waxed paper into the tartlet tin to make an impression. Cut out the tartlet's shape from the waxed paper, then trace these dimensions onto a piece of sturdy cardboard. Cut out the shape with a utility knife to finish the template.

3. Adjust rack to lower third of oven and preheat oven to 350 degrees F. Set oval tartlet tins close together on large baking sheets.

4. Roll the room-temperature dough on a lightly floured work surface until close to ¹⁄₁₆ inch thick. Using the template, trace shapes in the dough with a small paring knife. Set the cutouts on the tins. Dip a tin with the same dimensions and shape into the flour, then press the dough cutouts into the tins.

## DOUGH

½ recipe Miniature Tartlet Pastry (page 205)

## FILLING

Chocolate Butter Glaze

3 ounces unsalted butter

4 ounces semisweet chocolate, finely chopped

2 ounces unsweetened chocolate, finely chopped

Whipped Cream Filling

1 cup (8 ounces) heavy cream

2 tablespoons granulated sugar

1 tablespoon Amaretto liqueur

⅓ cup fragrant edible red rose petals, cut in chiffonade (thin strips)

## DECORATION

2 tablespoons fragrant edible red rose petals, minced

5. Bake for 12 to 15 minutes, or until the crust is light golden. Place baking sheet on a wire rack until the tins are cool enough to handle, about 10 minutes. Then turn each upside down, and let it drop into the palm of your hand. Set the pastries on a rack to cool completely. Transfer to a large tray or baking sheet.

6. Chocolate Butter Glaze: Place the butter and chocolates in a 1-quart bowl that fits snugly over a saucepan half filled with 120- to 130-degree-F water, to melt ingredients. Stir occasionally until smooth. If necessary, maintain the water's temperature over very low heat. Using a pastry brush, lightly coat each tartlet with melted chocolate butter. Set aside in a cool room until the chocolate sets.

7. Whipped Cream Filling: Whip the cream with the sugar and liqueur until soft peaks form; fold in the rose fragments. Using a pastry bag fitted with an open star tip (such as Ateco #2), pipe decorative swirls into the chocolate-coated shells.

8. Decoration: Sprinkle rose pieces over the whipped cream filling and refrigerate until serving.

9. These are at their best if served within 2 hours of filling and decorating.

STEP 2

STEP 4

# double chocolate tartlets

➤ **Makes 8 dozen 1½-inch round fluted tartlets**

. . . . . . . . . . . . . . . . . . . . . . . . . . . . . . . . . . . . .

Although figs are my favorite fresh fruit with this combination of tender chocolate short pastry and almond-chocolate filling, after tasting these tartlets, you'll find that variations with plums, pears, or peaches work well too.

1. Chocolate Miniature Tartlet Pastry: Put the flour, sugar, and cocoa powder in a food processor bowl. Process just to blend the ingredients. Scatter all the butter slices over the flour mixture, and process with on/off bursts until the mixture has the consistency of cornmeal.

2. Whisk the egg and vanilla together in a small bowl. With the motor on, pour the egg mixture down the feed tube. Process until the ingredients form a ball. Remove dough to the work surface, and with heel of your hand press the dough together until it is smooth and cohesive.

3. Adjust rack to lower third of oven and preheat oven to 350 degrees F. Arrange four dozen ungreased 1½-inch round fluted tins close together on a 12-x-15½-x-½-inch baking sheet.

4. Pinch off 1 teaspoon of the dough and drop it into a tin. Repeat until all the tins contain dough. One by one, roll each piece of dough into a ball in the palms of your hands. (This step aids in shaping the tartlets more evenly.) With index finger, press center of dough ball into the tin, then press dough up the sides while rotating tin to distribute the dough evenly.

5. Chocolate Frangipane Filling: Process all the filling ingredients in a food processor bowl until the mixture is smooth and free of lumps. Spoon about 1 teaspoon of it into each shell.

## CHOCOLATE MINIATURE TARTLET PASTRY

2 cups plus 1 tablespoon (297 grams) unsifted all-purpose flour

½ cup (100 grams) granulated sugar

⅓ cup (35 grams) unsifted cocoa powder

8 ounces (2 sticks) unsalted butter, chilled and cut into ¼-inch slices

1 large egg

1 teaspoon pure vanilla extract

6. Bake for 15 to 17 minutes, or until the crusts' edges appear dry and slightly firm to the touch. Place the baking sheet with tartlets on a wire rack for about 10 minutes, or until tins are cool enough to touch. Squeeze each tin between your thumb and forefinger, turn it upside down, and let the miniature tartlet drop into the palm of your hand. Place on rack to cool completely.

7. Repeat the filling and baking procedure with the remaining dough.

8. Decoration: Just before serving, place a thin fig slice on top of each tartlet.

9. Stack undecorated tartlets in an airtight sturdy plastic container and freeze up to 10 days. Store decorated tartlets in one layer in a covered foil-lined cardboard container, such as a cake box, at room temperature up to 3 hours.

## NOTE

When you're searching for a food gift, give just the baked tartlet shells neatly stacked in a decorative metal container with the recipe tucked inside.

### CHOCOLATE FRANGIPANE FILLING

4 ounces (1 stick) unsalted butter

½ cup (100 grams) granulated sugar

2 large eggs

1 teaspoon pure vanilla extract

4 ounces (¾ cup) blanched almonds, finely ground

1 ounce unsweetened chocolate, finely ground

### DECORATION

6 fresh figs, thinly sliced

# chocolate cherry chaps

➤ **Makes 4 dozen 1½-inch round fluted tartlets**

. . . . . . . . . . . . . . . . . . . . . . . . . .

A single chocolate-covered cherry in a sour cherry-glazed tender tartlet is similar to a piece of candy in its own edible paper case. After eating the sweet, juicy fruit dressed in semisweet chocolate, you'll agree: Chocolate never had it so good.

1. Pastry: Arrange the baked tartlet shells on a large tray or baking sheet.

2. Filling: Heat the jelly in a small saucepan just to warm and liquefy it. Using a pastry brush, coat each shell with a thin glaze of the jelly.

3. Dark Chocolate Fruit Glaze: Place the butter and chocolates in a 1-quart bowl that fits snugly over a saucepan half filled with 120- to 130-degree-F water, to melt ingredients. Stir occasionally until smooth. If necessary, maintain the water's temperature over very low heat.

4. Dip the cherries, one at a time, into the liquid chocolate glaze, and then set each cherry in a tartlet shell. With scissors, trim each cherry stem, leaving a stem between ½ inch and ¾ inch.

5. Store tartlets in one layer in a covered foil-lined cardboard container, such as a cake box, at room temperature up to 1 day.

## TECHNIQUE NOTE

Clipping the cherry stems decorates each tartlet uniformly *and* reminds the person eating it that the cherry contains a pit.

### PASTRY

4 dozen (½ recipe) baked Miniature Tartlet Pastry shells (page 205)

### FILLING

1 cup sour cherry jelly

### DARK CHOCOLATE FRUIT GLAZE

4 ounces (1 stick) unsalted butter

5 ounces semisweet chocolate, finely chopped

1 ounce unsweetened chocolate, finely chopped

4 dozen (1 pound) fresh bing cherries with stems, room temperature

# mazarine tartlets

➤ **Makes 4 dozen 1½-inch round fluted tartlets**

Wherever I travel, I always see versions of this tartlet. I think these are the best mini–fruit tarts you'll find. They're made with buttery pastry, sweet jam, nutty filling freshened with lemon, and a sparkling crown of assorted fresh fruits. Choose whatever is best: Small blueberries, stemmed red currants, champagne grapes, or tiny strawberries work especially well.

1. Arrange four dozen ungreased fluted 1½-inch tins close together on a 12-x-15½-x-½-inch baking sheet.

2. Dough: Pinch off 1 teaspoon of the dough and drop it into a tin. Repeat until all the tins contain dough. One by one, roll each piece of dough into a ball in the palms of your hands. With index finger, press center of dough ball into the tin, then press dough up the sides while rotating tin to distribute the dough evenly.

3. Adjust rack to lower third of oven and preheat oven to 350 degrees F.

4. Filling: Spoon, or pipe from a small handmade paper cone, a small dot of jam in the bottom of each tartlet.

5. Almond Filling: Process all the ingredients in a food processor bowl until the mixture is smooth, about 30 seconds. Spoon, or pipe with another handmade paper cone, about 1 teaspoon filling into each tartlet to cover the jam.

6. Bake for 15 to 20 minutes, or until the crusts' edges are light golden. Remove baking sheet from oven, and place on a rack to cool for 10 minutes.

CONTINUED ➤

## DOUGH

½ recipe Miniature Tartlet Pastry (page 205)

## FILLING

¼ cup strawberry jam

### Almond Filling

¼ cup (2 ounces) almond paste

1 ounce (2 tablespoons) unsalted butter

⅓ cup (30 grams) unsifted powdered sugar

1 egg yolk

1 teaspoon pure vanilla extract

1 teaspoon kirsch

½ teaspoon finely grated lemon zest

## DECORATION

1¼ cups assorted fresh fruit

⅓ cup red currant jelly

7. Squeeze each tin between your thumb and forefinger, turn it upside down, and let the tartlet drop into the palm of your hand. If it cannot be removed easily, it is either still too warm from the oven or underbaked. Return a few tartlets to oven to bake for 5 minutes more. Cool and remove. If these tartlets can be removed, then bake those remaining.

8. Decoration: Put the room-temperature fruit in a 3-quart mixing bowl. Heat the jelly just to warm and liquefy it, then pour it down the side of the bowl. Slide a rubber spatula under the fruit, and fold to lightly coat with the jelly. With fingertips, place fruit to top each tartlet.

9. Stack undecorated tartlets in an airtight sturdy plastic container and freeze up to 10 days. Store decorated tartlets in one layer in a covered foil-lined cardboard container, such as a cake box, at room temperature up to 12 hours.

# lemon meringue tartlets

➤ **Makes 8 dozen 1½-inch round fluted tartlets**

. . . . . . . . . . . . . . . . . . . . . . . . . . .

If your weakness is lemon meringue pie, these baby versions will break your willpower. The tangy creamy lemon, balanced by the sweet airy meringue, packs a great deal of flavor and texture in one small pastry package.

1. Pastry: Arrange the baked tartlet shells on two large baking sheets.

2. Lemon Curd: Combine the egg, yolks, and sugar in a 1½-quart heavy-bottomed saucepan. Stir in the juice and zest. Cook over medium-low heat, stirring occasionally, for 2 to 3 minutes, or until the mixture thickens to a hollandaise consistency. Pour into a bowl, cover the surface of the lemon curd with plastic, and refrigerate until chilled, or up to 3 days. Spoon or pipe from a 14-inch pastry bag fitted with a ¼-inch plain decorating tip (such as Ateco #2) the equivalent of ½ teaspoon lemon curd into each shell.

3. Adjust rack to lower third of oven and preheat oven to 375 degrees F.

4. Fluffy Meringue: In a large mixing bowl, blend the egg whites with the sugar. Place the bowl over another bowl of hot tap water and stir until the mixture is body temperature. Using an electric mixer, preferably with a whisk attachment, whip until the mixture has peaks that are thick and shiny, about 10 to 15 minutes.

## PASTRY

8 dozen (1 recipe) baked Miniature Tartlet Pastry shells (page 205)

## LEMON CURD

1 egg

2 egg yolks

½ cup (100 grams) granulated sugar

6 tablespoons (2 lemons) fresh lemon juice

2 teaspoons finely grated lemon zest

## FLUFFY MERINGUE

½ cup (about 4 large) egg whites

1 cup (200 grams) granulated sugar

5. Using another 14-inch pastry bag fitted with a ¼-inch open star decorating tip (such as Ateco #2), pipe a tall swirl on top of each tartlet. Bake for 3 to 4 minutes, or until the meringue is light golden. Place baking sheet on a wire rack until tartlets are cool. It's natural for the meringue to puff in the oven and deflate slightly during cooling. Piping tall swirls of meringue on each tartlet before baking maintains a dramatic appearance even with the meringue's adjusted height after baking.

6. Serve the same day the tartlets are filled and decorated.

## VARIATION NOTE

Look for fresh red currants in the produce department in June or July and substitute the fruit for the lemon cream filling. Then top the tartlets with the fluffy meringue.

# raspberry lemon tartlets

➤ **Makes 4 dozen 1½-inch round fluted tartlets**

This is one of the easiest tartlets in the miniature repertoire, but this ease of preparation certainly is not evident in the finished product. Fill tartlets with a simple lemon custard, and, after baking, decorate with a sweet red raspberry and mint leaf for a colorful and tasty garnish.

1. Adjust rack to lower third of oven and preheat oven to 350 degrees F. Arrange four dozen ungreased round fluted tartlet tins close together on a large baking sheet.

2. Dough: Pinch off the dough, 1 teaspoon at a time, and drop into tins. One by one, roll dough pieces into balls in the palms of your hands. With index finger, press center of dough ball into the tin, then press dough up the sides while rotating tin to distribute the dough evenly.

3. Lemon Custard Filling: In a small bowl, lightly whisk together all the filling ingredients just until blended. Spoon about ½ teaspoonful into each tartlet.

4. Bake for about 10 minutes, or until crust is light golden. Place baking sheet on a wire rack to cool. When the tins are cool enough to touch, squeeze each tin gently with your thumb and forefinger, turn it upside down, and let the miniature tartlet drop into the palm of your hand.

5. Decoration: Set a fresh mint leaf on top of each tartlet, then place a raspberry on each leaf, letting the leaf peek from under the berry.

6. Freeze undecorated tartlets in airtight sturdy plastic containers up to 10 days. Serve decorated tartlets the same day.

## DOUGH

½ recipe Miniature Tartlet Pastry (page 205)

## LEMON CUSTARD FILLING

2 egg yolks

3 tablespoons unsalted butter, melted and cooled to lukewarm

½ cup (50 grams) unsifted powdered sugar

1 tablespoon granulated sugar

2 tablespoons lemon juice

2 teaspoons finely grated lemon

## DECORATION

4 dozen fresh mint leaves

1 pint fresh raspberries

# scheherazade tartlets

➤ **Makes 8 dozen 1½-inch round fluted tartlets**

· · · · · · · · · · · · · · · · · · · · · · · · · · ·

A romantic name seems apropos for these tartlets filled with cranberries, America's rubies of the fruit world, and pomegranate seeds, famous as the fruit of love since ancient days.

1.  Pastry: Arrange the baked tartlet shells on two large trays or baking sheets.

2.  Chocolate Butter Glaze: Place the butter and chocolates in a 1-quart bowl that fits snugly over a saucepan half filled with 120- to 130-degree-F water, to melt ingredients. Stir occasionally until smooth. If necessary, maintain the water's temperature over very low heat. Using a pastry brush, apply a thin coating of glaze in each tartlet. Set aside in a cool room until the chocolate sets.

3.  Candied Cranberries: In a heavy 2½-quart saucepan over medium heat, combine the water and sugar. Stir occasionally, washing down any sugar crystals clinging to the sides of the pan with a brush dipped in cold water, until the sugar dissolves. Increase heat to medium-high and cook, without stirring, until the sugar syrup reaches 220 degrees F on a candy thermometer. Remove from heat. Stir in the cranberries. When the mixture has cooled to 115 degrees F, pour through a large medium-mesh sieve to separate the cranberries from the syrup. Discard the syrup.

4.  In a 3-quart bowl, gently toss the cranberries and pomegranate seeds together with a rubber spatula. Any syrup clinging to the cranberries will coat the pomegranate seeds to give the fruit a glazed appearance.

## PASTRY

8 dozen (1 recipe) baked Miniature Tartlet Pastry shells (page 205)

## FILLING

Chocolate Butter Glaze

3 ounces (¾ stick) unsalted butter

4 ounces semisweet chocolate, finely chopped

2 ounces unsweetened chocolate, finely chopped

Candied Cranberries

5 ounces water

1 cup plus 2 tablespoons (225 grams) granulated sugar

2 cups cranberries

⅓ cup fresh pomegranate seeds

5. With fingertips, gently lift the glazed fruit to fill each tartlet generously. For best flavor and appearance, serve the same day they are filled.

### BAKING NOTE

Look for pomegranates in the produce department, where they can be found sometimes as early as late August and usually through Christmas. To remove the crunchy seeds filled with tangy juice from the fruit, cut out the blossom end and score the skin in several places. Then, with your fingertips, break into the fruit in these places to release the seeds. Avoid cutting pomegranates, or you'll pierce the seeds and release their juice.

# jade buttercups

➤ **Makes 4 dozen 1½-inch round fluted tartlets**

. . . . . . . . . . . . . . . . . . . . . . . . . . . . . . . .

The freshness of kiwi and lemon, matched with the richness of butter-cream, gives this fruit tartlet distinction. Fill a small pastry shell with creamy lemon buttercream, put a slice of kiwi over the top, and brush with lemon gelée to produce a shimmering finish.

1. Pastry: Arrange the baked tartlet shells on a large baking sheet.

2. Lemon Curd Buttercream: Combine the egg, yolks, and sugar in a 1½-quart heavy-bottomed saucepan. Stir in the juice and zest. Stir constantly over medium-low heat for 2 to 3 minutes, or until the mixture thickens to a hollandaise consistency. Pour the lemon curd into a bowl, cover its surface with plastic, and refrigerate until chilled, or up to 3 days. In a 1½-quart mixing bowl, cream the butter with an electric mixer until light and fluffy. Add ½ cup of the lemon curd, 1 tablespoon at a time, beating until the mixture is airy and fully incorporated. Return the remaining lemon curd to the refrigerator for another use.

3. Spoon or pipe, using a 14-inch pastry bag fitted with a ¼-inch plain decorating tip (such as Ateco #2), about ½ teaspoon of the filling into each shell.

4. Lemon Gelée: Pour the water into a liquid-measure measuring cup. Sprinkle the gelatin over surface, and set aside until softened. Pour into a small saucepan, add the sugar, and heat over low heat just to dissolve the gelatin and sugar. Remove from heat, add the lemon juice, and pour into a 2-quart bowl; chill just until the mixture thickens to the consistency of egg whites, about 30 minutes.

### PASTRY

4 dozen (½ recipe) baked
Miniature Tartlet Pastry
shells (page 205)

### LEMON CURD BUTTERCREAM

1 egg

2 egg yolks

½ cup (100 grams)
granulated sugar

6 tablespoons (2 lemons)
fresh lemon juice

2 teaspoons finely
grated lemon zest

6 ounces (1½ sticks) unsalted
butter, room temperature

### DECORATION

Lemon Gelée

⅓ cup water

1 teaspoon gelatin

1 tablespoon sugar

1 tablespoon fresh
lemon juice, strained

5 kiwifruit

5. Using a serrated knife, cut the unpeeled kiwifruit into thin slices about 1/16 inch thick. With a 1 1/2-inch round cutter, cut a circle from each kiwi slice. Place a kiwi slice on top of each tartlet.

6. Brush the lemon gelée on top of each kiwi slice, and place baking sheet in refrigerator just to set the gelatin mixture.

7. These are best served within 2 hours of filling and decorating.

## VARIATION NOTE

You may substitute a white wine such as Gewürztraminer for the water and lemon juice in the lemon gelée.

# poirettes

➤ Makes 4 dozen 1½-inch round fluted tartlets

Tender tartlets bake with tiny pear pieces in an almond paste filling. The simple apricot and chocolate topping completes a sublime combination. When I want more chocolate flavor, I make the tartlets from the Chocolate Miniature Tartlet Pastry on page 214.

1. Arrange four dozen ungreased 1½-inch tins close together on a 12-x-15½-x-½-inch baking sheet.

2. Dough: Pinch off 1 teaspoon of the dough and drop it into a tin. Repeat until all the tins contain dough. One by one, roll each piece of dough into a ball in the palms of your hands. (This step aids in shaping the tartlets more evenly.) With index finger, press center of dough ball in the tin, then gradually press dough up the sides while rotating the tin to distribute the dough evenly.

3. Adjust rack to lower third of oven and preheat oven to 350 degrees F.

4. Drop one pear piece into each tartlet shell.

5. Almond Paste Frangipane: Process all the ingredients in a food processor bowl until the mixture is smooth. Spoon about 1 teaspoon of the filling into each shell to cover the pear.

6. Bake for 15 to 17 minutes, or until the crusts' edges are light golden. Place baking sheet with tartlets on a wire rack for about 10 minutes, or until tins are cool enough to touch. Squeeze each tin between your thumb and forefinger, turn upside down, and let the miniature tartlet drop into the palm of your hand. Place on rack to cool completely.

## DOUGH

½ recipe Miniature Tartlet Pastry (page 205)

## FILLING

1 poached pear, diced into ¼-inch cubes

Almond Paste Frangipane

4 ounces (⅓ cup plus 1 tablespoon) almond paste

⅓ cup (65 grams) granulated sugar

1 teaspoon rum

1 teaspoon pure vanilla extract

1 ounce (2 tablespoons) unsalted butter, room temperature

1 teaspoon finely grated lemon zest

2 large eggs

## DECORATION

½ cup strained apricot jam

4 ounces semisweet chocolate

7. Decoration: Heat the jam just to warm and liquefy it. Then brush over each tartlet. After glazing the pastries, place them on a rack.

8. Using a 2-inch paring knife, scrape the tip of the blade firmly but gently across the bar of chocolate to make fine flakes: Hold the chocolate bar close to the glazed pastries, so the fine shavings are sprinkled over each tartlet and stick to the glaze. You can shave the chocolate ahead of time. Freeze the shavings in an airtight container, then pick them up in a teaspoon, and sprinkle over each tartlet. Using a teaspoon keeps the chocolate from melting from the heat in your fingers.

9. Stack undecorated tartlets in an airtight sturdy plastic container and freeze up to 10 days. Store decorated tartlets in one layer in a covered foil-lined cardboard container, such as a cake box, at room temperature up to 1 day.

## BAKING NOTE

Sometimes I use 1 teaspoon grated fresh ginger in the filling to replace the rum and vanilla. For a more subtle ginger flavor, use 1 teaspoon fresh ginger juice. Rub a peeled portion of ginger along a stainless-steel box grater, put the grated ginger in a cloth towel, and twist to extract juice.

# lemon drops

➤ **Makes 4 dozen 1½-inch round fluted tartlets**

I adore the combination of tangy lemon and velvety caramel. These little pastries are glazed with rich caramel cream before being filled with a lemon curd lightened with whipped cream.

1. Pastry: Arrange the baked tartlet shells on a large baking sheet.

2. Lemon Curd: Combine the egg, yolks, and sugar in a 1½-quart heavy-bottomed saucepan. Stir in the juice and zest. Stir constantly over medium-low heat for 2 to 3 minutes, or until the mixture thickens to a hollandaise consistency. Pour the lemon curd into a bowl, cover its surface with plastic, and refrigerate until chilled, or up to 3 days.

3. Caramel Cream: Put the sugar in a 1½-quart heavy-bottomed saucepan or an unlined copper sugar pot over low heat. Stir occasionally with a small wooden spoon until the sugar dissolves. Increase heat to medium-high and cook, without stirring, until the melted sugar becomes amber in color, about 7 minutes. Turn off heat, add the butter, then the room-temperature cream. Be careful—the mixture bubbles madly. With the spoon, stir until the ingredients blend together smoothly.

4. Using a pastry brush, apply a thin coating of caramel cream to the shells. Dry at room temperature for 30 minutes, or up to 1 day.

5. Fold the whipped cream into ½ cup of chilled lemon curd. Refrigerate remaining lemon curd for another use. Using a 14-inch pastry bag fitted with a ¼-inch plain decorating tip (such as Ateco #2), pipe the filling decoratively into the caramel cream–glazed shells.

## PASTRY

4 dozen (½ recipe) baked Miniature Tartlet Pastry shells (page 205)

## FILLING

Lemon Curd

1 egg

2 egg yolks

½ cup (100 grams) granulated sugar

6 tablespoons (2 lemons) fresh lemon juice

2 teaspoons finely grated lemon zest

Caramel Cream

½ cup (100 grams) granulated sugar

1 ounce (2 tablespoons) unsalted butter

⅓ cup (2½ ounces) heavy cream, room temperature

½ cup (4 ounces) heavy cream, whipped to soft peaks

## DECORATION

4 dozen candied lilacs

6. Decoration: Top each tartlet with a candied lilac.

7. Store glazed shells in one layer in covered foil-lined cardboard containers, such as cake boxes, at room temperature up to 1 day. These are best served within 2 hours after filling.

## VARIATION NOTES

It's easy to mix lemon curd with other ingredients. These Lemon Drops combine lemon curd with whipped cream, the Jade Buttercups (page 224) combine lemon curd with butter to make buttercream, and the Lemon Meringue Tartlets (page 219) combine the sharp lemon filling with a fluffy meringue.

The caramel cream is as versatile as the lemon curd. It is combined with butter and ground nuts for a buttercream in Caramel Carmenitas (page 207) or just mixed with nuts and a bit of honey in Swiss Bettinas (page 230). Caramel cream and chocolate taste divine in Midas Cups (page 231), or the cream can even glaze tartlet shells, as in this recipe.

# swiss bettinas

➤ **Makes 4 dozen 1½-inch round fluted tartlets**

The crunchy toasted walnuts, smothered in a rich creamy caramel, that fill each tender tartlet shell remind me of a luscious version of these tartlets I sampled in a charming pastry shop in Zurich, Switzerland.

1. Pastry: Arrange the baked tartlet shells on a large tray or baking sheet.

2. Engadiner Cream: Put the sugar in a 1 ½-quart heavy-bottomed saucepan or an unlined copper sugar pot over low heat. Stir occasionally with a small wooden spoon until the sugar dissolves. Increase heat to medium-high and cook, without stirring, until the melted sugar reaches an amber color, about 7 minutes. Turn off heat, add the butter, then the cream. Be careful—the mixture bubbles madly. With the spoon, stir until the ingredients blend together smoothly. Stir the walnuts and honey into the caramel cream while hot. Cool 30 minutes, and then spoon 1 teaspoonful of filling into each baked shell.

3. Decoration: Top each tartlet with a chocolate coffee bean candy.

4. Store in one layer in a covered foil-lined cardboard container, such as a cake box, at room temperature up to 2 days.

PASTRY

4 dozen (½ recipe) baked Miniature Tartlet Pastry shells (page 205)

ENGADINER CREAM

½ cup (100 grams) granulated sugar

1 ounce (2 tablespoons) unsalted butter

⅓ cup heavy cream, room temperature

½ cup walnuts, toasted and chopped

2 teaspoons honey

DECORATION

48 chocolate coffee bean candies

# midas cups

➤ **Makes 4 dozen 1½-inch round fluted tartlets**

A flake of gold leaf sparkling on top of an extravagant chocolate-caramel tart signals the eye that this sweet is truly special. The silky chocolate caramel cream gives a perfect balance of flavors to the toasty caramelized sugar, heavy cream, and semisweet chocolate. Sheets of edible 24-karat gold leaf are available at specialty cookware stores or artists' supply stores.

1. Pastry: Arrange the baked tartlet shells on a large tray or baking sheet.

2. Chocolate Caramel Cream: Place the chopped chocolate in a medium bowl. Put the sugar in a 1½-quart heavy-bottomed saucepan or an unlined copper sugar pot over low heat. Stir occasionally with a small wooden spoon until the sugar dissolves. Increase heat to medium-high and cook, without stirring, until the melted sugar reaches an amber color, about 7 minutes. Turn off heat, add the butter, then the cream. Be careful—the mixture bubbles madly. With the spoon, stir until the ingredients blend together smoothly. When the caramel cream's bubbling subsides, pour it into bowl with the chocolate. Stir until the chocolate has melted and the mixture is smooth and shiny. Cool 30 minutes, and then spoon 1 teaspoonful of filling into each shell. Put aside until chocolate filling is set, about an hour.

3. Decoration: With tweezers, pluck off a tiny piece of gold leaf, the size of an oatmeal flake, and deposit it on top of the glossy chocolate filling for decoration. With fingertip, press the gold lightly to anchor it to the filling and to capture the gold's sparkle.

4. Store in one layer in a covered foil-lined cardboard container, such as a cake box, at room temperature up to 2 days.

## PASTRY

4 dozen (½ recipe) baked Miniature Tartlet Pastry shells (page 205)

## CHOCOLATE CARAMEL CREAM

3 ounces semisweet chocolate, chopped

½ cup (100 grams) granulated sugar

1 ounce (2 tablespoons) unsalted butter

⅓ cup heavy cream, room temperature

## DECORATION

24-karat gold leaf

# flaky miniatures

sour cream pastry . . . . . . . . . . . . . . . . . . . . . . . . . . . .235

sweet cheese puffs . . . . . . . . . . . . . . . . . . . . . . . . . . .236

pumpkin pastries . . . . . . . . . . . . . . . . . . . . . . . . . . . .238

eccles tarts . . . . . . . . . . . . . . . . . . . . . . . . . . . . . . . . .240

heartovers . . . . . . . . . . . . . . . . . . . . . . . . . . . . . . . . . .242

shreveshire tarts . . . . . . . . . . . . . . . . . . . . . . . . . . . . .244

eva deutsch's almond slices . . . . . . . . . . . . . . . . . .246

cottage cheese dough . . . . . . . . . . . . . . . . . . . . . . . .248

four-star rugelach . . . . . . . . . . . . . . . . . . . . . . . . . . .249

cinnamon twists . . . . . . . . . . . . . . . . . . . . . . . . . . . .250

cream cheese pastry . . . . . . . . . . . . . . . . . . . . . . . . .251

sweet ravioli . . . . . . . . . . . . . . . . . . . . . . . . . . . . . . . .252

california rolls . . . . . . . . . . . . . . . . . . . . . . . . . . . . . . .254

dried fruit pastry strips . . . . . . . . . . . . . . . . . . . . . .255

heavy cream flaky pastry . . . . . . . . . . . . . . . . . . . . .257

flaky windmills . . . . . . . . . . . . . . . . . . . . . . . . . . . . .258

pecan strudel . . . . . . . . . . . . . . . . . . . . . . . . . . . . . . .260

miniature caramel cream vol-au-vents . . . . . . . .262

fig pastry rolls . . . . . . . . . . . . . . . . . . . . . . . . . . . . . .264

blitz puff pastry . . . . . . . . . . . . . . . . . . . . . . . . . . . . .266

florentine pastry strips . . . . . . . . . . . . . . . . . . . . . .269

streusel pastry strips . . . . . . . . . . . . . . . . . . . . . . . .271

phyllo accordions . . . . . . . . . . . . . . . . . . . . . . . . . . .273

flaky cheesecake turnovers . . . . . . . . . . . . . . . . . . .275

# sour cream pastry

➤ **Makes 1 ⅓ pounds**

. . . . . . . . . . . . . . . . . . . . . . . . . . . . . . . . .

Utopia for a baker is a foolproof pastry, one that never gets tough no matter how much you handle it. Look no further than this page: Sour Cream Pastry is a dream to work with and heaven to eat. The star ingredient in the pastry is a thick liquid—sour cream. Its acid tenderizes; its fat contributes flakiness. You can make it easily in a food processor, but I prefer making it by hand for a flakier pastry.

1. Put the flour and salt in a 3-quart bowl; stir to blend. Scatter the butter slices over the flour, and cut in with a pastry blender until the mixture consists of particles that vary in size from small peas to bread crumbs.

2. Stir in the sour cream with a fork. The pastry will appear dry, because the sour cream is thick and doesn't disperse easily. With your hands, manipulate the dough into a ball.

3. Divide in half, or as recipe directs. Wrap in plastic, and refrigerate until cold and firm, at least 4 hours, and up to 3 days; or freeze, well wrapped, up to 1 month.

## BAKING NOTE

I love to experiment in baking. This "What if?" makes it possible for me never to stop learning. A good example was when I substituted another thick liquid, unflavored low-fat yogurt, for the sour cream in this recipe. It led to Yogurt Pastry, which is just as flaky and delicious as the Sour Cream Pastry. The difference in taste is subtle: The Yogurt Pastry is not as tangy as the Sour Cream Pastry.

2 cups (280 grams) unsifted all-purpose flour

⅛ teaspoon salt

8 ounces (2 sticks) unsalted butter, chilled and cut into ¼-inch slices

½ cup (5 ounces) sour cream

# sweet cheese puffs

➤ **Makes 2 ½ to 3 dozen 1 ½-inch puffs**

. . . . . . . . . . . . . . . . . . . . . . . . . . . . . . . . . . . . . .

If I were to become famous for any of my creations, I hope it would be for the Sweet Cheese Puffs. A dollop of lemon-and-vanilla-flavored cream cheese is encased in Sour Cream Pastry and pinched at the top, much like a "beggar's purse"; during baking the pastries blossom open. The taste is equally as wonderful as the look, like cheesecake wrapped in rich flaky pastry.

1. Dough: Divide the pastry into three equal pieces. Shape each into a 5-inch square about ⅝ inch thick. Wrap in plastic, and refrigerate until cold and firm, at least 4 hours.

2. Cream Cheese Filling: Process all the filling ingredients in a food processor bowl until the mixture is smooth.

3. Remove one pastry square from refrigerator. Set aside for 10 minutes before rolling it. On a floured surface, roll the pastry into a rectangle slightly less than ⅛ inch thick. With a ruler and a pastry wheel, trim the ragged edges; then measure and cut the pastry into 3-inch squares.

4. Lay the pastry squares across the top of ungreased 12-cup miniature muffin pans, each cup measuring 1⅞ inches across and ¾ inch deep, centering each square over one cup. Spoon 1 heaping teaspoon of filling on each square; then bring opposite corners to the center, and press lightly to seal. This process will also ease the pastry into each cup. Refrigerate for at least 30 minutes. Roll and shape the remaining pastry squares in the same fashion.

5. Adjust rack to lower third of oven; preheat oven to 375 degrees F.

## DOUGH

1 recipe Sour Cream Pastry
(page 235)

## CREAM CHEESE FILLING

8 ounces cream cheese

1 large egg

½ cup (100 grams)
granulated sugar

1 teaspoon pure vanilla extract

1 teaspoon finely
grated lemon zest

## DECORATION

½ cup (50 grams)
unsifted powdered sugar

6. Bake two to three pans at a time for about 20 to 25 minutes, or until pastries are light brown. Remove pan from oven to a wire rack for about 10 minutes. Remove pastries from pan to a wire rack to cool completely.

7. Decoration: Sprinkle with powdered sugar before serving at room temperature.

8. If not serving the same day baked, stack undecorated pastries in airtight sturdy plastic containers and freeze up to 2 weeks. To serve, reheat to freshen in a 325-degree-F preheated oven for about 7 to 12 minutes, or until warm; cool slightly, then sprinkle with the powdered sugar.

STEP 4

## VARIATION NOTE

If you feel like embellishing the cheese filling a bit, it's nice to add ½ cup diced poached apple or pear pieces. In the fall, I suggest you look for quinces in the produce section of the supermarket. Add ½ cup poached and diced quince to the cream cheese filling. Though it is a richly flavored fruit, it is not as popular as the apple or pear. In my opinion, seeing the quince's golden peach color, inhaling its distinct scent, and tasting its concentrated perfume is culinary magnificence.

# pumpkin pastries

➤ **Makes 2½ to 3 dozen 1½-inch pastries**

Pair a flaky, buttery pastry with a filling similar to pumpkin cheesecake, and even people who swear the flavor of pumpkin will never make it on their hit parade list will convert.

1. Dough: Divide the pastry into three 5-inch squares about ⅝ inch thick. Wrap in plastic, and refrigerate until cold and firm, at least 4 hours.

2. Pumpkin Cream Cheese Filling: Process all the filling ingredients in a food processor bowl until the mixture is smooth and well blended.

3. Remove one pastry square from refrigerator. Set aside for 10 minutes before rolling it. On a floured work surface, roll the pastry into a rectangle until less than ⅛ inch thick. With a ruler and a pastry wheel, trim the ragged edges; then measure and cut pastry into 3-inch squares.

4. Lay the pastry squares across the top of ungreased 12-cup miniature muffin pans, each cup measuring 1⅞ inches across and ¾ inch deep, centering each square over one cup. Spoon 1 heaping teaspoon of filling on each square; then bring opposite corners to the center, and press lightly to seal. This process will also ease the pastry into each cup. Refrigerate for at least 30 minutes. Roll and shape the remaining pastry squares in the same fashion.

5. Adjust rack to lower third of oven; preheat oven to 375 degrees F.

6. Bake two to three pans at a time for about 20 to 25 minutes, or until pastries are light brown. Remove pans from oven to a wire rack for about 10 minutes. Remove pastries from pans to a wire rack to cool completely.

## DOUGH

1 recipe Sour Cream Pastry (page 235)

## PUMPKIN CREAM CHEESE FILLING

6 ounces cream cheese

¼ cup pumpkin purée, fresh or canned

1 large egg

½ cup (100 grams) packed light brown sugar

½ teaspoon finely grated orange zest

## DECORATION

½ cup (50 grams) unsifted powdered sugar

½ teaspoon ground cinnamon

7. Decoration: Sift the powdered sugar and cinnamon together; sprinkle pastries before serving at room temperature.

8. If not serving the same day baked, stack undecorated pastries in airtight sturdy plastic containers and freeze up to 2 weeks. To serve, reheat to freshen in a 325-degree-F preheated oven for about 7 to 12 minutes, or until warm; cool slightly, then sprinkle with the powdered sugar and cinnamon.

# eccles tarts

➤ **Makes 3½ dozen 1-x-2-inch pastries**

Sample these lemon-scented flaky pastries with a freshly brewed cup of your favorite tea. These pastries were inspired by the traditional English tarts of the same name.

1. Dough: Divide the pastry into three equal pieces. Shape each into a 4-inch square about ½ inch thick. Wrap in plastic and refrigerate until firm, at least 4 hours.

2. Dried Fruit Filling: In a 1½-quart bowl, toss all the filling ingredients to blend together. On a cutting board, coarsely chop them. The additional chopping makes this group of ingredients more uniform in size. Transfer the ingredients back into a bowl, tossing with fingertips to mix them and break up any large clumps of fruit sticking together.

3. Adjust rack to lower third of oven and preheat oven to 375 degrees F. Line two large cool baking sheets with parchment paper.

4. Remove one pastry square from refrigerator. Set aside for about 10 minutes before rolling. In a small bowl, whisk the egg until smooth.

5. Roll out the pastry on a lightly floured surface until it is ¹⁄₁₆ inch thick. Using a 2¾-inch round cutter, cut out shapes in the dough. Using a small pastry brush, lightly coat each circle with the egg wash. Spoon about ¾ teaspoonful of filling in the center of each pastry circle. Lift one-half of the pastry over the filling as though you were forming a turnover. Press the edges together to seal. With fingertips, hold this half-circle pastry at the seam, perpendicular to the work surface, with the folded edge touching the work surface. Still using your fingertips, press down to flatten the pastry and

## DOUGH

1 recipe Sour Cream Pastry
(page 235)

## DRIED FRUIT FILLING

1 tablespoon unsalted
butter, melted

1 tablespoon granulated sugar

1 teaspoon finely
grated lemon zest

¼ cup fresh bread crumbs
(about 1 thin slice bread,
crusts removed)

1 ounce (scant 3 tablespoons)
dried currants

1 ounce (2 tablespoons)
golden raisins

1 ounce (2 tablespoons)
glacé citron, finely chopped

1 ounce (¼ cup) walnuts,
toasted and coarsely chopped

## EGG WASH

1 large egg

## DECORATION

½ cup (100 grams)
granulated sugar

manipulate into an oval shape. Turn pastry over with its seam side down. This technique sounds more difficult than it really is. Lightly coat pastries with the egg wash and, to decorate, sprinkle with the sugar. With the tip of a small sharp paring knife, cut an *X* in the pastry as a vent and decoration. Roll and shape the remaining pastry squares in the same fashion.

STEP 5

6. Bake, one sheet at a time, for 12 to 15 minutes, or until golden. Using a metal spatula, lift pastries off the parchment to a wire rack to cool.

7. These are best eaten at room temperature the same day baked, or stack in an airtight sturdy plastic container and freeze up to 2 weeks. To serve, reheat to freshen in a 325-degree-F preheated oven for about 5 minutes, or until warm; serve at room temperature.

# heartovers

➤ **Makes 6 dozen 1½-inch pastries (or 3 dozen pairs)**

. . . . . . . . . . . . . . . . . . . . . . . . . .

These pastries begin as heart-shaped cutouts. Then, one side of the pastry is folded over to enclose the filling and form a turnover. Generally, a turnover starts as a circle before it becomes a semicircle. But in this case, the cutout is a heart that transforms into a half heart—thus the name Heartovers. For a novel presentation, match one Heartover next to another to form a pair—or a heart.

   For these Heartovers, it's nice to use two fillings—one half of a pair, apricot-pistachio; the other half, apple (page 252).

1. Dough: Form half the pastry into two 4-inch squares, each ½ inch thick. Wrap in plastic and refrigerate until firm, at least 4 hours.

2. Apricot-Pistachio Filling: In a 1-quart saucepan, bring the apricots, juice, and sugar to a boil. Reduce heat to medium-low, and simmer until almost all the liquid is evaporated, about 7 minutes. Stir in the butter; pour on a heatproof plate to cool. When cool, chop coarsely; stir in the pistachios.

3. Adjust rack to lower third of oven and preheat oven to 375 degrees F. Line a large cool baking sheet with parchment paper.

4. Remove one pastry square from refrigerator. Set aside for 10 minutes before rolling it. In a small bowl, whisk the egg until smooth.

## DOUGH

½ recipe Sour Cream Pastry
   (page 235)

## APRICOT-PISTACHIO FILLING

3 ounces dried apricots

⅓ cup fresh orange juice

1 tablespoon packed
   light brown sugar

1 tablespoon unsalted butter

½ ounce (2 tablespoons)
   pistachios, toasted and
   finely chopped

## EGG WASH

1 large egg

## DECORATION

½ cup fresh egg-bread
   crumbs (about 2 thin slices,
   crusts removed)

5. Roll out the dough on a lightly floured surface until it is ⅟₁₆ inch thick. Using a 2-inch heart cutter, cut out shapes in dough. Using a small pastry brush, apply a light coating of egg wash over each heart cutout. Pipe or spoon ½ teaspoon filling in the center of each pastry. Lift one-half of the pastry over the filling. Using the tines of a fork, press the edges together to seal. Space 1 inch apart on the baking sheet and refrigerate about 15 minutes to firm the pastries and make it easier to handle them to decorate them. Repeat procedure with the remaining square of dough.

6. Remove the pastries on the baking sheet from the refrigerator and apply a thin coat of egg wash on top of each pastry. Dip one at a time in the bread crumbs. Bake for 10 to 13 minutes, or until light golden brown. Using a metal spatula, lift the pastries off the parchment to a wire rack to cool.

7. These are best eaten at room temperature the same day baked, or stack in an airtight sturdy plastic container and freeze up to 2 weeks. To serve, reheat to freshen in a 325-degree F preheated oven for about 5 minutes or until warm; serve at room temperature.

# shreveshire tarts

➤ **Makes 3½ dozen 1-x-2-inch pastries**

. . . . . . . . . . . . . . . . . . . . . . . . . . . . . .

If you like pastry with a little spirit, try these tarts. A flaky pastry surrounds a filling flavored with fresh mint and orange zest. These tarts remind me of a pastry I ate on a recent visit to London, thus the name.

1. Dough: Divide the pastry into three equal pieces. Shape each into a 4-inch round about ½ inch thick. Wrap in plastic and refrigerate until firm, at least 4 hours.

2. Dried Currant Filling: In a 1½-quart bowl, toss all the filling ingredients to blend together. On a cutting board, coarsely chop them; return ingredients to bowl.

3. Adjust rack to lower third of oven and preheat oven to 375 degrees F. Line two large cool baking sheets with parchment paper.

4. Remove one pastry disk from refrigerator. Set aside for about 10 minutes before rolling. In a small bowl, whisk the egg until smooth.

5. Roll out the pastry on a lightly floured surface to a ¹⁄₁₆-inch-thick circle, about 14 inches in diameter. Using a 2¾-inch round cutter, cut out shapes in the dough. Using a small pastry brush, lightly coat each circle with some of the egg wash. Spoon about ¾ teaspoonful of filling in the center of each pastry circle. Lift one-half of the pastry over the filling as though you were forming a turnover. Press the edges together to seal. With fingertips, hold this half-circle pastry at the seam, perpendicular to the work surface, with the folded portion touching the work surface. Still using your fingertips, press down to flatten the pastry and manipulate into an oval shape. Turn pastry over with its seam side down. This technique sounds more difficult than it really is. Lightly coat pastries

## DOUGH

1 recipe Sour Cream Pastry (page 235)

## DRIED CURRANT FILLING

1 tablespoon unsalted butter, melted

1 tablespoon granulated sugar

1 teaspoon honey

1 teaspoon finely grated orange zest

1 tablespoon fresh mint, finely minced

2½ ounces (½ cup) dried currants

## EGG WASH

1 large egg

## DECORATION

½ cup (100 grams) granulated sugar

with more of the egg wash and sprinkle with the sugar. With the tip of a small sharp paring knife, cut two slits diagonally in the pastry, both as a vent and as decoration. Roll and shape the remaining pastry squares in the same fashion.

6. Bake, one sheet at a time, for about 12 to 15 minutes, or until golden. Using a metal spatula, lift pastries off the parchment to a wire rack to cool.

7. These are best eaten at room temperature the same day baked; or stack in a sturdy airtight plastic container and freeze up to 2 weeks. To serve, reheat to freshen in a 325-degree-F preheated oven for about 5 minutes, or until warm; serve at room temperature.

# eva deutsch's almond slices

➤ Makes 4½ dozen 1-inch slices

. . . . . . . . . . . . . . . . . . . . . . . . . . . . . . . .

Seattle's Eva Deutsch was the mother of one of my best friends, and she was probably the best cookie maker I've ever known, something you'll discover when you try her rich Almond Slices. Tender, flaky Sour Cream Pastry is rolled around a filling of almond paste, hazelnuts, and lemon zest, before being baked and sliced. The not-too-sweet pastries are absolutely delicious.

1. Dough: Form the pastry into two 4-inch squares, each about ½ inch thick. Wrap in plastic and refrigerate until firm, at least 4 hours.

2. Almond-Hazelnut Filling: Put all the ingredients in a food processor bowl and process until the mixture comes together in a smooth mass.

3. Divide the filling into four equal portions, each about ¼ cup. Roll each portion back and forth on a floured surface with the lightly floured fingertips of both hands into a rope about 13 inches long. Set aside while you roll out the pastry.

4. Adjust rack to lower third of oven and preheat oven to 375 degrees F. Line a large cool baking sheet with parchment paper.

5. Remove one portion of dough from the refrigerator. Set aside for 10 minutes before rolling it. To make the egg wash, in a small bowl, whisk the egg until smooth.

**DOUGH**

½ recipe Sour Cream Pastry (page 235)

**ALMOND-HAZELNUT FILLING**

8 ounces (1 scant cup) almond paste, room temperature

1 ounce (3 tablespoons) hazelnuts, toasted and ground to yield ⅓ cup

2 tablespoons (25 grams) granulated sugar

2 tablespoons (25 grams) packed light brown sugar

2 teaspoons finely grated lemon zest

⅛ teaspoon ground cinnamon

1 large egg

**EGG WASH**

1 large egg

**DECORATION**

1½ ounces (¼ cup) unblanched almonds, split in half at seam

½ cup (100 grams) granulated sugar

6. On a lightly floured surface, roll the dough into a 6½-x-15-inch rectangle ⅟₁₆ inch thick. With a ruler and pastry wheel, trim the edges to measure about 6 inches wide and 14½ inches long. Lightly brush the pastry with the egg wash.

7. With a ruler and pastry wheel, cut the pastry strip in half to create two strips, each about 2¾ x 14½ inches.

8. Center a rope of filling on one pastry strip. Flatten it with your fingertips, then lift one side of the pastry to the center of the filling; lift the other side of pastry to overlap the other side and cover the filling. Press with fingertips again to seal the pastry layers together and to flatten the roll to ⅜ inch thick and 1½ inches wide. Place seam side up on the cool baking sheet. Repeat with the other pastry strip, and space the pastry rolls 1½ inches apart on the baking sheet.

9. Repeat the procedure with the other portion of pastry and place the assembled pastry rolls parallel to the others on the baking sheet. Lightly brush each roll with the egg wash, then decorate by pressing the almond halves 1 inch apart along the seams. Sprinkle lightly with the sugar. Bake for 12 to 15 minutes, or until pastries are light golden brown and flaky. Using a metal spatula, lift them off the parchment to a wire rack to cool.

10. When the pastries are cool, cut them, between the almonds, into 1-inch slices with a sharp knife.

11. These are best eaten at room temperature the same day baked; or stack in sturdy airtight plastic containers and freeze up to 2 weeks. To serve, reheat to freshen in a 325-degree-F preheated oven for about 7 minutes, or until warm; serve at room temperature.

# cottage cheese dough

➤ **Makes 1⅓ pounds**

. . . . . . . . . . . . . . . . . . . . . . . . . . . . . . . . .

The cottage cheese adds its distinctive tangy flavor to this pastry.

1. Spoon the cottage cheese into a sieve over a bowl and allow it to drain for at least 2 hours. Using a rubber spatula, toss the cottage cheese occasionally. Remove 1 cup of the drained cottage cheese for the dough. Reserve the remaining cheese for another use.

2. Process the flour and salt in a food processor just to combine. Scatter all the butter slices over the flour mixture and process with on/off pulses until the butter appears to disappear into the mixture. Scatter 1 cup of the cottage cheese over the mixture and process with on/off pulses just until mixture comes together into a cohesive ball.

3. Divide the dough into quarters; shape each into a flat disk. Wrap in plastic and refrigerate until firm, at least 4 hours; or freeze, well wrapped, up to 1 month.

1 pint small curd cottage cheese (4% milkfat)

2 cups (280 grams) unsifted all-purpose flour

⅛ teaspoon salt

8 ounces (2 sticks) unsalted butter, chilled and cut into ¼-inch slices

# four-star rugelach

➤ **Makes 5 dozen 1½-inch crescents**

. . . . . . . . . . . . . . . . . . . . . . . . . . . . . . . . . .

Rugelach (roog-uh-luh), popular croissant-shaped cookies, are flaky and rich, but not overly sweet.

1. Dough: Divide the dough into quarters; shape each into a flat disk. Wrap in plastic and refrigerate until firm, at least 4 hours.

2. Filling: Adjust rack to lower third of oven and preheat oven to 350 degrees F. Line a large baking sheet with aluminum foil. In a small bowl, combine the sugar and cinnamon.

3. Remove one dough package at a time from refrigerator. Set aside for 10 minutes before rolling it. On a lightly floured surface, roll the dough into a 10- to 11-inch circle, ⅛ inch thick. With a small metal spatula, spread only 1 tablespoon jam very thinly over dough. Sprinkle with 2 tablespoons cinnamon sugar, then with ¼ cup of the ground nuts and 2 tablespoons of the currants, if desired. With rolling pin, lightly roll to press filling ingredients into the dough.

4. Using a sharp knife, cut the circle into 16 pie-shaped wedges; roll each one up, beginning at the wide end. Place rolls 1 inch apart, point down, on foil-lined baking sheet. Bake for 15 to 20 minutes, or until golden brown. If the pastries are browning too much on the bottom from the jam oozing out, move them off the jam to a clean spot on the baking sheet. Continue to bake until done. Remove pan to a rack to cool for 5 minutes. Then, with a metal spatula, transfer rugelach to a wire rack to cool. Repeat shaping and baking procedure with the remaining dough and filling.

5. These are best eaten the same day baked. Store in a covered foil-lined cardboard container at room temperature for up to 2 days; or stack in an airtight sturdy plastic container and freeze up to 2 weeks. To serve, defrost at room temperature and reheat to freshen in a 300-degree-F preheated oven for about 5 to 7 minutes; serve cool.

## DOUGH

1 recipe Cottage Cheese Dough (facing page)

## FILLING

½ cup (100 grams) granulated sugar

1 teaspoon ground cinnamon

4 tablespoons strained apricot jam

1 cup (4 ounces) finely chopped walnuts

2½ ounces (½ cup) dried currants (optional)

# cinnamon twists

➤ **Makes 4 dozen 2-inch-long twists**

Long, slender pastry straws, flavored with cinnamon sugar, are handsome on a plate of fresh fruit or assorted ice creams.

1. Dough: Prepare the dough and divide it into quarters. Wrap individually in plastic and refrigerate until firm. (These Cinnamon Twists use just two of the dough packages; reserve the remaining two for another recipe.)

2. Adjust rack to lower third of oven and preheat oven to 350 degrees F. Center an 8-inch-wide strip of aluminum foil on a baking sheet, leaving at least an inch of the sheet uncovered on either side of the foil.

3. Cinnamon Sugar: In a small bowl, stir to combine the sugar and cinnamon. Sprinkle ¼ cup of the cinnamon sugar on a work surface, and roll out one-quarter of the dough on it into an 11-x-12-inch rectangle, about ⅛ inch thick. As you roll, turn the dough over and continue to roll it out so that both sides are coated with the sugar.

4. Cut ½-inch-wide strips, each about 11 inches long. To twist a strip, hold each end between thumb and forefinger. Turn one end toward you and the other one away until twisted three or four times. (It's best to twist strip loosely rather than too tight.) Place strips, 1 inch apart, across the aluminum foil strip on the baking sheet. Press the ends of the strips that extend beyond the foil onto the sheet to anchor them.

5. Bake for 15 minutes, or until light golden brown. Cool in pan on a rack. Trim ends and cut into 2-inch-long pieces. Repeat shaping and baking procedure with the remaining dough and cinnamon.

6. Store in an airtight tin at room temperature up to 1 week.

## DOUGH

1 recipe Cottage Cheese Dough (page 248)

## CINNAMON SUGAR

½ cup unsifted powdered sugar

½ teaspoon ground cinnamon

# cream cheese pastry

➤ **Makes 1½ pounds**

Here is another rich, flaky pastry, a bit sweeter and somewhat less flaky than the Sour Cream Pastry (page 235). Both the Sour Cream Pastry and the Cream Cheese Pastry are foolproof and provide only the most delicious results.

1. Process the flour, sugar, lemon zest, and salt in the food processor bowl a few seconds just to mix ingredients. Scatter the butter slices over the flour mixture, and process with on/off bursts until the mixture has the consistency of cornmeal. Scatter the cheese cubes over mixture and process just until the ingredients come together in a ball.

2. Divide the dough in half. Shape into two 5-inch squares, each about ¾ inch thick. Wrap in plastic and refrigerate until firm, for at least 4 hours or up to 3 days; or freeze, well wrapped, up to 2 weeks.

2 ¼ cups (315 grams) unsifted all-purpose flour

2 tablespoons granulated sugar

1 teaspoon finely grated lemon zest

⅛ teaspoon salt

8 ounces (2 sticks) unsalted butter, chilled and cut into ¼-inch slices

6 ounces cream cheese, cut into small cubes

# sweet ravioli

➤ **Makes 4 dozen 1½-inch pastries**

. . . . . . . . . . . . . . . . . . . . . . . .

These look like Italian ravioli and taste like mini apple pies. The "pasta" is made from tender Cream Cheese Pastry and the filling from an intensely flavored apple mixture with a hint of Cheddar cheese.

1. Apple Filling: In a 2½-quart heavy saucepan, melt the butter. Add the apple pieces, sprinkle with the sugar, and cook over medium heat for about 20 minutes, or until the apples are soft and the liquid is thick and caramelized. With a wooden spoon, stir occasionally, and mash the apples during cooking, to form a mixture similar to caramelized applesauce. Remove from heat and stir in the lemon zest. Spread the mixture on a heatproof plate to cool quickly. When completely cool, add the cheese, if desired.

2. Adjust rack to lower third of oven and preheat oven to 375 degrees F. Line a large cool baking sheet with parchment paper.

3. Dough: Remove the dough squares from refrigerator. Set aside for 10 minutes before rolling them out. In a small bowl, whisk the egg until smooth.

4. Roll out one portion of pastry on a lightly floured surface until it is ⅛ inch thick. With the edge of a ruler, mark faint indentations 1½ inches apart in the dough. With a pastry brush, apply a light coating of the egg wash to the dough. Spoon or pipe out, using a pastry bag fitted with a ½-inch plain decorating tip (such as Ateco #6), small mounds of filling equivalent to ¾ teaspoon on the indentations marked in the dough.

## APPLE FILLING

1 ounce (2 tablespoons)
unsalted butter

1 pound (about 3) Gravenstein
or Golden Delicious apples,
peeled, cored, and quartered

¼ cup (50 grams)
granulated sugar

½ teaspoon finely
grated lemon zest

1 ounce finely grated sharp
Cheddar cheese (optional)

## DOUGH

1 recipe Cream Cheese Pastry
(page 251)

## EGG WASH

1 large egg

## DECORATION

½ cup (100 grams)
granulated sugar

5. Roll out the remaining portion of dough to the same dimensions as the first. Cover the filled sheet of pastry with the dough and press the sheets of pastry together firmly around each mound of filling. Cut the ravioli into 1½-inch squares with a fluted pastry wheel. Check that each square's edges are sealed.

6. Transfer the ravioli to the baking sheet. Lightly coat with the remaining egg wash, sprinkle with the sugar to decorate, and cut a small vent in the center of each square. Bake for 12 to 15 minutes, or until puffed and light golden brown. Using a metal spatula, lift the ravioli off the parchment to a wire rack to cool.

7. These taste best served at room temperature the same day baked, or stack in an airtight sturdy plastic container and freeze up to 2 weeks. To serve, reheat to freshen in a 325-degree-F preheated oven for about 5 minutes, or until warm; serve at room temperature.

## TECHNIQUE NOTE

Making these sweet ravioli employs a time-saving technique for forming many small pastries quickly.

## VARIATION NOTES

### Fresh Plum Filling

Cut fresh French or Italian pitted plums in quarters, dip into the flour, and substitute for the Apple Filling recipe.

### Fresh Quince Filling

Substitute ½ pound quince for half of the apples in the Apple Filling recipe.

# california rolls

➤**Makes 3 dozen 1¼-inch rolls**

Though these are similar to rugelach, the shape and filling are different. You can substitute dried cherries or dried cranberries for the apricots and golden raisins—and even brown sugar for the granulated sugar.

1. Dough: Prepare the dough and divide it into quarters. Wrap individually in plastic and refrigerate until firm. (California Rolls use two of the dough packages; reserve the remaining two for another recipe.)

2. Adjust rack to the lower third of the oven and preheat oven to 350 degrees F. Line baking sheet with aluminum foil.

3. Filling: Combine the sugar and cinnamon in a small bowl.

4. Remove one dough package from the refrigerator 10 minutes before rolling it. On a lightly floured surface, roll the dough into an 11-x-12-inch rectangle, ⅛ inch thick. Using a small metal spatula, spread 1 tablespoon of the jam very thinly over dough. Sprinkle with 2 tablespoons cinnamon sugar, then with 2 tablespoons *each* raisins, apricots, and pistachios. With rolling pin, lightly roll to press the filling ingredients into the dough.

5. Using a sharp knife, cut the rectangle in half so that each strip measures 5½ x 12 inches. Roll up each one lengthwise. With a sharp knife, cut 1¼-inch-wide slices from each long roll. Place the small rolls 1 inch apart, flap down, on the foil-lined baking sheet. Bake for 15 to 20 minutes, or until golden brown. If the pastries are browning too much on the bottom from jam oozing out, move them off the jam to a clean spot on the baking sheet. Continue to bake them until done. Remove pan to a rack to cool for 5 minutes. Then, with a metal spatula, transfer rolls to a wire rack. Repeat shaping and baking procedure with the remaining dough and filling.

DOUGH

1 recipe Cottage Cheese Dough
   (page 248)

FILLING

¼ cup granulated sugar

½ teaspoon ground cinnamon

2 tablespoons strained apricot jam

¼ cup golden raisins,
   finely chopped

¼ cup dried apricots,
   finely chopped

¼ cup pistachios, finely chopped

# dried fruit pastry strips

➤ **Makes 3 dozen 1-x-2-inch slices**

To create this pastry, fold rich cream cheese pastry around a dried fruit mixture and bake. Then cut into strips to reveal filling and layers of pastry. The combination of tangy dried fruit and flaky pastry is irresistible. When I need several dozen assorted cookies to feed a crowd, this recipe is perfect, since Dried Fruit Pastry Strips are easy to assemble.

1. Adjust rack to lower third of oven and preheat oven to 375 degrees F. Line a large cool baking sheet with parchment paper.

2. Dough: Remove the pastry from the refrigerator. Set aside for 10 minutes before rolling it. In a small bowl, whisk the egg until smooth.

3. Dried Currant Filling: In a 1½-quart bowl, toss all the filling ingredients to blend together. On a cutting board, coarsely chop ingredients; return to bowl.

4. On a lightly floured surface, roll the dough into a 14½-x-11½-inch rectangle. Using a ruler and pastry wheel, trim the edges to measure approximately 14 inches long x 11 inches wide. Lightly brush the pastry with the egg wash.

5. With a ruler and pastry wheel, cut the pastry into thirds to create three strips about 4½ inches wide and 11 inches long. Spoon about ½ cup of the filling lengthwise down two thirds of each dough strip. Spread the filling to within about ½ inch of the shorter edges. Fold the unfilled third over half the filling, then lift this portion and fold it over so the edges meet. Press edges on the short sides and along the seam to seal.

CONTINUED ➤

## DOUGH

½ recipe Cream Cheese Pastry (page 251)

## EGG WASH

1 large egg

## DRIED CURRANT FILLING

2 tablespoons unsalted butter, melted

2 tablespoons granulated sugar

2 teaspoons honey

2 teaspoons finely grated orange zest

2 tablespoons fresh mint leaves, finely minced

5 ounces (1 cup) dried currants

## DECORATION

3 tablespoons granulated sugar

6.  Transfer the pastry strip, seam side down, onto baking sheet. With fingertips, flatten the pastry slightly to evenly distribute the filling and realign the rectangular shape. Repeat the procedure with the remaining strips of dough. Set them on the baking sheet parallel to each other and 2 inches apart. Brush the rolls with the egg wash, and, using the tines of a fork or the tip of a paring knife, score the pastry surface to decorate it.

7.  Decoration: Sprinkle pastry lightly with the granulated sugar.

8.  Bake for 12 minutes, then reduce oven temperature to 350 degrees F and bake about 5 to 6 minutes more, or until golden brown. Lift the strips on the parchment paper to a wire rack until cool. Using a sharp knife, cut diagonally into 1-inch slices.

9.  These taste best at room temperature the same day baked. Or store, unsliced, well wrapped in aluminum foil, at room temperature up to 2 days. Cut into slices as needed.

## VARIATION NOTE

Substitute other fillings such as the Apricot-Pistachio Filling (page 242), the Dried Fruit Filling (page 240), or even the Fig Filling (page 264) for the Dried Currant Filling. If you've never baked with dried tart red cherries, this recipe offers the perfect opportunity. Substitute them for the dried currants in the filling above.

# heavy cream flaky pastry

➤ **Makes 1 ⅓ pounds**

2 cups (280 grams)
  unsifted all-purpose flour

¼ teaspoon salt

8 ounces (2 sticks) unsalted
  butter, chilled and diced into
  small cubes

½ cup (4 ounces) heavy
  cream, chilled

This easy-to-make pastry puffs in the oven much like puff pastry, but it is more delicate and tender. Making the pastry by hand rather than with a machine gives flakier results. Applying a simple rolling and folding technique makes a cohesive, layered dough. It's these layers that lift the pastry magically and evenly while baking.

1. Put the flour and salt in a 3-quart mixing bowl; stir to blend. With a pastry blender, cut in the butter until particles are the size of small peas. With a fork, gradually stir in the cream until the mixture comes together into a cohesive dough. If it seems too dry to come together, you need not add more cream. Just use your hands to press it against the sides of the bowl to form a cohesive mass.

2. On a lightly floured board, roll the dough to form a 9-x-7-inch rectangle; fold in half to form a 4½-x-7-inch rectangle. Rotate the dough 90 degrees and roll out again to a 9-x-7-inch rectangle, and again fold in half to form a 4½-x-7-inch rectangle. Wrap in plastic and refrigerate until firm and cold, at least 3 hours or up to 2 days; or freeze, well wrapped, up to 1 week.

# flaky windmills

➤ **Makes 2 dozen 1½-inch pastries**

. . . . . . . . . . . . . . . . . .

When I need a cookie with an unusual twist for an interesting assortment on a petits fours tray, I make these high-tech windmill designs from leftover pastry scraps that I patch together. Shape scraps into a disk, wrap in plastic wrap, and refrigerate to firm butter and relax dough before rerolling.

1. Adjust rack to lower third of oven and preheat oven to 375 degrees F. Line a large cool baking sheet with parchment.

2. Royal Icing: Whip the ingredients in a deep mixing bowl with an electric mixer at medium speed until the mixture has a creamy, marshmallow-like consistency, about 5 minutes.

3. Dough: Remove the dough from refrigerator and roll it on a lightly floured surface until it is ³⁄₁₆ inch thick. Trim to a rectangle approximately 8 x 12 inches. With a small metal spatula, spread a very thin layer of Royal Icing over the pastry. With a ruler and pastry wheel, trim the ragged edges; then measure and cut pastry into 2-inch squares. Space the pastry squares 1 inch apart on the cool baking sheet. With a small paring knife, cut 1-inch slashes at each corner toward the center. Fold alternate corners into center in pinwheel fashion; press gently in the center. Using a small handmade paper cone, pipe a tiny dot of the Royal Icing in the center of each pastry.

4. Bake for 10 minutes, reduce temperature to 350 degrees F, and bake 4 minutes longer, or until light golden brown. Place the baking sheet on a wire rack for 5 minutes, then lift pastries off the parchment to a rack to cool.

## ROYAL ICING

1 cup (100 grams) unsifted powdered sugar

2 tablespoons (1 large) egg white

⅛ teaspoon cream of tartar

## DOUGH

10 ounces Heavy Cream Flaky Pastry scraps (page 257)

5. These are best eaten at room temperature the same day baked. Store in one layer in a covered foil-lined cardboard container, such as a cake box, in a dry room at room temperature up to 1 day; or stack in an airtight sturdy plastic container and freeze up to 2 weeks. To serve, reheat to freshen in a 325-degree-F preheated oven for about 5 minutes, or until warm; serve cool.

# pecan strudel

➤ **Makes 4 dozen ½-inch slices**

. . . . . . . . . . . . . . . . . . . . . . . . . . . . . . . . . . . .

I can't say enough about this pastry, one of my all-time favorite taste treats. It's a straightforward combination of flaky pastry wrapped around a luscious not-too-sweet pecan filling. It's rolled strudel-fashion and sliced into individual servings. To dress up the small slices, I often use a tiny stencil and paint a design with Glossy Chocolate Ganache Glaze (page 171) on each piece. Thanks to Joan Chamberlain for giving me the recipe for this luscious pecan filling.

1.  Pecan Filling: Beat the butter and sugar together in an electric mixer until creamy. Add the egg and beat until creamy and smooth. Stir in the pecans and flour.

2.  Adjust rack to lower third of oven and preheat oven to 375 degrees F. Line a large cool baking sheet with parchment paper.

3.  Dough: Remove the dough from refrigerator. Divide it in half, refrigerate one portion, and set aside the other for 10 minutes before rolling it. In a small bowl, whisk the egg for the egg wash until smooth.

4.  On a lightly floured surface, roll the dough into a 12-x-6-x-¹⁄₁₆-inch-thick rectangle. Using a ruler and pastry wheel, trim the edges to measure approximately 12 inches long x 5¾ inches wide. Lightly brush with some of the egg wash.

5.  Spoon half the filling lengthwise down the center of the pastry to within ½ inch of the edges on the short ends. With fingertips, pat the filling to shape it to resemble a sausage. Lift one long side of the dough lengthwise over the filling. Lift the other portion so the pastry overlaps, and press to seal. Press the ends together to seal.

## PECAN FILLING

3 ounces (¾ stick) unsalted butter, room temperature

½ cup (100 grams) granulated sugar

1 large egg

8 ounces (2 cups) pecans, finely chopped to yield 2 cups (see Baking Note)

3 tablespoons unsifted all-purpose flour

## DOUGH

½ recipe Heavy Cream Flaky Pastry (page 257)

## EGG WASH

1 large egg

6. Gently transfer the pastry to the baking sheet, sealed-seam side down. With fingers, reshape pastry into a rectangular log, about 12 inches long, 2 inches wide, and ¾ inch high. Brush the entire surface with more of the egg wash. With the tines of a fork or the tip of a paring knife, lightly score the pastry with intersecting lines, or shapes such as leaves, for decoration. Repeat the procedure for the remaining dough and filling. Set this pastry parallel to the first one, about 3 inches apart.

7. Bake for 25 to 30 minutes, or until golden brown. Lift the pastries, on the parchment paper, from the baking sheet to a wire rack to cool.

8. Transfer the pastry rolls to a cutting board. Using a sharp knife, cut them diagonally into ½-inch slices.

9. These are best eaten at room temperature the same day baked; or freeze unsliced and undecorated, well wrapped in aluminum foil, up to 1 week. To serve, reheat to freshen in a 325-degree-F preheated oven for about 10 minutes, or until warm; cool before slicing and decorating.

### BAKING NOTE

Because the nuts provide structure as well as flavor in this filling recipe, it is important to measure the chopped nut pieces as accurately as possible. With a food processor, through variations of brand, speed, blade, timing, and force, you can grind a given weight of nuts into widely varying volumes of chopped nuts. A nut mill grinds nuts into the same volume every time, so for this recipe use a nut mill to chop the nuts to yield 2 cups.

# miniature caramel cream vol-au-vents

➤ Makes 3½ dozen 1½-inch miniature vol-au-vents

. . . . . . . . . . . . . . . . . . . . . . . .

Small circles of Heavy Cream Flaky Pastry, each with a tiny circular cut in the center, bake into a flaky pastry container to fill with the ultimate caramel filling. If you don't want to make the pastry, the filling is fabulous drizzled over ice cream or poached fruit, such as peaches or pears.

1. Caramel Syrup Filling: In a 1½-quart heavy-bottomed saucepan, heat the corn syrup and sugar over low heat until the sugar is dissolved. Then, increase heat to medium-high and boil the mixture until the caramel is light amber-colored, about 10 minutes. Remove from heat, and pour in the cream all at once. The mixture will foam. Carefully stir mixture with a wooden spoon to distribute the heat and blend the ingredients together. Pour into a small bowl to thicken and cool thoroughly before filling pastries, about 2 hours.

2. Adjust rack to lower third of oven and preheat oven to 375 degrees F. Line a large cool baking sheet with parchment paper.

3. Dough: Divide the dough in half, refrigerate one half, and roll out the other on a lightly floured surface to form a rectangle 12 inches long, 8 inches wide, and ⅛ inch thick. Using a 1¾-inch scalloped round cutter, cut shapes from the dough. With a ¾-inch round cutter, stamp each pastry center, without cutting all the way through the dough. Space the circles 1 inch apart on baking sheet.

4. Bake for 12 to 13 minutes, or until light golden brown. Transfer baking sheet to a wire rack to cool for 5 minutes. Using the tip of a paring knife, carefully remove the small pastry circle marked in the center. (Some pastry should remain under each small circle.) Allow the shells to cool completely before filling.

## CARAMEL SYRUP FILLING

⅓ cup light corn syrup

⅔ cup (130 grams) granulated sugar

½ cup (4 ounces) heavy cream, room temperature

## DOUGH

1 recipe Heavy Cream Flaky Pastry (page 257)

## DECORATION

42 candied lilacs, finely chopped

5. Repeat this procedure with the other portion of dough. Shape scraps into a disk, wrap in plastic wrap, and refrigerate to firm butter and relax dough before rerolling for another recipe, such as Flaky Windmills (page 258).

6. Spoon the caramel syrup filling, a teaspoon at a time, into each pastry shell. Sprinkle the candied lilacs over pastries.

7. These are best eaten at room temperature the same day baked and filled; or store in one layer in a covered foil-lined cardboard container, such as a cake box, in a dry room at room temperature up to 1 day. Stack unfilled pastries in an airtight sturdy plastic container and freeze up to 2 weeks. To serve, reheat to freshen in a 325-degree-F preheated oven for about 5 minutes, or until warm; add the caramel filling and lilacs, and serve at room temperature.

TECHNIQUE NOTE

If the caramel forms lumps when you add the cream, put the saucepan back over a very low flame and slowly stir until smooth.

# fig pastry rolls

➤ Makes 4 dozen ½-inch slices

Dried figs have never tasted better. Here's my contemporary version of that old favorite, fig bars.

1. Fig Filling: In a 1½-quart heavy-bottomed saucepan, combine the figs, sugar, and water. Simmer over medium heat, stirring constantly, just until thick. Remove from heat, and stir in the butter. Cool to room temperature. Add the lemon juice and vanilla. Place in bowl of food processor and pulse just until the mixture forms a purée.

2. Adjust rack to lower third of oven and preheat oven to 375 degrees F. Line a large cool baking sheet with parchment paper.

3. Dough: Remove the dough from the refrigerator. Divide it in half, refrigerate one portion, and set aside the other for 10 minutes before rolling it. In a small bowl, whisk the egg until smooth.

4. On a lightly floured surface, roll the dough into a 12-x-6-x-¹⁄₁₆-inch-thick rectangle. Using a ruler and pastry wheel, trim the edges to measure about 12 inches long x 5¾ inches wide. Lightly brush with some of the egg wash.

5. Spoon half the filling lengthwise down the center of the pastry, to within ½ inch of the edges on the short ends. With fingertips, pat the filling to shape it to resemble a sausage. Lift one long side of the dough over the filling. Lift the other portion, allowing the pastry to overlap, and press to seal. Press the ends together to seal.

## DOUGH

½ recipe Heavy Cream
  Flaky Pastry (page 257)

## FIG FILLING

1 cup (6 ounces) dried figs,
  stems removed, chopped

3 tablespoons granulated sugar

½ cup water

1 ounce (2 tablespoons)
  unsalted butter

1 tablespoon fresh lemon juice

1 teaspoon pure vanilla extract

## EGG WASH

1 large egg

6. Gently transfer the pastry to baking sheet, sealed-seam side down. With fingers, reshape pastry into a rectangular log, about 12 inches long, 2 inches wide, and ¾ inch high. Brush the entire surface lightly with more of the egg wash. Using the tines of a fork or the tip of a paring knife, decorate pastry surface with lines or shapes. Repeat the procedure for the remaining dough and filling. Set this pastry parallel to the first one, about 3 inches apart.

7. Bake for 25 to 30 minutes, or until golden brown. Lift the pastries, on the parchment paper, from the baking sheet to a wire rack to cool.

8. Transfer the pastry rolls to a cutting board. Using a sharp knife, cut them diagonally into ½-inch slices.

9. These are best at room temperature the same day baked; or freeze unsliced, well wrapped in aluminum foil, up to 1 week. To serve, reheat to freshen in a 325-degree-F preheated oven for about 10 minutes or until warm; cool before cutting into slices.

# blitz puff pastry

➤ **Makes about 2 pounds**

A blitz puff pastry recipe, written with careful details to guarantee successful results, resembles a pie crust recipe. Both recipes call for a lot of fat and require attention when working with it to achieve a proper flaky texture. Though the blitz variety is easier and quicker to make than classic puff pastry, it's important that the butter be well chilled after cutting it into ½-inch-thick slices. Chilled butter withstands the rolling of the dough a few times to create layers. If the butter is too soft, the dough absorbs the butter, while too firm butter breaks through the dough and prevents any layer formation.

1. Cut the sticks of butter into ½-inch-thick slices; then cut each slice in half lengthwise to give you 12 to 16 oblong chunks per stick of butter. Since it takes time to cut the butter into pieces, place them on a baking sheet and refrigerate for at least 10 minutes to rechill and firm after handling.

2. Scatter the butter pieces over the flour in the bowl of a heavy-duty mixer; with a rubber spatula, toss them briefly to coat with the flour.

3. Add the salt to the ice water in a liquid-measure measuring cup; stir to dissolve it.

4. With the paddle attachment, mix the butter and flour on the lowest speed just long enough for the flour to coat the butter pieces lightly, about 10 seconds (or as long as it takes to say "perfect puff pastry" five times). The majority of chunks should remain the size of walnuts.

1 pound (4 sticks)
   unsalted butter, chilled

1 pound (3 ¼ cups)
   unsifted all-purpose flour

¾ teaspoon salt

1 cup ice water

5. Resume the mixer's lowest speed while pouring the ice water on the flour mixture in a steady stream, not too slowly or too quickly. As soon as all the water has been added, stop the mixer. Most of the butter chunks should look almost the way they did when you began the blending process. The mixture will appear messy and uncohesive, and there will still be loose flour particles in the bottom of the bowl.

6. Using your fingertips, scoop up a large portion of the dry flour particles from the bottom of the bowl and place them on the messy uncohesive mass; press them together in an attempt to form a dough. Don't be concerned if some dry particles remain.

7. Cover the dough with plastic wrap; press the wrap down onto the surface of the dough to prevent its drying. Refrigerate for 15 minutes, allowing the butter chunks to rechill and dough to relax and mellow.

8. Dust work surface lightly with flour. To layer the dough, pat it into a 10-x-6-inch rectangle 1 inch thick. If it resembles potato salad, you're doing just fine.

9. Roll the dough into a rectangle about 16 x 8 inches and ½ inch thick, dusting with flour if necessary. A short end of the dough is closest to you; it won't be completely cohesive. Brush off any excess flour with a brush. Fold the bottom third up over the center; next, fold the top third down over the bottom until it resembles a business letter. This is a single fold, and the dough still isn't smooth.

10. Rotate the dough 90 degrees to the right so its top flap opens like a page in a book. Again lightly flour the work surface and the pastry, and roll into a rectangle measuring 16 x 8 inches and ½ inch thick. Brush off any excess flour; then, with the short end closest to you, fold it into the center of the rectangle. Fold the other short end so that the two short ends meet in the center. Fold the dough in half again, forming a double fold consisting of four layers. Now the mixture is beginning to look like a dough.

CONTINUED ➤

11. Wrap in foil; refrigerate for 20 minutes. You have just completed one single fold and one double fold in a short time, so remember the resting period is approximate. If at any time the dough resists rolling or the butter becomes too soft, a longer refrigeration period may be needed.

12. Lightly dust the work surface and dough with flour, and place the refrigerated dough so that the last fold is at a right angle to you and the flap on top opens like a book. Roll again into a 16-x-8-inch rectangle. Brush off any excess flour; then, fold the short end closest to you into the center of the rectangle. Fold the other short end so that the two short ends meet in the center. Now fold the dough in half again, forming another double fold. You'll notice the pastry is beginning to take form. Rewrap in the foil, and return to refrigerator for 20 minutes more. Remember, this is the third turn.

13. Position the dough so that the last fold is at a right angle to you and the top flap opens like a book. Repeat the rolling and folding as directed for the third turn in step 12. This is the fourth and final turn. Rewrap in the foil, and refrigerate for at least 1 hour before shaping for use.

14. After the puff pastry has rested, roll it into a more manageable shape, a 13-x-8-inch rectangle.

15. Refrigerate it up to 2 days; or freeze, well wrapped, up to 2 months.

## VARIATION NOTES

It's easy to make Blitz Puff Pastry with whole-wheat pastry flour: Substitute 2 cups unsifted whole-wheat pastry flour for 2 cups (280 grams) of the unsifted all-purpose flour.

Whole-wheat pastry flour is available in most health food stores.

# florentine pastry strips

➤ **Makes 6 dozen 1-x-2-inch rectangular strips**

Puff pastry is baked until flaky and golden; then a syrupy almond, honey, and butter mixture is spread on top and the pastry is returned to the oven briefly before it is cut into rectangles. Every bite is as seductive as a sticky bun.

1. Dough: Roll the dough into an ⅛-inch-thick 14-inch square; transfer to a large baking sheet, such as one 17 x 14 x ½ inches. Cover completely with plastic wrap, pressing the plastic directly onto the dough. Refrigerate for at least 30 minutes before baking.

2. Adjust rack to lower third of oven and preheat oven to 425 degrees F. Line a large cool baking sheet with parchment paper. Transfer the chilled dough from refrigerator to baking sheet; prick entire surface with fork tines. Trim off ⅟₁₆ inch from all edges to encourage an even, uninhibited rise in the pastry while baking.

3. Bake for 10 minutes; then reduce temperature to 375 degrees F, and bake for 10 minutes longer. After the initial 10 to 15 minutes of baking, check occasionally to see if the puff pastry is lifting evenly. Prick any uneven area with a skewer to release trapped air before the outer portion of pastry sets.

4. A high lift is not important, so if almost the entire pastry sheet has lifted, place a baking sheet on top to weight it. Bake for 1 minute; then remove the baking sheet from the top of the pastry.

5. Reduce the oven temperature to 325 degrees F, and bake for 12 to 17 minutes longer, or until the pastry is golden brown and sounds and feels crisp when pierced with a skewer or toothpick in four or five places. Place the baking sheet on a wire rack to cool completely.

CONTINUED ➤

## DOUGH

½ pound (about ¼ recipe)
Blitz Puff Pastry (page 266)

## DECORATIVE TOPPING

⅓ cup (65 grams)
granulated sugar

2 tablespoons heavy cream

1 tablespoon light corn syrup

1 tablespoon honey

1½ ounces (3 tablespoons)
unsalted butter

3 ounces (1 cup) sliced almonds

6. Decorative Topping: Combine the sugar, cream, corn syrup, honey, and butter in a 1-quart heavy-bottomed saucepan. Place over low heat, and stir often until sugar dissolves and butter melts, about 3 minutes. Bring the mixture to a boil, and remove from heat. Add the almonds, and stir to blend. Set aside for 5 to 10 minutes to cool and thicken slightly.

7. Adjust the rack 7 to 8 inches from the broiling element; preheat broiler.

8. Pour the slightly cooled topping onto the pastry, spreading evenly with a rubber spatula until surface is covered. Place under broiler for about 30 to 60 seconds, or until the top is bubbly and the nuts are golden. Place the baking sheet on a wire rack to cool slightly.

9. With a ruler and a sharp knife, cut about thirteen 1-inch-wide strips about 13 inches long. Cut each strip into rectangles about 2 inches long.

10. These are best eaten the same day they are baked; or stack in airtight sturdy plastic containers and freeze up to 2 weeks. To serve, reheat to freshen in a 325-degree-F preheated oven for about 7 minutes, or until warm; serve at room temperature.

## BAKING NOTE

Puff pastry scraps work beautifully for this recipe.

# streusel pastry strips

➤ Makes 6 dozen 1-x-2-inch strips

Cover puff pastry with a streusel to create these crisp, sweet, flaky puff pastry strips. They're a perfect accompaniment to scrambled eggs for a special breakfast, or with a serving of morning fruit, such as grapefruit.

1. Dough: Roll the dough into an ⅛-inch-thick 14-inch square; transfer to a large baking sheet, such as one 17 x 14 x ½ inches. Cover completely with plastic wrap, pressing the plastic directly on the dough. Refrigerate for at least 30 minutes before baking.

2. Streusel: Combine the sugars and flour in a 1½-quart bowl with a pastry blender. Scatter the butter pieces over the dry ingredients, and work the butter in with fingertips until the mixture resembles coarse crumbs.

3. Adjust rack to lower third of oven and preheat oven to 425 degrees F. Line a large cool baking sheet with parchment paper. Transfer the chilled dough to the baking sheet; prick entire surface with fork tines. Trim off ¹⁄₁₆ inch from all edges to encourage an even, uninhibited rise in the pastry while baking. Brush a thin film of water over the pastry. Sprinkle the streusel over the pastry, and gently press it so it will stick.

4. Bake for 10 minutes, then reduce temperature to 375 degrees F, and bake for 10 minutes longer. After the initial 10 to 15 minutes of baking, check occasionally to see if the puff pastry is baking evenly. Prick any uneven area with a skewer to release trapped air.

CONTINUED ➤

## DOUGH

½ pound (about ¼ recipe) Blitz Puff Pastry (page 266)

## STREUSEL

½ cup (50 grams) unsifted powdered sugar

¼ cup (50 grams) granulated sugar

1 cup plus 2 tablespoons (160 grams) unsifted all-purpose flour

4 ounces (1 stick) unsalted butter, room temperature, cut into 8 pieces

## DECORATION

½ cup (50 grams) unsifted powdered sugar

5.  A high lift is not important, so if almost the entire pastry sheet has lifted, place a baking sheet on top to weight it. Bake for 1 minute; then remove the baking sheet from the top of the pastry.

6.  Reduce temperature to 325 degrees F, and bake for 12 to 17 minutes longer, or until the pastry is golden brown and sounds and feels crisp when pierced with a skewer or toothpick in four or five places. Place baking sheet on a wire rack to cool completely.

7.  Decoration: Lightly dust entire surface with the powdered sugar. With a ruler and a sharp knife or pastry wheel, cut about thirteen 1-inch-wide strips about 13 inches long. Cut each strip into rectangles about 2 inches long.

8.  These are best eaten the same day they are baked; or stack in airtight sturdy plastic containers and freeze up to 2 weeks. To serve, reheat to freshen in a 325-degree-F preheated oven for about 7 minutes or until warm; serve at room temperature.

## BAKING NOTE

Puff pastry scraps work beautifully for this recipe.

# phyllo accordions

➤ Makes 4 dozen 2-inch pastries

. . . . . . . . . . . . . . . . . . . . . . . . . . . . . . .

Bring these easy-to-prepare flaky pastries to a party and I guarantee your dance card will be full all evening. Actually, invite a friend to make these with you, since four hands are always better than two when working with phyllo. Four hands speed up the process of forming the pastries and assist in keeping the phyllo under wraps to ensure it does not dry in the air.

1. Adjust rack to lower third of oven; preheat oven to 325 degrees F. Line two cool large baking sheets with parchment paper.

2. Pastry: Mix the chopped nuts, sesame seeds, and sugar in a small bowl; set aside.

3. Place the phyllo sheets on the work surface. Using a sharp knife or scissors, cut sheets in half to make them 12 x 8 inches; cut again to make them 6 x 8 inches. Stack quarter sheets together; cover with a strip of plastic wrap, then with a damp towel.

4. Remove two sheets at a time; brush top sheet lightly with melted butter. Sprinkle with 1 tablespoon of the nut mixture.

5. Roll the sheets lengthwise, beginning loosely, around a long wooden spoon handle or 14-inch wooden dowel, ½ inch in diameter. Brush the phyllo pastry lightly with melted butter again. With fingertips, gently push in both ends of pastry to wrinkle and condense it from 8 inches to 3½ or 4 inches. Then, holding the pastry at one end with fingertips, carefully pull the wooden stick out. Place seam side down on the baking sheet. Cover with plastic wrap.

6. Repeat procedure with the remaining phyllo sheets, spacing pastries 1 inch apart.

   CONTINUED ➤

## PASTRY

4 ounces (1 cup) walnuts, finely chopped

4 ounces (1 cup) pecans, finely chopped

¼ cup each sesame seeds and granulated sugar

12 sheets (½ pound) phyllo dough, approximately 16 x 12 inches, room temperature

8 ounces (2 sticks) unsalted butter, melted and cooled to tepid

## HONEY BUTTER GLAZE

½ cup water

1 cup (200 grams) granulated sugar

¼ cup honey

1 ounce (2 tablespoons) unsalted butter

1 tablespoon finely grated lemon zest

1 tablespoon fresh lemon juice

7.  Remove plastic and bake until crisp and golden, about 20 minutes. Using a metal spatula, lift pastries off the parchment to a wire rack to cool. Cut rolls crosswise in half or thirds.

8.  Honey Butter Glaze: Combine all the ingredients except the lemon juice in a 1½-quart saucepan. Heat over low heat just until sugar is dissolved. Raise heat and cook for 5 minutes. Remove from heat, and stir in the lemon juice. Cool for 10 minutes. Then, brush over the pastries just to glaze them.

9.  Stack unglazed pastries in an airtight metal container at room temperature up to 3 days. Serve glazed pastries at room temperature the same day baked.

STEP 5

## TECHNIQUE NOTE

The late Loni Kuhn, the well-known cooking professional and a dear friend, had a great tip: If possible, work with phyllo dough when the weather is humid. This way, there's less risk that the phyllo will dry out so quickly.

## BAKING NOTE

If you have the time, clarify the butter to ensure that the pastries bake evenly without burning. Clarifying removes the milk solids, the liquid in butter that can make phyllo dough soggy, and leaves an oil with a nutty, sweet butterfat flavor.

The clarifying process is simple: In a 1-quart heavy-bottomed saucepan, melt the butter over very low heat. Turn off heat, skim off the foamy particles on top. Slowly pour the oil into a glass jar; be careful to leave the milky solids behind in the saucepan. Cover the jar and refrigerate until needed.

# flaky cheesecake turnovers

➤ **Makes 3 ½ dozen 1 ½-inch triangles**

Here's a favorite filling I've used many times for my miniature tartlets. Using up leftovers can lead the way to a delicious treat. In this case, the filling and phyllo dough combine to make flaky, crunchy pastries on the outside with a creamy, smooth almond paste cheesecake inside.

1. Adjust rack to lower third of oven and preheat oven to 350 degrees F. Line two baking sheets with parchment paper.

2. Filling: In a medium bowl, mix together the almond paste and sugar. Beat in the cream cheese, then the egg and lemon zest, until creamy and smooth.

3. Pastry: Place stacked sheets of the phyllo on work surface. Cut the rectangular sheets into five equal strips about 3 inches wide by 12 inches long. Take two strips from a stack, leaving one on top of the other, and brush just the top portion with melted butter. While working, keep the rest of the phyllo strips covered with plastic wrap.

4. Spoon 1 rounded teaspoon of the cheesecake filling in the center of one narrow end of a double-thickness strip, an inch from the edge of the dough. Starting from lower right, fold the right bottom corner over the filling on an angle, to form a triangle. Fold over on line created by the top edge, and continue folding back and forth to the end of the strip to make one multilayered triangle. (Fold each strip as you would a flag.) Set the pastry seam side down on the baking sheet and brush with melted butter. Keep the triangles covered with plastic wrap until baking. Prepare the remaining strips in the same way.

CONTINUED ➤

## FILLING

4 ounces (⅓ cup plus 1 tablespoon) almond paste

¼ cup granulated sugar

8 ounces cream cheese, room temperature

1 large egg

1 teaspoon finely grated lemon zest

## PASTRY

16 sheets (¾ pound) phyllo dough, approximately 16 x 12 inches

8 ounces (2 sticks) unsalted butter, melted and cooled to tepid

5.  Remove plastic wrap and bake for 15 minutes, or until golden.
    Using a metal spatula, lift the triangles off the parchment to a wire
    rack to cool.

6.  To assemble ahead, set the pastries on parchment-lined baking
    sheets, and place in freezer, uncovered, just 30 minutes to solidify
    the butter coating. Remove from freezer just to cover the sheets
    with plastic; overwrap with aluminum foil. Return to freezer. Bake
    pastries while frozen, but first transfer them, on the parchment,
    to another parchment-lined baking sheet to prevent the pan from
    buckling in the preheated oven. Bake the frozen pastries a few
    minutes longer than unfrozen ones.

STEP 4

## TECHNIQUE NOTES

My good friend and fellow cookbook author Louise Fiszer has great
advice about phyllo dough: Work with phyllo only when it has reached
room temperature—then it will behave as though it were silk, easy to
maneuver and not brittle. Remove the unwrapped box of phyllo from the
refrigerator about 1 hour before you intend to use it.

There is a reason for forming the triangular pastries with a double thickness of phyllo: It makes them extra flaky.

# miniature cakes

These cakes are not so rich
that they can't be enhanced by
buttercreams or chocolate,
or just simply glazed

The Genoise Sheet Cake (page 283), the Butter Cake (page 294), and the Almond Cake (page 300) provide versatile foundations from which to create stunning miniature cakes. These simple yet flavorful cakes are not so rich that they can't be enhanced by buttercreams or chocolate, or just simply glazed with apricot jam.

## MIXING MINIATURE CAKES

The Genoise Sheet Cake (page 283) begins as a thick, foamy foundation of whipped eggs and sugar before a small amount of flour and a minimum of melted butter are folded in. It is light yet firm enough to cut into individual shapes for Parisers (page 289), and at the same time thin and flexible enough for rolling Calypso Minirolls (page 292).

The other cakes are denser in texture, not as light or spongy as the genoise, because they contain an abundance of butter and flour. Their solid foundations make them easy to cut without crumbling. Miniatures such as Dominoes (page 294) and Polka Dot Minicakes (page 300) are perfectly suited to dipping or glazing, since they don't leave behind a number of crumbs each time a piece is dipped or glazed.

## CUTTING MINIATURE CAKES

Large cakes such as the Genoise Sheet Cake (page 283) and the Butter Cake (page 294) are ideal for providing many portions without spending a lot of time baking and decorating.

You can glaze and decorate each portion individually as you do when making the Honey Bee Minicakes (page 286) or Parisers (page 289), or you can decorate the entire cake as demonstrated in the Pistachio Petits Fours (page 283) and cut it into daintier portions later.

Another simple procedure is to mark portions on the cake, decorate each one identically, and later cut the cake where marked.

It's possible to cut any shape or design to create a variety of miniature cakes. Straight edges are easier to cut and less wasteful of cake than rounded edges. Round cutters, such as circles and flower shapes, usually aren't as sharp as a knife that cuts straight-edged portions.

I've designed the miniature cake recipes so that you can conveniently and easily make an assorted variety from only one cake. For example, from one Genoise Sheet Cake (page 283), you can fashion Honey Bee Minicakes (page 286). I've also provided a recipe for Punsch Cakelets (page 305) that is ideal for using those trimmings left over from the Genoise Sheet Cake (page 283), Butter Cake (page 294), and Almond Cake (page 300). To accumulate the necessary amount of trimmings for these cakelets, keep the leftovers, well covered, in a sturdy plastic container in the freezer.

Follow these tips for cutting precision shapes and sizes and you'll find it's easier to achieve uniform results for daintier, more finished-looking miniature cakes.

➤ Partially freezing the cake, about 30 minutes, makes cutting easier.

➤ When cutting genoise cake, use a serrated knife. Cut with a sawing motion. Sometimes scissors are quicker than a knife for cutting and do the job even better. When cutting cakes with a closer texture, such as the Butter Cake (page 294) and Almond Cake (page 300), use a sharp paring knife.

➤ If using a cookie cutter, select one with a sharp edge. Press into the cake and wiggle slightly to the right and left. Don't force straight through the cake, or the sides will be ragged and crumbly.

## PART IV

# cake miniatures

pistachio petits fours . . . . . . . . . . . . . . . . . . . . . . . . .283

honey bee minicakes . . . . . . . . . . . . . . . . . . . . . . . .286

parisers . . . . . . . . . . . . . . . . . . . . . . . . . . . . . . . . . . . . .289

calypso minirolls . . . . . . . . . . . . . . . . . . . . . . . . . . .292

dominoes . . . . . . . . . . . . . . . . . . . . . . . . . . . . . . . . . . .294

jewel fruit prisms . . . . . . . . . . . . . . . . . . . . . . . . . .296

s'more squares . . . . . . . . . . . . . . . . . . . . . . . . . . . . . .298

miniature fruit meringues . . . . . . . . . . . . . . . . . .299

polka dot minicakes . . . . . . . . . . . . . . . . . . . . . . . .300

chocolate-pistachio tigrés . . . . . . . . . . . . . . . . . . .303

punsch cakelets . . . . . . . . . . . . . . . . . . . . . . . . . . . . .305

# pistachio petits fours

➤ **Makes 6 dozen 1½-inch triangles**

· · · · · · · · · · · · · · · · · · · · · · · · · · · · · · · · ·

I adore pistachios, and when used in this miniature I love them all the more. A sandwich of spongy genoise and silken, nutty buttercream is frozen after assembling to make cutting into small triangles easy.

1. Adjust rack to lower third of oven and preheat oven to 450 degrees F. Line a 12-x-15½-x-½-inch baking sheet with aluminum foil, leaving a 2-inch overhang on short ends. Fold overhangs under the ends of the pan. Grease and flour aluminum foil; tap out excess flour.

2. Genoise Sheet Cake Batter: Sift the flour, 1 tablespoon sugar, and salt on a sheet of waxed paper; set aside. In a large mixing bowl, using a whisk, stir the eggs, yolks, and the ½ cup sugar over a shallow pan of hot water until the mixture is body temperature. Remove the bowl from hot water and, using an electric mixer, preferably with a whisk attachment, whip the egg mixture at medium speed until it has cooled and increased considerably in volume. Add the vanilla during the final moments of whipping. When the mixture is thick enough that when the whisk is lifted, some of the mixture falls from the whisk into the bowl in ribbons and remains on the surface, fold in the dry ingredients with a rubber spatula.

3. Gently pour the batter down the center of the pan, spreading as evenly as possible, using the pan's sides as a guide: The batter should be level with the sides of the pan. Bake until the cake springs back when lightly touched near its center and has a light golden color, about 5 minutes.

CONTINUED ➤

## GENOISE SHEET CAKE BATTER

½ cup plus 1 tablespoon (56 grams) sifted cake flour

1 tablespoon granulated sugar

⅛ teaspoon salt

3 large eggs

2 egg yolks

½ cup (100 grams) granulated sugar

1 teaspoon pure vanilla extract

## PISTACHIO SILK BUTTERCREAM

4 egg yolks

¼ cup water

½ cup (100 grams) granulated sugar

8 ounces (2 sticks) unsalted butter, room temperature

2 ounces (½ cup) sliced almonds, toasted and chopped

4 ounces (¾ cup) pistachios, blanched, toasted, and chopped to yield 1 cup

½ teaspoon almond extract

Green liquid food coloring

4. Remove the pan from the oven, and place it on a wire rack. Using a knife, gently release any portion of the cake sticking to the sides of pan. Cover the cake with another baking sheet, and invert. Remove the original baking sheet, and peel off the foil carefully to avoid tearing the cake; then turn foil over so that the sticky side faces up, and reposition it on the cake. Cover with a large wire rack, and invert right side up. Cool completely.

5. Using your fingertips or a small paring knife, carefully peel off the soft, brown, paper-thin crust from the cake's surface. Now the cake is more flexible when rolling, more porous when moistened with flavored syrups, and more attractive when sliced since the cake layer and its filling form a pattern.

6. Cut the cake in half to make two 12-x-7½-inch pieces. Lift one portion of cake onto a clean baking sheet.

7. Pistachio Silk Buttercream: In the large bowl of an electric mixer, whip the egg yolks until light and fluffy, about 4 minutes. Remove bowl from mixer stand. Combine the water and sugar in a 1-quart heavy saucepan over low heat. Stir occasionally, washing down any sugar crystals clinging to the sides of the pan with a brush dipped in cold water, until the sugar is dissolved. Increase heat and cook the syrup, without stirring, until it registers 238 degrees F on a candy thermometer. Pour into the center of the yolks and quickly whisk vigorously to combine. Return bowl to electric mixer, and whip at medium speed until the mixture thickens and cools to body temperature, about 5 minutes. Maintaining medium speed, add the butter to the cooled egg yolk mixture, 2 tablespoons at a time. Continue mixing until all the butter has been incorporated and the buttercream is smooth and homogeneous.

8. When the buttercream is soft and smooth, stir in the nuts, almond extract, and 2 drops green food coloring until thoroughly combined. Reserve 3 tablespoons of the buttercream for finishing.

DECORATION

½ cup (50 grams) unsifted powdered sugar

1 ounce (3 tablespoons) blanched pistachios, split

9. Spread the buttercream evenly over the cake on the baking sheet. Gently press the other half of the cake on top to sandwich the buttercream. Spread the reserved buttercream over the top of the cake to provide a thin coating. Cover the cake's surface with plastic wrap and freeze until buttercream has firmed, or up to 2 weeks.

10. One hour before serving, remove cake from freezer. Using a sharp knife, trim edges evenly. With the aid of a ruler, measure and cut five 1½-inch-wide strips, each 12 inches long. Cut each strip into eight 1½-inch squares. Then, while still frozen and firm, cut each square in half to form triangles. Dip the knife in hot water and wipe it before each cut to make cutting easier and neater.

11. Transfer the frozen pastries to a jelly-roll pan or a covered foil-lined cardboard container, such as a cake box. To decorate, sprinkle with the powdered sugar and center a pistachio half on top of each triangle before serving at room temperature.

### TECHNIQUE NOTES

Freezing the cake with its filling firms the cake and buttercream so it's easier to cut neat portions carefully. The precise pattern of the cake and buttercream when sliced is important.

How to Blanch Shelled Pistachios: Bring a small pot of water to a boil. In a small saucepan, pour enough boiling water over the pistachios to cover them by 2 inches. Over medium heat, bring water back to a boil; turn off heat and let stand 1 minute. Pour the mixture through a mesh strainer. While the pistachios are warm, slip off skins. Spread blanched pistachios onto a baking sheet and set in a preheated very low oven (150 to 200 degrees F). Leave in oven just until nuts are dry, about 20 minutes. Drying the pistachios slowly in a low oven enhances their flavor without changing their beautiful color.

# honey bee minicakes

➤ **Makes 3 dozen 2-inch sticks**

. . . . . . . . . . . . . . . . . . . . . . . . . . . . .

Luscious sticks of spongy genoise and silken honey buttercream are glazed with dark chocolate before crowning with a cheery buttercream bee.

1. Transfer the cake to a large baking sheet.

2. Honey Silk Buttercream: In the large bowl of an electric mixer, whip the egg yolks until light and fluffy, about 4 minutes. Remove bowl from mixer stand. Combine the water and sugar in a 1-quart heavy saucepan over low heat. Stir occasionally, washing down any sugar crystals clinging to the sides of the pan with a brush dipped in cold water, until sugar is dissolved. Increase heat and cook the syrup, without stirring, until it registers 238 degrees F on a candy thermometer. Pour into the center of the yolks and quickly whisk vigorously to combine. Return bowl to electric mixer, and whip at medium speed until the egg yolk mixture thickens and cools to body temperature, about 5 minutes. Maintaining medium speed, add the butter to the cooled egg yolk mixture, 2 tablespoons at a time. Continue mixing until all the butter has been incorporated and the buttercream is smooth and homogeneous. Whip in the honey.

3. Using a flexible metal icing spatula, spread 2 tablespoons of the buttercream evenly over top of cake to give it a smooth finish.

4. Using a pastry bag fitted with a ½-inch plain decorating tip (such as Ateco #6), pipe ½-inch-thick strings of buttercream lengthwise on the cake in parallel lines about ⅛ inch apart. Place in freezer, uncovered, for about 1 hour to partially freeze the pastry to facilitate cutting easily into individual sticks.

## CAKE

⅓ Genoise Sheet Cake,
   12 x 5 inches (page 283)

## DECORATION

**Honey Silk Buttercream**

4 egg yolks

¼ cup water

½ cup (100 grams)
   granulated sugar

8 ounces (2 sticks) unsalted
   butter, room temperature

2 tablespoons honey

**Dark Chocolate Satin Glaze**

¼ cup (1½ ounces) solid
   vegetable shortening

1 pound semisweet
   chocolate, chopped

1 ounce (¼ cup) sliced almonds

5. Dark Chocolate Satin Glaze: Combine the shortening and chocolate in a 3-quart bowl. Place it over a saucepan filled with enough hot water (120 to 130 degrees F) to reach the bottom of the bowl. Stir the mixture occasionally until the glaze is liquid and smooth and registers 110 degrees F on a candy thermometer. If water cools while melting the chocolate, maintain the 120-degree-F temperature over very low heat. Set aside.

6. To make Buttercream Bees: Slip a ¼-inch plain decorating tip (such as Ateco #2) *over* the ½-inch plain decorating tip. Hold the tip in place with one hand, and with the other hand squeeze the bag and pipe out thirty-six ¾-inch-long ovals on a sheet of aluminum foil. Stick a sliced almond on each side of a buttercream oval to serve as wings for the bees. Using a small handmade paper cone, pipe stripes of chocolate glaze over the bee bodies. Place bees, on the foil, in freezer.

7. Remove the cake from freezer. With a sharp knife, cut between the strings of buttercream. Then cut each strip into 2-inch-long pieces. Transfer the small cake strips to wire racks, spacing them 1 inch apart. Place racks over a jelly-roll pan to catch drips when glazing.

8. Ladle about 2 tablespoons of the glaze over each pastry, masking it completely. When no glaze remains in the bowl, pour the glaze from the jelly-roll pan back into the bowl, set over hot water, and reheat. It's useful to pour the glaze through a sieve before reheating, since some cake crumbs may have fallen into it during the masking.

9. After coating all the pastries, move each pastry gently from its base with a small metal spatula so that any drips are cut from its underside while the glaze is liquid. This neat finish also keeps the pastries from sticking to the rack.

CONTINUED ➤

STEP 4

STEP 7

10. The warm glaze sets up rather quickly after touching the cold, firm buttercream, leaving a gorgeous sheen. When the coating firms, it will not stick to your fingers as you lift the pastries.

11. Remove the bees from freezer; lift one at a time off the foil to place on top of each chocolate-coated honey stick.

12. Carefully lift the pastries, one by one, with a small metal spatula, and transfer them to a foil-lined cardboard container, such as a cake box. Store, uncovered, in a cool room up to 1 day.

# parisers

➤ **Makes 2 dozen 1¼-inch round cakes**

A Pariser looks like a bonbon, but it is actually a coin of genoise mounded with a decadent chocolate buttercream and encased in a satiny, dark chocolate glaze. To make it look as appealing as it tastes, I pipe a pale yellow buttercream flower and a pair of pale green buttercream leaves on top.

1. Cake: Put the cake on a cutting board, and, using the wide end of a ½-inch plain decorating tip (such as Ateco #6) as a cutter, cut out 1¼-inch circles. (Partially freezing the cake before cutting it facilitates neater shapes.) Transfer the cake circles to a clean baking sheet.

2. Chocolate Silk Buttercream: In the large bowl of an electric mixer, whip the egg yolks until light and fluffy, about 4 minutes. Remove bowl from mixer stand. Combine the water and sugar in a 1-quart heavy saucepan over low heat. Stir occasionally, washing down any sugar crystals clinging to the sides of the pan with a brush dipped in cold water, until the sugar is dissolved. Increase heat and cook the syrup, without stirring, until it registers 238 degrees F on a candy thermometer. Pour into the center of the yolks and quickly whisk vigorously to combine. Return bowl to electric mixer, and whip at medium speed until the egg yolk mixture thickens and cools to body temperature, about 5 minutes. Maintaining medium speed, add the butter to the cooled egg yolk mixture, 2 tablespoons at a time. Continue mixing until all the butter has been incorporated and the buttercream is smooth and homogeneous.

3. Spoon 1½ cups of the buttercream into a large bowl and stir until soft and smooth. (Save the remaining buttercream for another miniature.) Stir about ½ cup of the buttercream into the melted chocolate until well blended; add to the bowl of buttercream, stirring until smooth.

CONTINUED ➤

## CAKE

½ Genoise Sheet Cake,
   12 x 7½ inches (page 283)

## DECORATION

**Chocolate Silk Buttercream**

4 egg yolks

¼ cup water

½ cup (100 grams) granulated sugar

8 ounces (2 sticks) unsalted
   butter, room temperature

2 ounces unsweetened
   chocolate, melted

**Dark Chocolate Satin Glaze**

¼ cup (1½ ounces)
   solid shortening

1 pound semisweet
   chocolate, chopped

**Decorative Icing**

1 cup (100 grams)
   unsifted powdered sugar

3½ ounces (7 tablespoons)
   unsalted butter, room
   temperature

⅛ teaspoon salt

½ teaspoon almond extract

½ teaspoon pure vanilla extract

Green and yellow liquid food coloring

4. Using a pastry bag fitted with a ½-inch plain decorating tip (such as Ateco #6), pipe out a bulb of buttercream on top of each cake circle. Refrigerate to firm the buttercream, about 1 to 2 hours.

5. Place the chilled pastries on wire racks, spacing them 1 inch apart. Glaze one rack at a time, keeping the remaining pastries on racks in refrigerator. When ready to glaze, place rack over a jelly-roll pan to catch drips.

6. Dark Chocolate Satin Glaze: Combine the shortening and chocolate in a 3-quart bowl. Place it over a saucepan filled with enough hot water (120 to 130 degrees F) to reach the bottom of the bowl. Stir the mixture occasionally until the glaze is liquid and smooth and registers 110 degrees F on a candy thermometer. If water cools while melting the chocolate, maintain the 120-degree-F temperature over very low heat.

7. Ladle about 2 tablespoons of the chocolate glaze over each pastry, masking it completely. Repeat with the remaining racks of pastries. When no glaze remains in the bowl, pour the glaze from the jelly-roll pan back into the bowl, set over hot water, and reheat. It's useful to pour the glaze through a sieve before reheating, since some cake crumbs may have fallen into it during the masking.

8. After all the pastries have been coated, move each pastry gently from its base with a small metal spatula so that any drips are cut from its underside while the coating is liquid. This neat finish also keeps the pastries from sticking to the rack when they are removed. The warm coating sets up rather quickly after touching the cold, firm buttercream, leaving a gorgeous sheen. When the coating firms, it will not stick to your fingers as you lift the pastries.

STEP 4

9. Decorative Icing: Sift the powdered sugar onto a sheet of waxed paper. In a medium mixing bowl, mix the butter, salt, and about one-half of the sugar until smooth and creamy. Gradually add the remaining sugar, then the extracts, beating until smooth and creamy.

10. When the glaze has set, color small portions of the decorative icing in shades of pastel yellow and green with the food coloring. Using two small handmade paper cones, pipe yellow flower-like shapes on each pastry and two green leaves on opposite sides of each flower.

11. Carefully lift the pastries, one by one, with a small metal spatula, and transfer them to a foil-lined cardboard container, such as a cake box. Store, covered, in a cool room up to 1 day.

## VARIATION NOTE

For shaping flowers and leaves, you can substitute butter royal icing for the decorative icing. Beat 1 ⅓ cups powdered sugar with 1 egg white and 1 tablespoon soft unsalted butter until smooth and glossy. If too thin to pipe, beat until stiffer or add more powdered sugar; if too thick, add water, drop by drop.

# calypso minirolls

➤ **Makes 3 dozen 2-inch-long minirolls**

The toasty quality of caramel is accented by the sweet tang of fresh orange in these bite-sized jelly rolls. Small strips of genoise, flavored with orange juice and a buttery caramel filling, are rolled to create cakes that are ideal for an afternoon tea or with coffee after a meal.

1. Cake: Trim the cake of any crisp edges. Roll a rolling pin over the cake to compress it. Brush the orange juice over the cake with a pastry brush.

2. Caramel Filling: Combine the water, sugar, and butter in a 1-quart heavy-bottomed saucepan. Over medium-high heat, bring to a boil and cook, stirring occasionally, until light tan in color, about 7 minutes. Turn off heat, add the cream, stirring until blended. Cool no longer than 30 to 40 minutes, to thicken. Using a metal icing spatula, spread the filling thinly over the cake.

3. Using a ruler and sharp serrated knife, cut six 2-inch-wide strips, each about 12 inches long. Cut each strip into three 2½-inch pieces.

4. With fingertips, roll up each cake portion and place the minirolls seam side down on a clean baking sheet. Cover the minirolls with plastic wrap.

5. Decoration: Sprinkle lightly with the powdered sugar and stick a candied lilac on top of each roll before serving.

6. Store in a covered foil-lined cardboard container, such as a cake box, at room temperature up to 1 day.

## CAKE

1 Genoise Sheet Cake (page 283)

## FILLING

¼ cup fresh orange juice

Caramel Filling

¼ cup water

½ cup (100 grams) granulated sugar

2 ounces (4 tablespoons) unsalted butter

¼ cup heavy cream

## DECORATION

¼ cup (25 grams) powdered sugar

36 candied lilacs

## VARIATION NOTE

### Swiss Tea Cakes

For a shape variation, spread the cake with the caramel filling as the recipe specifies, then cut cake into 2-inch squares. Fold each square in half, almost corner to corner, but slightly off center, short of corners meeting and just short of forming a perfect triangle. Stick a candied lilac in the apex of each pastry's imperfect triangle for decoration.

STEP 2

VARIATION

# dominoes

➤ **Makes 6 dozen 1-x-2-inch cakes**

. . . . . . . . . . . . . . . . . . . . . . . . . . . . .

These butter cake petits fours, with thin layers of apricot, marzipan, and chocolate, are playful recreations of the domino tiles. They are easy to make for a crowd.

1. Adjust rack to lower third of oven and preheat oven to 375 degrees F. Grease and flour a 10-x-15-x-1-inch baking pan.

2. Butter Cake Batter: Sift the flour, baking powder, and salt on a sheet of waxed paper; set aside. In the large bowl of an electric mixer, cream the butter at medium speed until it is creamy, smooth, and lighter in color, about 45 seconds. Beat in the sugar until creamy. Add the eggs, one at a time, beating until light and fluffy. With a rubber spatula, scrape the mixture clinging to the sides into the center of the bowl when necessary. Add the orange zest, then lower mixer speed and blend in the flour mixture in three additions. Mix just until smooth and thoroughly combined.

3. Spread the batter evenly over the baking pan. Bake for 20 to 22 minutes, or until the cake springs back when lightly touched near the center and has a light golden color. Remove to a wire rack until cool.

4. Decoration: Heat the apricot jam just to warm and liquefy it. Spread thinly over the cake.

5. With a rolling pin, roll out the marzipan to about 1/16 inch thick on a surface lightly sprinkled with powdered sugar. Drape over rolling pin and place on the cake. With fingertips, gently push the marzipan to extend it to completely cover the cake. The jam underneath makes it easy to slide the marzipan over the cake. Be gentle, as the marzipan tears.

## BUTTER CAKE BATTER

2 cups (200 grams) sifted cake flour

1 teaspoon baking powder

¼ teaspoon salt

9 ounces (2¼ sticks) unsalted butter, room temperature

1½ cups (300 grams) granulated sugar

4 large eggs, room temperature

1 tablespoon finely grated orange zest

## DECORATION

⅓ cup strained apricot jam

12 ounces marzipan

Powdered sugar

Dark Chocolate Satin Glaze

¼ cup (1½ ounces) solid vegetable shortening

1 pound semisweet chocolate, chopped

## ROYAL ICING

½ cup (50 grams) unsifted powdered sugar

2 teaspoons egg white

6. Using a ruler as a guide, cut the cake into five 2-inch-wide strips, each 15 inches long. Cut each strip into fifteen 1-inch rectangles.

7. Dark Chocolate Satin Glaze: Combine the shortening and chocolate in a 3-quart bowl. Place it over a saucepan filled with enough hot water (120 to 130 degrees F) to reach the bottom of the bowl. Stir occasionally until the glaze is liquid and smooth and registers close to 110 degrees F on a candy thermometer. If water cools while melting the chocolate, maintain the 120-degree-F temperature over very low heat.

8. Transfer the pastries to wire racks, spacing them 1 inch apart. Place racks over a jelly-roll pan to catch drips when glazing. Ladle about 2 tablespoons of the glaze over each pastry, masking it completely.

9. When no more glaze remains in the bowl, pour the glaze from the jelly-roll pan into the double boiler, and reheat. It's useful to pour the glaze through a sieve before reheating, since some cake crumbs may have fallen into it during the masking of the pastries.

10. After masking all the pastries, move each pastry gently from its base with a small metal spatula to remove any chocolate drips from its underside while the glaze is liquid. This neat finish also keeps the pastries from sticking to the rack.

11. Royal Icing: Combine the sugar and egg white in a small bowl. Mix together until the icing is creamy and thick, and forms a string when poured from a spoon.

12. When the glaze has set, using a small handmade paper cone, pipe a domino pattern with Royal Icing on each pastry. (The glaze has set when it does not stick to your fingers as you lift the pastries.)

13. Carefully lift the pastries, one by one, with a small metal spatula, and transfer them to a foil-lined cardboard container, such as a cake box. Store, covered, in a cool room up to 1 day. When ready to serve, place the pastries in small paper cases, if you prefer.

# jewel fruit prisms

➤ **Makes 3 dozen 1-inch cakes**

. . . . . . . . . . . . . . . . . . . . . . . . .

As the name implies, these small butter cakes sparkle like jewels. The effect is achieved by making a wine jelly from orange muscat wine and cutting it into tiny squares, then scattering them over the cake. The results are moist and refreshing. Eating a game aspic garnish with a chilled duck terrine gave me the idea for the fruity wine jelly. It flavors and decorates these little cakes beautifully.

1. Cake: Place the cake on a large clean baking sheet.

2. Wine Jelly: Pour the wine into a liquid-measure measuring cup. Sprinkle the gelatin over the surface, and set aside until softened. Then pour into a small saucepan, add the sugar, and heat over low heat just to dissolve the gelatin and sugar. Remove from heat and pour into a shallow Pyrex baking dish, about 9 x 13 inches. The wine mixture should be ⅛ inch deep. Refrigerate to gel.

3. Remove the jelly from refrigerator, and, with the tip of a paring knife, cut lines close to ⅛ inch apart in both directions (the pattern looks like graph paper) to form wine jewels.

4. With a spatula, lift the jelly from the pan to break the cut pieces apart. With a serving spoon, arrange over the cake. Refrigerate for 30 minutes.

5. With a ruler and a sharp knife, cut the cake into 1-inch squares. To cut neat and precise squares, cut straight down with the knife; don't pull the blade through the cake each time you cut. Wipe the knife clean after each cut.

## CAKE

½ Butter Cake, 10 x 7½ inches (page 294)

## WINE JELLY

⅔ cup Essencia (Quady California Orange Muscat)

2 teaspoons gelatin

2 tablespoons sugar

6. Cover cake with aluminum foil, taking care that the foil does not rest directly on the topping, and return the cake on its tray to refrigerator until 1 hour before serving.

## VARIATION NOTES

For variety, substitute an extra-dry champagne, dessert Sauterne, or even fresh orange juice for the wine in the jelly.

Fold 1 cup fresh room-temperature blueberries into the Butter Cake batter to add a fruity flavor to this simply luscious cake.

# s'more squares

➤ **Makes about 4 dozen 1½-inch squares**

You don't need a campfire to make this version of the classic S'more. It has all the luscious ingredients in a petit four–sized morsel.

1. Adjust rack to lower third of oven and preheat oven to 325 degrees F. Press a sheet of aluminum foil to cover outside the bottom and sides of a 9-inch square pan. Invert pan and gently press aluminum form into pan to fit contours; set aside.

2. Crust: In a large bowl, blend the graham cracker crumbs and the sugar. Add the butter and blend thoroughly. Press the crumbs into foil-lined pan; set aside.

3. Filling: Sift the flour, salt, and baking soda onto a piece of waxed paper; set aside. In a small saucepan, melt the chocolate and butter over low heat, stirring occasionally. Turn off heat, stir in the water. Pour the mixture into a large bowl and let cool for about 5 minutes. Stir in the sugar, then the eggs and vanilla, just until thoroughly blended. Add the flour mixture, stirring just until combined. Pour filling into crumb-lined pan, spreading evenly.

4. Bake for 30 minutes only. Remove pan from oven to a rack, and cool in the pan.

5. Topping: To serve, remove the cake from the pan to a cutting board by lifting the foil by its edges. Pour the chocolate into a small hand-made paper cone and pipe zigzag lines over the filling's surface. Cut into 1½-inch squares. Center a mini marshmallow on each square, and pipe a tiny dot of chocolate in the center of each marshmallow.

6. Store in one layer in a covered foil-lined cardboard container, such as a cake box, at room temperature up to 2 days.

## CRUST

1½ cups (5½ ounces) graham cracker crumbs

¼ cup (50 grams) packed light brown sugar

7 tablespoons (3½ ounces) unsalted butter, melted

## FILLING

⅔ cup (100 grams) unsifted all-purpose flour

¼ teaspoon salt

⅛ teaspoon baking soda

2 ounces unsweetened chocolate, chopped

6 tablespoons (3 ounces) unsalted butter

1 tablespoon water

1 cup (200 grams) granulated sugar

2 large eggs

2 teaspoons pure vanilla extract

## TOPPING

2 ounces milk chocolate, melted

4 dozen mini marshmallows

# miniature fruit meringues

➤ **Makes 3 dozen 1-inch cakes**

. . . . . . . . . . . . . . . . . . . . . . . . . . . . . . . . . . .

This is my interpretation of the classic Baked Alaska, without the ice cream, so it's easy to serve.

1. Cake: Place the cake on a large clean baking sheet. In a large bowl, toss the fruit for decoration to mix.

2. Adjust oven rack 6 to 7 inches from broiler, and preheat it.

3. Fluffy Meringue: In a large mixing bowl, blend the egg whites with the sugar. Place the mixture over another bowl of hot tap water and stir until mixture is body temperature. Remove from water, and using an electric mixer, preferably with a whisk attachment, whip until mixture has peaks that are thick and shiny, about 10 to 15 minutes.

4. Spread about ½ cup of the meringue evenly over the cake to cover. Sprinkle the fruit over meringue. With fingertips, press fruit into meringue to anchor in place. With a metal icing spatula, spread the remaining meringue over the fruit to cover.

5. Place baking sheet under broiler just until the meringue's surface is light golden in color. Place baking sheet on a wire rack to cool.

6. With a ruler and a sharp knife, cut the cake into 1-inch squares. To cut neat and precise squares, cut straight down with the knife; don't pull the blade through the cake each time you cut. Wipe knife clean after each cut.

7. Serve these at room temperature the same day they are baked.

## BAKING NOTE

Freshly separated egg whites, rather than leftover ones, are best for helping this meringue cut easily and neatly without sticking to the knife blade.

## CAKE

½ Butter Cake, 10 x 7½ inches (page 294)

## DECORATION

2 cups assorted small fresh fruits, such as raspberries, blueberries, and strawberries

## FLUFFY MERINGUE

½ cup (about 4 large) egg whites

1 cup (200 grams) granulated sugar

# polka dot minicakes

➤ **Makes 2 dozen 1½-inch minicakes**

The elegant appearance of these minicakes belies their easy decoration. Cover little rounds of almond cake with a creamy white chocolate glaze, then apply several tiny dark chocolate polka dots on top before the glaze sets.

1. Adjust rack to lower third of oven and preheat oven to 350 degrees F. Grease and flour a 7-inch square baking pan. (Check the bottom measurement of your 8-inch square pans—most pans measure only 7 inches square on the bottom.)

2. Almond Cake Batter: In the large bowl of an electric mixer, beat the almond paste at low speed just to break it up, about 30 seconds. Add the sugar in a steady stream, and beat until incorporated. Add the eggs, one at a time, and continue beating until the mixture is light and fluffy. Add the zest. Using a rubber spatula, scrape the mixture from the sides into the center of the bowl when necessary. Lower speed, and blend in the flour until mixture is smooth and thoroughly combined. Spread evenly into pan.

3. Bake for 25 minutes or until center springs back when lightly touched. Remove pan to a wire rack until completely cool.

4. White Chocolate Glaze: Melt the butter, shortening, and white chocolate in a bowl that fits snugly over a pan of 120-degree-F water. Stir until the glaze is smooth and liquid.

5. Using a 1½-inch round cutter, cut out rounds from the cake in the baking pan. Transfer the cake cutouts to wire racks, spacing them 1 inch apart. Place racks over a jelly-roll pan to catch drips when glazing. Ladle about 2 tablespoons of the glaze over each pastry, masking it completely.

## ALMOND CAKE BATTER

8 ounces (1 scant cup) almond paste, room temperature

¼ cup (50 grams) granulated sugar

3 large eggs, room temperature

1 teaspoon lemon zest

⅓ cup plus 1 tablespoon (36 grams) sifted cake flour

## DECORATION

White Chocolate Glaze

4 ounces (1 stick) unsalted butter, diced

1 tablespoon vegetable shortening

8 ounces white chocolate, finely chopped

1 ounce semisweet chocolate, finely chopped

6. When no more glaze remains in the bowl, pour the glaze from the jelly-roll pan back into the bowl, and reheat over hot water. It's useful to pour the glaze through a sieve before reheating, since some cake crumbs may have fallen into it during the masking.

7. After all the pastries have been coated, move each pastry gently from its base with a small metal spatula so that any drips are cut from its underside while the coating is liquid. This neat finish also keeps the pastries from sticking to the rack.

8. Melt the semisweet chocolate in a small bowl set over a pan of 120-degree-F water. Half fill a small handmade paper cone with the dark chocolate glaze. Before the white chocolate glaze sets on the pastries, pipe several tiny polka dots on the minicakes with the darker chocolate glaze. Stir ¼ cup of the remaining white chocolate glaze into the melted chocolate. Replace bowl over hot water and stir until smooth and liquid.

9. When the glaze has set, carefully lift the pastries, one by one, with a small metal spatula, and transfer them to a foil-lined cardboard container, such as a cake box. Store, covered, in a cool room up to 1 day. When ready to serve, place the pastries in small paper cases, if you prefer.

## VARIATION NOTES

### Cranberry Almond Cake

Fold ½ cup fresh cranberries into the almond cake batter. After baking and cooling the cake, sprinkle with powdered sugar instead of the white chocolate glaze with polka dots.

CONTINUED ➤

## Limoges Petits Fours

When you remove the almond cake from the oven, cool 10 minutes, then invert onto a rack to cool further. Set rack over a jelly-roll pan.

Prepare the white chocolate glaze as directed above. Heat ¼ cup currant jelly just until warm and smooth. Spoon into a small handmade paper cone and set aside. Pour the glaze onto center of cake and spread evenly using a metal spatula. Sides of cake need not be glazed. Snip off tip of cone, and pipe thin lines of jelly between ¼ and ½ inch apart diagonally across the glaze. Set cake aside at room temperature until the glaze sets, at least 1 hour.

Transfer cake to a cutting board and trim the edges with a long, sharp knife. Using a ruler and the knife, cut into 1-inch squares. To make squares neat, dip the knife blade into hot water and wipe it with paper towels after each cut. Makes 4 dozen 1-inch square petits fours.

# chocolate-pistachio tigrés

➤ **Makes about 5 dozen 2-inch round tigrés**

On a trip to France, I tasted Tigrés at every pastry shop I visited. Made with a financier batter, they have spots—not stripes as the name would imply—of chocolate. The best are tender and buttery; I added the richness of pistachios.

1. Adjust rack to lower third of oven and preheat oven to 350 degrees F. Brush miniature nonstick 2-inch round molds with an indentation in the center with the 3 tablespoons melted butter. (If molds do not have a nonstick finish, butter and dust with flour.)

2. Batter: In a large bowl, combine the ground pistachios, sugar, and flour. In another large bowl, whisk the egg whites just until foamy. Add the flour mixture and stir until combined. Gradually stir in the 7½ ounces melted butter to blend thoroughly. Stir in the vanilla and almond extracts and mini chocolate chips. Let the batter rest at room temperature for about 30 minutes, or until slightly thickened.

3. Using a 16-inch pastry bag fitted with a 7/16-inch plain decorating tip (such as Ateco #5), pipe or spoon the batter into molds (covering the indentation) about two-thirds full. Bake for about 8 to 10 minutes, or just until the edges are golden, the surface is dull, and the cakes appear set and spring back when lightly pressed. After baking, remove mini cakes from molds and set them to cool on a wire rack. (Tigrés may be stored at this point in airtight plastic containers at room temperature for up to 2 days, or frozen for up to 10 days.)

CONTINUED ➤

## BATTER

3 tablespoons unsalted butter, melted for greasing the molds

½ cup (2¾ ounces) shelled raw pistachios, finely ground to yield 3/4 cup

2 cups (200 grams) unsifted powdered sugar

½ cup plus 2 tablespoons unsifted all-purpose flour

¾ cup (about 5 to 6) large egg whites

7½ ounces (1 stick plus 7 tablespoons) unsalted butter, melted

1 teaspoon pure vanilla extract

¼ teaspoon pure almond or pistachio extract

⅓ cup mini chocolate chips, finely chopped

## DARK CHOCOLATE GANACHE

2½ ounces semisweet or bittersweet chocolate, finely chopped

3 tablespoons heavy cream

4.  Dark Chocolate Ganache: Place the chocolate in a medium bowl. In a small saucepan, heat the cream until boiling. Pour cream over chocolate and let sit 30 seconds. Whisk together until smooth and creamy. Set aside at room temperature just until the mixture cools a bit and begins to thicken.

5.  Set Tigrés upside down on a baking sheet. Spoon, or pipe using a small pastry bag fitted with a ¼-inch plain decorating tip (such as Ateco #2), enough of the chocolate ganache to fill each indentation.

6.  Store in one layer in a covered foil-lined cardboard container, such as a cake box, at room temperature for up to 2 days.

# punsch cakelets

➤ **Makes 4 dozen 1½-inch squares**

Here's a perfect way to use the trimmings from the Genoise Sheet Cake (page 283), Butter Cake (page 294), and Almond Cake (page 300). I always freeze the scraps of cake in a sturdy plastic container until I have enough to make this recipe.

This is my version in miniature of the Punschtortes I've tasted in Germany and Austria. As the name suggests, these are bite-sized punch-flavored cakelets. Cake cubes are tossed with a punch of orange and lemon juice, jam, and dark rum. When assembling this no-bake cake, a simple technique compresses the mixture in a foil-lined pan to make it easy to remove the multicolored layer cake cubes before topping each one with a glistening red raspberry.

1.  Cake: Cut the cake trimmings into ½- to 1-inch cubes and transfer to a 3-quart bowl. Line a 9-x-13-inch pan with aluminum foil.

2.  Punch Filling: Rub each side of four of the sugar cubes against the orange skin to capture the flavor from the fruit's oil. Rub each side of the remaining four sugar cubes over the lemon. In a 3-cup heavy saucepan, combine the sugar cubes (to produce a more intense citrus flavor) with the water and sugar over low heat. Stir occasionally, washing down any sugar clinging to the sides of the pan with a brush dipped in cold water, until the sugar is dissolved. Increase the heat and cook the syrup, without stirring, until it reaches 230 degrees F on a candy thermometer. Stir in the apricot jam and remove from heat to cool. Stir in the juices and rum.

CONTINUED ➤

## CAKE

8 cups cake trimmings, loosely packed

## PUNCH FILLING

8 small sugar cubes

1 orange

1 lemon

½ cup water

⅓ cup (65 grams) granulated sugar

⅓ cup strained apricot jam

⅔ cup fresh orange juice

2 tablespoons fresh lemon juice

2 tablespoons dark rum

1 cup (½ pint) fresh raspberries

## DECORATION

1 cup (½ pint) fresh raspberries

3 tablespoons red currant jelly

3. Using a rubber spatula, toss the raspberries with the cake pieces. Gradually add ¾ cup of the punsch filling, tossing to coat and moisten the cake cubes. Continue to add more punsch filling just until cake pieces feel moist but not wet.

4. Spread the moistened cake cubes and fruit in the pan. Fit a sheet of aluminum foil on top of the cake mixture, and set a pan the same size as the one below on top of the aluminum foil. Put a 5-pound bag of sugar or something comparable in weight on top to condense the mixture. Refrigerate, keeping the weight in place, for at least 8 hours or until the cake is firm and compact enough to slice without crumbling. During this period, the mixture absorbs the punsch filling evenly to form a moist cake layer.

5. To serve, use a knife and ruler to cut cake into 1½-inch cubes.

6. Decoration: Put the raspberries in a 3-quart bowl. Heat the currant jelly just until smooth and liquid but not hot. Pour jelly down one side of the bowl and, using a rubber spatula, gently toss just to coat the berries. Top each small cake cube with a raspberry. Using a small offset metal spatula makes lifting each piece out of the pan easy. Before serving, place each cakelet into a paper mini muffin cup, preferably aluminum foil or silicone-treated.

## BAKING NOTES

Different cakes soak up varying amounts of punsch filling. For example, a spongy texture absorbs more of the filling than a buttery pound cake. For this recipe, 8 cups leftover sponge cake (about 17 ounces) works well.

Unlike a cake from a batter, which may include flour, eggs, ground nuts, or even chocolate to build its structure, these small cakes remain fragile, since only the moisture from the filling holds the unbaked mixture together.

## VARIATION NOTES

Punsch Cakelets are delicious as a filling for Chocolate Thimbles (page 168). After preparing the Chocolate Thimbles, cut the cakelets to fit.

### Punsch Balls

A German variation of this recipe forms walnut-sized balls from the cake-fruit mixture. Scoop up small portions with a spoon and form into compact balls with the palms of your hands. Dip the Punsch Balls into Dark Chocolate Satin Glaze (page 104), and let sit on aluminum foil until the chocolate sets up.

# miniature sweets

There's nothing like the
taste of candy made with the
freshest, best ingredients

My first kitchen experience involved making vinegar taffy candy with a babysitter. It was easy to assemble and measure the ingredients, entertaining to watch the mixture cook, even suspenseful—would pulling it with buttered hands really produce taffy? Yet the most fun was finally eating the results. This incident ignited my passion for making candy.

When I want to give a gift from my kitchen, many times I rely on candy. There's nothing like the taste of candy made with the freshest, best ingredients.

Candy is the perfect ending to a meal. Serving it after dessert with coffee is a tradition around the world. Candy is a symbol of hospitality—small, stunning jewels arranged on a simple dish welcome guests to help themselves. I search out candies to taste wherever I travel, sampling candies from around the world every chance I get, and there are many splendid, mouthwatering varieties. But for me, nothing tastes better or is more charming than a box of homemade candies.

Chocolate and candy may seem synonymous, but though I'm a big fan of chocolate my sweet tooth mandates that not all candies be chocolate. So here is an assortment, similar to one you might find in a candy box: chewy caramels, crunchy toffee, vibrant fruit jellies, spiced marshmallows, silky truffles, and juicy apples.

Candy making does not have to be time-consuming. For example, the actual working time for making the Golden Caramels (page 326) is about 45 minutes; the Blood Orange Jellies (page 329), about 15 minutes; the Five-Spice Marshmallows (page 332), about 40 minutes; and the Express Method for tempering chocolate (page 315) is about 30 minutes. After that, it's hands-off from 30 minutes to 8 hours while candies cool and set.

Preparing the candies in this chapter doesn't require a lot of expensive, fancy equipment, but the right tools make candy making neater, more accurate, and less time-consuming. A 4-quart, heavy-bottomed saucepan about 5½ inches deep provides the proper dimensions for mixtures like Golden Caramels (page 326), Blood Orange Jellies (page 329), and Raspberry Jellies (page 334), which bubble up while cooking. A microwave oven (I tested on an 800-watt model with a turntable) is a terrific time-saver when melting and tempering chocolate. Reusable rubberized-silicone mats, Silpat or Exopat or Super Parchment (an ultrathin reusable 13-x-17-inch sheet), provide a nonstick surface for sheet pans so that sticky candies like Golden Caramels (page 326) and Five-Spice Marshmallows (page 332), as well as baked goods, release easily. Instant-read meat/yeast and candy thermometers indicate accurately the stages of tempering chocolate and candy making. Disposable decorating bags (10- and 18-inch sizes) save time by eliminating messy clean-up, and a new generation of rubber spatulas are heat resistant to temperatures up to 500 degrees F.

Two items that are nice to have but are not necessary are a plastic or metal candy maker's funnel, somewhat like an unbendable pastry bag, which very efficiently forms candies like the Chocolate Wafers (page 330), and a cooking thermometer/timer with a probe to insert in the mixture as it cooks so that it automatically sounds an alarm when the desired temperature is reached.

Most candy recipes have a short ingredient list, and you'll often see the same ingredients called for in many recipes: corn syrup, sugar, chocolate, heavy cream, vanilla, and, of course, butter. Their physical properties are the foundations you build upon when making candy.

For example, corn syrup sweetens and controls crystallization of sugar in the candy. A relatively large proportion of corn syrup prevents the sugar syrup from crystallizing. There's no need to wash down the sides of the pan or take any other precautions against crystallization, as you do with candy making using other ingredients.

For consistently good results, use cane sugar (it says cane on the package), which is more stable than beet sugar, especially when caramelizing sugar.

Choose brands of chocolate that have at least 50 percent cocoa mass (a few American brands and most European brands indicate percentage on the wrapper) for the most intense flavor and for reliability when tempering.

## MELTING CHOCOLATE

Melting chocolate to a creamy, smooth liquid as an ingredient for glazes, batters, and doughs must be done in a gentle manner in order to avoid scorching the chocolate and sacrificing its flavor and texture. For semi-sweet or bittersweet chocolate, wait to stir the melting chocolate until it appears to be liquefying. Milk proteins in milk or white chocolate are more sensitive to heat, which makes the melting process tricky. Stirring milk or white chocolate more often than dark chocolate ensures a shiny, smooth liquid without tiny lumps or graininess. Three-quarters of a pound (12 ounces) of solid chocolate yields 1 cup of melted chocolate.

### Water-Bath (Bain-marie) Method

Chop the chocolate into ⅛-inch-thick matchstick-size pieces on a dry cutting board with a chef's knife or cleaver. Place the chocolate in a bowl that fits snugly over a saucepan or container half filled with water at 120 degrees F (tap water: hot to the hand). When chocolate begins to melt, stir until creamy, smooth. When melting a large quantity of chocolate, the water will have to be replaced as the water cools.

### Microwave Method

Chop the chocolate into ¼-inch-thick matchstick-size pieces on a dry cutting board with a chef's knife or cleaver. Place chopped chocolate in a microwave-safe plastic bowl, such as a Rubbermaid or Tupperware bowl. I avoid microwave-safe glass bowls, since they retain heat and can scorch the chocolate.

Microwave the bowl of chocolate, uncovered, at 50 percent (medium) power until the chocolate appears shiny, about 1 to 4 minutes (depending on the type of microwave and the amount, brand, and type of chocolate). Remove container from microwave and stir the chocolate until melted. If any unmelted chocolate remains, microwave at additional 15-second intervals, stirring until smooth. Watch milk and white chocolates closely, and stir more often than dark chocolates to prevent overheating. (I tested with an 800-watt microwave oven; however, microwave ovens vary, so stop and check often as the chocolate melts.)

Remember that some brands of chocolate retain their shape as they melt in the microwave. How liquid the chocolate is can best be known when you stir it. However, stirring too soon can slow the melting process. If there is no sign of liquefying, press the chocolate with the blade of a dry rubber spatula to "see" where it is soft and liquid. Stir the chocolate slowly and evenly, allowing the liquid chocolate to melt the soft.

### TEMPERING CHOCOLATE ON THE FAST TRACK

For some recipes in this chapter, you need to temper melted chocolate so it will be stable and will set properly. Like the Traditional Method (page 168), the Express Method (page 315) depends on accuracy to stabilize the cocoa butter in the chocolate to produce a glossy, smooth, firm result suitable for molding, dipping, coating, or piping.

The Traditional Method is based on a more precise way of tempering melted chocolate and uses water baths for heating and cooling the chocolate along with more specific temperatures. This method takes more time than the Express Method, as the name implies. If the chocolate you select is not in temper, the Traditional Method is the ideal one.

The Express Method, an easy way to temper chocolate, is especially apropos to the candies in this chapter. The Express Method does not rely on exact temperatures as much as the Traditional Method, and requires no water baths and no water changes. Though you can gauge the chocolate's temperature with an instant-read meat thermometer, this method

| AMOUNT OF CHOCOLATE | BOWL SIZE |
| --- | --- |
| up to 4 ounces | 1.2-quart microwave-safe plastic bowl |
| 4 to 24 ounces (4 ounces to 1½ pounds) | 1.9- to 2-quart microwave-safe plastic bowl |
| 24 to 42 ounces (1½ to 2½ pounds) | 2.5- to 3-quart microwave-safe plastic bowl |

Note: When a recipe calls for a larger amount of tempered chocolate than you think necessary (e.g., Candied Almond Clusters, page 322), it's because the tempered chocolate's temperature is more easily maintained with a larger mass. Spread the leftover chocolate over a sheet of aluminum foil, keep it in a cool place until set, break it into pieces, and store it in an airtight sturdy plastic container at room temperature to use another time. If the extra chocolate sets up with white streaks or a grainy texture then it has lost its temper. Use this chocolate in recipes that call for melted chocolate, such as Dark Chocolate Satin Glaze (page 104) and Glossy Chocolate Ganache Glaze (page 171) or retemper it using the Traditional Method (page 168) for piping, dipping, or molding, as in Candied Almond Clusters (page 322) and Chocolate Thimbles (page 168).

relies on your senses too—does a dab placed just below your lip feel cool or warm? However, you must begin the process with tempered chocolate.

The goal is to melt about two-thirds of the chocolate in the bowl, leaving the remainder unmelted or softened. As you stir the unmelted or softened chocolate into the melted chocolate, it cools the chocolate and at the same time distributes the cocoa butter crystals throughout. This allows the chocolate to recrystallize in a stable form—its original tempered state—so it will set up when put in a cool place or refrigerated briefly. The result is melted, tempered chocolate that is ready to use. (Chocolate that sets up slowly or doesn't set up at all is not tempered properly. In this case remelt the chocolate and temper it again using the Traditional Method, page 168.)

### EXPRESS METHOD IN SEVEN EASY STEPS

1. Select a chocolate with a flavor you like and one that has at least 50 percent cocoa mass (a range of 50 percent to 70 percent is best). The chocolate you select for the Express Method must be in temper (i.e., have a surface with a glossy sheen, and be smooth in texture and snappy firm when you break it).

2. Using a chef's knife or cleaver, cut the chocolate into matchstick pieces, about ¼-inch thick (it's natural for some chocolates to shatter when cutting the sticks), reserving some chunks of chocolate. You can use these chunks to lower the melted chocolate's temperature should dark chocolate heat above 90 degrees F or white or milk above 88 degrees F (step 7, page 316).

3. Place chopped chocolate in a microwave-safe plastic bowl, such as a Rubbermaid or Tupperware bowl. (Avoid microwave-safe glass bowls, since they retain heat and can overheat or scorch the chocolate.)

4. Microwave the bowl of chocolate, uncovered, at 50 percent (medium) power until about two-thirds of the chocolate appears shiny, about 1 to 4 minutes (depending on the microwave oven and the amount,

| AMOUNT OF CHOCOLATE | CHOCOLATE TO RESERVE |
| --- | --- |
| up to 8 ounces | 1 chunk (½ ounce) |
| 8 to 16 ounces | 2 chunks (½ ounce each) |
| 16 to 24 ounces (1 to 1½ pounds) | 2 chunks (1 ounce each) |

brand, and type of chocolate). Remove container from microwave and with a dry rubber spatula, stir the chocolate slowly and evenly, allowing the liquid chocolate to melt the soft or unmelted chocolate that remains.

5. Check the temperature with an instant-read meat/yeast thermometer to see if it has reached 86 to 90 degrees F for dark chocolate, 84 to 88 degrees F for white or milk chocolate. Wipe the stem of the thermometer after each measurement. Make sure the probe is deep enough into the chocolate to give an accurate reading. A small indentation on the stem of the thermometer shows you how far to insert it; hold thermometer at an angle if tempering a small amount of chocolate.

   Alternatively, dip a rubber spatula into the chocolate and place a small dab just below your lip. If it feels cool it's probably ready to use, but to be on the safe side, do a temper test before proceeding.

6. Temper Test: Whichever way you test—either with a thermometer, a chocolate dab below your lip, or both, always spread a small sample of the chocolate on a piece of aluminum foil and refrigerate it for about 3 minutes. If it's glossy and firm and releases easily from the foil, then the chocolate is in temper and ready to use.

7. Rescue: If the melted chocolate exceeds 90 degrees F or fails the temper test, add a chunk of reserved chocolate and stir until the chocolate is 86 to 90 degrees F for semisweet and bittersweet chocolates or 84 to 88 degrees F for milk and white chocolates. If there are two chunks of reserved chocolate, and the first chunk melts into the chocolate before the desired range of temperatures, add the second chocolate chunk to further lower the chocolate's temperature.

   When the chocolate has cooled to the desired temperature, remove what is left of the chocolate chunk to a piece of aluminum foil, and put it in a cool place to set up. Then wrap in the foil, label it, and save for another time or another use.

| AMOUNT OF CHOCOLATE | BOWL SIZE |
|---|---|
| 4 to 24 ounces (4 ounces to 1½ pounds) | 1.9- to 2-quart microwave-safe plastic bowl |
| 24 to 42 ounces (1½ to 2½ pounds) | 2.5- to 3-quart microwave-safe plastic bowl |

## PART V

# miniature sweets

toffee butter crunch ........................319

candied almond clusters ...................322

truffle lollipops ...........................324

golden caramels ...........................326

candied lady apples ......................328

blood orange jellies ........................329

chocolate wafers...........................330

five-spice marshmallows ...................332

raspberry jellies ...........................334

candied kumquat circles ...................336

# toffee butter crunch

➤ **Makes about 2 pounds 1½-inch-square crunch bits**

. . . . . . . . . . . . . . . . . . . . . . . .

The nicest gift you can give me is a recipe. Marge Sternlieb, a friend and former caterer, sent me this one years ago, and I think of her fondly every time I make this thin, easy-to-chew, delectable toffee.

For the neatest shapes a mallet or rolling pin helps make uniform cuts, or just break into random pieces with your hands. For an attractive presentation, stand three pieces on their cut side in 2½-inch paper candy cases.

Substitute 2 cups (10½ ounces) blanched almonds or 2 cups (9 ounces) slivered almonds for the hazelnuts, if you wish. After chopping the nuts, shake them in a sieve to eliminate the minuscule nut particles. Use fine powder as part of the flour for a cookie, brownie, or cake.

1. Line a 10-x-15-x-1-inch baking pan with aluminum foil and lightly coat with an unflavored vegetable oil or spray; set aside.

2. In a heavy-bottomed 2½-quart saucepan, melt the butter. Add the sugar, corn syrup, and water, stirring to blend. Bring to a boil over medium heat, stirring occasionally. Reduce heat to low, and continue to cook; mixture will return to a boil (a slow, steady bubbling on the surface). Let it boil, stirring occasionally until a candy thermometer registers 300 degrees F, about 17 to 20 minutes. If candy syrup does not cover thermometer completely, tilt the saucepan briefly to get an accurate reading. (At close to 250 degrees F the mixture becomes light tan in color, and by the time it registers 300 degrees F it changes to a rich deep tan.) Quickly stir in 1 cup of the chopped nuts; pour into lined pan, without scraping the saucepan. Spread evenly (the light coating of oil makes this easy). Lift the toffee by both ends of the foil and transfer to a cooling rack; set aside for about 5 minutes, or until toffee is firm but still hot.

CONTINUED ➤

8 ounces (2 sticks) unsalted butter

1⅓ cups (265 grams) granulated sugar

1 tablespoon light corn syrup

3 tablespoons water

10 ounces (2 cups) toasted hazelnuts, chopped to yield 2 cups

4 ounces semisweet or bittersweet chocolate, finely chopped

3.  Sprinkle the chocolate over the toffee's surface (the heat of the toffee will melt the chocolate right away). Using a metal decorating spatula, spread the chocolate thinly over the toffee. Without delay, sprinkle the remaining 1 cup of the nuts over the chocolate, gently pressing the nuts into the melted chocolate with the palm of your hand. Place toffee still in the pan in refrigerator for 5 to 7 minutes, or just until the chocolate appears set. Remove from refrigerator to a cool place for at least an hour. Wrap securely in aluminum foil until ready to cut into pieces.

4.  Gently lift the toffee from its foil to a cutting board. To cut strips, place a cleaver or large sharp knife 1½ inches in from edge of toffee. With a single motion, gently tap top blunt edge of knife with a mallet or the curved portion of a rolling pin. Repeat to cut remaining toffee into 1½-inch strips. With the cleaver or knife (you no longer need the mallet), cut strips crosswise into 1½ inches square.

5.  Store in layers, separated by strips of aluminum foil in an airtight metal or plastic container for up to 2 weeks.

## TECHNIQUE NOTES

To toast hazelnuts, place them on a baking sheet and bake in a preheated 350-degree-F oven for 10 minutes, or until skins split and the nuts are straw to pale golden in color; shake the sheet occasionally. Wrap the nuts in a cloth towel for about 10 minutes, then rub them to remove as much skin as possible.

For this recipe you want the nuts chopped somewhere between fine and coarse. You can achieve this best by using a nut mill (see page 17).

## VARIATION NOTE

To coat both sides of the toffee with chocolate, you need to temper the chocolate. Whichever chocolate you use—dark, milk, or white—is your choice; you will need 9 ounces. Using a cleaver or chef's knife, cut chocolate into matchstick pieces, about ¼ inch thick, reserving two chunks of chocolate that each weighs about ½ ounce. Melt and temper the chocolate pieces in a 1.9- or 2-quart microwave-safe plastic bowl, such as a Rubbermaid or Tupperware bowl (see Express Method, page 315), or a 3-quart stainless steel bowl (see Traditional Method, page 168).

Spread half the chocolate over one side of the toffee, sprinkle with 1 cup toasted, chopped nuts, and press them into the chocolate. Gently turn the toffee over and spread the remaining chocolate over this side, sprinkle with an additional cup of toasted, chopped nuts, and press them into the chocolate. Refrigerate for 5 to 10 minutes only to begin setting the chocolate. Remove from refrigerator and set in a cool place. To cut and store the toffee, proceed as directed above.

# candied almond clusters

➤ **Makes 3½ dozen 1½-inch clusters**

These chewy candies, spiked with bits of crystallized ginger, are partially dipped in bittersweet chocolate.

1. Adjust rack to lower third of oven and preheat oven to 350 degrees F. Line two large cool baking sheets with parchment paper.

2. Place the egg white in a large bowl, add the brown sugar, and whisk just to combine. Place this bowl over another bowl filled with just enough hot water to touch the bottom and sides of the container without floating it. Stir the mixture just until the sugar is dissolved. Add the almonds and ginger and stir with a rubber spatula to coat the nuts.

3. Drop rounded teaspoons of the mixture, one at a time (use a teaspoon measure), 1 inch apart on a baking sheet.

4. Bake one sheet at a time, for 8 to 10 minutes, or just until the nuts are golden. Clusters will feel soft, but become crisp as they cool. Remove baking sheets from the oven to a cooling rack. Candied Almond Clusters may be made 2 days ahead, stacked in a metal or plastic container, and stored at room temperature before coating with chocolate.

5. Cover a baking sheet with aluminum foil, or use a large Silpat or Exopat mat or other nonstick material (see Equipment, page 21), textured surface up; set nearby.

6. Using a cleaver or chef's knife, cut the chocolate into matchstick pieces, about ¼-inch thick, reserving two chunks of chocolate that each weigh about ½ ounce.

1 large (2 tablespoons) egg white

⅓ cup (65 grams) packed light brown sugar

2 cups (6 ounces) sliced almonds

⅓ cup (2 ounces) chopped crystallized ginger

8 ounces semisweet or bittersweet chocolate, for tempering

7. Melt and temper the chocolate pieces in a 1.9- or 2-quart microwave-safe plastic bowl, such as a Rubbermaid or Tupperware bowl (see Express Method, page 315), or a 3-quart stainless steel bowl (see Traditional Method, page 168).

8. To coat the bottom of the clusters with a thin film of chocolate, lift each cluster, one by one, with fingertips and dip the base ¼ inch up the cluster. Shake off or gently scrape clusters against the side of the bowl to remove any excess chocolate from each cluster. Set the clusters on a strip of foil or on the Silpat or Exopat mat. Repeat to coat the remaining clusters.

9. Set in a cool place until chocolate is shiny and firm.

10. Layer between sheets of foil in an airtight metal or plastic container and store in a cool place for up to 10 days.

## TECHNIQUE NOTE

By setting the chocolate-dipped clusters on a Silpat or Exopat mat, rough side up, you create a professional-looking textured pattern on the bottom of the clusters.

# truffle lollipops

➤ **Makes about 2½ dozen 1¼-inch nut-coated truffles**

. . . . . . . . . . . . . . . . . . . . . . . . . . . . .

These whimsical truffles that look like lollipops are actually two candies stuck together. Enjoy them plain or rolled in crumbs. For best flavor, eat these at room temperature. Here's your perfect food gift—they're easy to make and shape, and though creamy, they're firm enough to store unrefrigerated.

1. Dark Chocolate Truffles: Put the chocolate in a medium bowl. In a small saucepan, heat the cream just to the boil. Remove from heat. Pour over the chocolate; whisk until chocolate melts and mixture is smooth and shiny. Stir in the sour cream, corn syrup, and vanilla and almond extracts.

2. Using an ice cream scoop (1-teaspoon capacity) or a melon baller (1-teaspoon capacity), deposit rounded mounds of the chocolate mixture, spaced about ½-inch apart, onto a baking sheet lined with aluminum foil. (Or, place mixture in a pastry bag fitted with a ½-inch plain decorating tip, such as Ateco #6, and pipe 1-inch dollops of the truffle mixture onto a baking sheet lined with aluminum foil.) Set in a cool place until truffles are just firm enough to hold their shape, about 1½ hours.

3. Florentine Lollipop Sticks: Prepare the Florentine squares according to the recipe (page 114), with the following exception in step 4: While mixture is still warm but no longer liquid, cut half the mixture into 3-x-½-inch rectangles using a pastry wheel.

4. Florentine Crumbs: When the other half of the Florentine mixture is firm, remove it from the foil, break up into pieces, and chop finely on a cutting board with a chef's knife.

**DARK CHOCOLATE TRUFFLES**

6 ounces semisweet or bittersweet chocolate, finely chopped

⅓ cup heavy cream

2 tablespoons commercial sour cream

1 teaspoon light corn syrup

½ teaspoon pure vanilla extract

½ teaspoon pure almond extract

**FLORENTINE LOLLIPOP STICKS AND CRUMBS** (page 114)

5. Spread the Florentine Crumbs on a large plate. Using your palms, shape one scoop of chocolate mixture at a time into a ball, then roll in the crumbs until coated. Remove the Florentine Lollipop Sticks from the foil and poke one candy stick into the center of each truffle. Serve the truffles with the candy-like sticks facing up.

6. Store assembled Truffle Lollipops in a foil-lined cardboard container, such as a cake box, in a cool place for up to 1 week. Or store Dark Chocolate Truffles, Florentine Lollipop Sticks, and Florentine Crumbs individually. Layer Dark Chocolate Truffles between sheets of foil in an airtight plastic container and store in a cool place for up to 1 week, or refrigerate for up to 2 weeks. Store Florentine Lollipop Sticks in an airtight plastic container at room temperature for up to 2 weeks. Store Florentine Crumbs in a small airtight plastic container for up to 2 weeks.

## VARIATION NOTE

For raspberry truffles, press a fresh raspberry into the center of the chocolate mixture in the scoop before depositing it onto the foil-lined baking sheet.

# golden caramels

➤ **Makes about 2 pounds 3 ounces**

. . . . . . . . . . . . . . . . . . . . . . . . . . . . . . . . . . .

Golden Caramels—literally, that's what these are in taste, color, and decoration. Decorate each caramel square with a bit of 24-karat gold. It's simple to make richly flavored Dark Chocolate Caramels from this same recipe: just add 6 ounces bittersweet chocolate (such as Valrhona, Scharffen Berger, or Callebaut), coarsely chopped, to the sugar and corn syrup in step 3. Mmmmm, delicious!

    Wrap caramels in clear cellophane or chocolate-coat them—just dip them, one by one, into tempered chocolate, shake off excess, and transfer to a sheet of aluminum foil until the chocolate sets up.

1. Line bottom and sides of a 9-inch square pan with parchment paper; set aside.

2. Split the vanilla bean in half with a small paring knife, and scrape out the seeds; discard the pod. Add the seeds to the cream in a 1½-quart saucepan; scald the cream and keep the saucepan near the stove so that if the cream cools too much when needed, you can reheat it briefly.

3. In a deep, heavy-bottomed 4-quart saucepan over low heat, blend the corn syrup and the sugar, stirring occasionally until the mixture becomes more fluid and most of the sugar appears dissolved.

4. Stop stirring, raise heat to medium-high, and gently boil until a candy thermometer registers 305 degrees F (hard-crack stage), about 9 to 10 minutes.

1 vanilla bean

2 cups (1 pint) heavy cream

1 cup light corn syrup

2 cups (400 grams) granulated sugar

2 ounces (½ stick) unsalted butter, softened and cut into 4 pieces

½ teaspoon salt

24-karat gold leaf

5. Add the butter and salt to the sugar mixture, stirring constantly. Pour in the warm vanilla-flavored cream in a slow but steady stream without letting the boiling stop (be careful—mixture foams up and is steamy). Lower heat to medium and continue to boil gently until the thermometer registers about 248 degrees F, stirring occasionally to prevent scorching, about 14 to 15 minutes.

6. Let the candy stand about 3 minutes to allow bubbling to subside, then pour into the prepared pan without scraping the saucepan; allow to cool at least 5 hours.

7. Invert onto a clean cutting board and cut into ½-inch-wide strips; then cut across the strips to form ½-inch squares. To apply a patch of gold leaf to each square, use a small artist's brush. With the brush, lift a tiny patch about the size of an oatmeal flake of gold leaf and deposit it on top of the caramels for decoration.

8. Cut caramels tend to stick together and not hold their shape unless individually wrapped, so for easiest storage wrap the block of caramel in aluminum foil and cut off portions as needed. Store cut caramels in layers, separated by aluminum foil in an airtight metal or plastic container in a cool place for up to 3 weeks.

**VARIATION NOTE**

For a chewier caramel, boil the mixture to 248 degrees F in step 5.

# candied lady apples

➤ **Makes about 3 dozen candied apples**

· · · · · · · · · · · · · · · · · · · · · · · · · · · · · · · · · ·

There's nothing that can't be miniaturized—even candied apples. Start with lady apples; the versatile coating can also cover Seckel pears or even strawberries.

1. Have the apples at room temperature. Insert a lollipop stick into the stem end of each apple. Set apples on a baking sheet lined with aluminum foil, a Silpat or Exopat mat, or other nonstick material.

2. Combine the water, corn syrup, and granulated sugar in a 1½-quart heavy-bottomed saucepan over medium-low heat. Cook, stirring occasionally, until the sugar is dissolved.

3. Raise heat and bring mixture to a boil. Boil, without stirring, until a candy thermometer registers 300 degrees F (hard-crack stage).

4. Remove pan from heat and let stand until bubbling subsides, about 1 minute. Gently stir in the food coloring and cinnamon oil.

5. Holding the stick, dip an apple into the hot syrup. Allow any excess to drip back into the saucepan, then set apple onto the lined baking sheet. Repeat to coat remaining apples.

6. Allow the syrup to cool and harden, about 1 hour. Wrap each candied apple in cellophane. Store in a cool, dry room.

36 (1½ pounds) lady apples, rinsed and dried

36 lollipop sticks

1 cup water

⅔ cup light corn syrup

2 cups (400 grams) granulated sugar

½ teaspoon red liquid food coloring

½ teaspoon cinnamon oil

# blood orange jellies

➤ **Makes about 5 dozen 1-inch square or round jellies**

. . . . . . . . . . . . . . . . . . . . . . . . . . . . . . . .

Not as chewy as a gum drop, these are colored and flavored by vibrant blood orange juice. For a delicious alternative when blood oranges are not available, substitute orange juice.

1. Line bottom and sides of a 9-inch square pan with parchment paper; set aside. Place each pouch of the pectin in a glass and snip the tops; set near the cooking area.

2. In a deep, heavy-bottomed 4-quart saucepan, over low heat, blend the juice, sugar, and zest. Bring to a boil over medium-high heat, and boil (mixture foams up), stirring occasionally, for 6 minutes only. Remove from heat and whisk in the pectin until well combined. Without delay, pour into parchment-paper-lined pan. Allow the jelly to sit at room temperature until set, about 3 hours.

3. Invert the jelly onto a sheet of parchment paper. Cut into 1-inch strips, then cut across the strips to form 1-inch squares. Or without cutting into strips, cut out 1-inch circles using a 1-inch round cookie cutter.

4. Place about 1 cup additional sugar on a plate and coat all sides of each jelly with the sugar. Add more sugar as needed.

5. Store in one layer in a covered foil-lined cardboard container, such as a cake box, in a cool place at room temperature up to 5 days.

Two 3-ounce pouches liquid pectin

1 cup plus 2 tablespoons fresh blood orange juice

2½ cups (500 grams) granulated sugar

1 tablespoon finely grated orange zest

Additional granulated sugar for coating jellies

# chocolate wafers

➤ **Makes 4 dozen 1½-inch wafers**

. . . . . . . . . . . . . . . . . . . . . . . . . . . . .

9 ounces semisweet or bittersweet chocolate, for tempering

48 whole dried Bing or sweet-tart cherries

The French are known for these stunning chocolate candies. They are simply small, thin discs of chocolate topped with three or four items, usually an assortment of toasted whole nuts and/or dried fruits. For this recipe, I center a single plump dried cherry on each Chocolate Wafer.

Your options are many—toasted walnuts, pecans, blanched almonds, pistachios, or hazelnuts are just a sampling of nuts you might use; small pieces of dried apricot, crystallized ginger chips, a sprinkling of pearl sugar, or even finely chopped cocoa nibs (the seed of the cacao bean) are other choices.

Phil Ogiela, former executive pastry chef at the now closed 231 Ellsworth Restaurant in San Mateo, California, is one of the most inspiring pastry chefs I know. He takes these wafers a step further by depositing each dollop of melted, tempered chocolate on top of a pressed mint leaf (fresh leaves pressed between two sheets of parchment paper and heavily weighted with books for 5 days)—sublime!

You can use a candy maker's funnel (at least 1 cup capacity) for this recipe instead of a pastry bag. A candy maker's funnel is easy to use and makes perfect discs of the melted, tempered chocolate.

1. Line a large baking sheet with aluminum foil, or a large Silpat or Exopat mat or other nonstick material (see Equipment, page 21), textured surface up. Set upright in a large glass or bowl, a 16-inch pastry bag fitted with a ⁷⁄₁₆-inch plain decorating tip (such as Ateco #5), or an 18-inch disposable decorating bag fitted with a ⁷⁄₁₆-inch plain decorating tip (such as Ateco #5).

2. Using a cleaver or chef's knife, cut the chocolate into matchstick pieces, about ¼-inch thick, reserving two chunks of chocolate that each weighs about ½ ounce.

3. Melt and temper the chocolate pieces in a 1.9- or 2-quart microwave-safe plastic bowl, such as a Rubbermaid or Tupperware bowl (see Express Method, page 315), or a 3-quart stainless steel bowl (Traditional Method, page 168).

4. Fill pastry bag with the chocolate, and pipe small dollops about 1 inch apart onto the prepared sheet pan. To pipe, position the pastry tip perpendicular to the baking sheet, about ¼ inch above it, each time you pipe small candy "kiss" dollops (each a scant ½ measuring teaspoon). Space them about 1 inch apart. If a thin string of chocolate trails between dollops, it's natural, because it's difficult to stop the flow of chocolate completely before piping again. Once the chocolate sets, it's easy to lift the Chocolate Wafer from its surface without the chocolate string.

5. After piping out the chocolate, without delay, firmly rap the baking sheet on the work surface, thereby transforming the dollops of chocolate into thin wafers. Center a dried cherry on top of each chocolate wafer. Set in the refrigerator for 5 minutes, then remove to a cool place until chocolate wafers are completely firm.

6. To store, layer between sheets of plastic wrap in an airtight metal or plastic container in a cool place for up to 10 days.

## TECHNIQUE NOTE

By setting the chocolate-dipped clusters on a Silpat or Exopat mat, rough side up, you create a professional-looking textured pattern on the bottom of the clusters.

# five-spice marshmallows

➤ **Makes 6 dozen 1 ½ inch rosettes**

. . . . . . . . . . . . . . . . . . . . . . . . . . . . . . . .

Flavors of Chinese five-spice, vanilla, and lemon zest are the ideal foil for these chewy yet tender sweet marshmallows. There are a variety of ground five-spice blends available in supermarket spice sections. I use one that combines anise, fennel, cloves, cinnamon, and ginger. You can pipe this marshmallow mixture directly into Chocolate Thimbles (page 168).

1. Line two large baking sheets with Silpat or Exopat mats or other nonstick material, or aluminum foil, lightly coated with unflavored oil or spray, then lightly sprinkled with powdered sugar. Fit a 16-inch pastry bag with a large star decorating tip (such as Ateco #8).

2. Pour the ½ cup water into the bowl of a heavy-duty mixer. Sprinkle the gelatin over the water and set aside for 15 minutes to soften.

3. In a heavy-bottomed 1 ½-quart saucepan, pour in the ¾ cup water, corn syrup, and sugar. Over low heat, dissolve the sugar. Raise heat to medium-high and cook, uncovered, until mixture reaches 235 degrees F on a candy thermometer. Pour the hot mixture over the gelatin and stir to combine. Set aside to cool until 130 degrees F, about 15 minutes.

4. Add the vanilla, lemon zest, and five-spice, and with a whisk attachment whip on medium speed until the mixture has increased about four times in volume and is white and fluffy, about 10 minutes.

5. Fill a pastry bag with the mixture, and pipe small rosettes onto the prepared sheet pan. To pipe, position the pastry tip perpendicular to the baking sheet, about ½ inch above it, each time you pipe a candy "kiss" dollop. Space the dollops about 1 inch apart. If a thin string of marshmallow mixture trails between them, it's natural, because

½ cup water

4 teaspoons (1 package plus 1 ½ teaspoons) unflavored gelatin

¾ cup water

1 tablespoon light corn syrup

2 cups (400 grams) granulated sugar

1 teaspoon pure vanilla extract

1 teaspoon finely grated lemon zest

½ teaspoon ground Chinese five-spice

1 cup unsifted powdered sugar

it's difficult to stop the flow of the mixture completely before piping again. Let stand at room temperature for at least 4 hours. Once the marshmallow sets, use a small paring knife (lightly oiled or sprayed with an unflavored vegetable oil) and cut the strings from the base of the marshmallow rosettes.

6. Sift a light coating of the powdered sugar over the tops of the rosettes. Wipe the blade of a small metal spatula with an unflavored vegetable oil or a spray. Slip the spatula under each rosette to release from the nonstick mat or foil. (Reapply oil to the spatula as needed.)

7. Line a cardboard container, such as a cake box, with a sheet of aluminum foil, lightly coat the foil with powdered sugar, and store the rosettes in one layer in the container, covered at room temperature, for up to 3 days.

## VARIATION NOTE

For a stiffer, chewier marshmallow use 2 whole packages (5 teaspoons) unflavored gelatin.

# raspberry jellies

➤ Makes about 5 dozen 1-inch square or round jellies

. . . . . . . . . . . . . . . . . . . . . . . . . . . . . .

These tender, chewy bites are so intensely flavored you might think you're eating fresh raspberries. However, the jellies will taste only as good as the raspberries you select. Taste the fruit before using. If fresh raspberries are not available, substitute with one 12-ounce package frozen red raspberries, preferably ones with no sugar added. If sugar has been added, taste one, then, depending on their sweetness, decrease sugar in the recipe from 2½ cups to at least 2¼ cups. Thaw the raspberries, purée them in a food processor, then pour the mixture through a strainer to remove seeds until you have the required ⅔ cup purée for the recipe.

1. Purée the raspberries in the food processor; pour through a fine-mesh strainer set over a bowl. Using a rubber spatula, push the mixture through the strainer to remove seeds and to yield ⅔ cup purée.

2. Line bottom and sides of a 9-inch square pan with parchment paper; set aside. Place each pouch of pectin in a glass and snip the tops; set near the cooking area.

3. In a deep, heavy-bottomed 4-quart saucepan, over low heat, blend the purée, water, 2½ cups sugar, and zest. Bring to a boil over medium-high heat, and boil (mixture foams up), stirring occasionally, for 5 minutes only. Remove from heat and whisk in the pectin until well combined. Without delay, pour into the parchment-paper-lined pan. Allow jelly to sit at room temperature until set, about 3 hours.

1½ pints (about 2½ cups) fresh raspberries

Two 3-ounce pouches liquid pectin

½ cup water

2½ cups (500 grams) granulated sugar

1 tablespoon finely grated orange zest

Additional granulated sugar for coating jellies

4.  Invert the jelly onto a sheet of parchment paper. Cut into 1-inch strips, then cut across the strips to form 1-inch squares. Or, without cutting into strips, cut out 1-inch circles using a 1-inch round cookie cutter.

5.  Place about 1 cup sugar on a plate to coat all sides of each jelly. Add more sugar as needed.

6.  Store in one layer in a covered foil-lined cardboard container, such as a cake box, in a cool place at room temperature up to 5 days.

# candied kumquat circles

➤ **Makes 6 dozen ½-inch-thick slices**

. . . . . . . . . . . . . . . . . . . . . . . . . . . . .

Kumquats are unusual, not like most citrus fruits—the peel is sweet and full of flavor and the flesh is sour, whereas the orange's peel is sour and the flesh sweet. Their unique flavor makes their use ideal for candying.

1. Wipe or spray a large cooling rack with unflavored vegetable oil and set the rack over a large sheet of aluminum foil or baking sheet; set aside.

2. Using a small serrated knife, cut off the tips of the kumquats at each end, and discard. Slice the remaining portion in half, cross-wise; remove all seeds.

3. In a 2½-quart heavy-bottomed saucepan, combine the water, corn syrup, and 2 cups sugar; bring to a boil over medium-low heat. Add the kumquat slices to the sugar syrup. Reduce heat and simmer slices until tender, about 1 hour.

4. Raise heat and cook until the syrup registers 222 degrees F on a candy thermometer.

5. Turn off heat, remove the kumquat slices with a slotted spoon, and transfer them to the wire rack to drain off the syrup. Allow to dry at room temperature for 1 to 3 days before storing or coating in sugar. You may store candied slices before coating in sugar in a metal container at room temperature for up to 3 weeks.

6. To finish, place about 1 cup sugar on a plate and toss the slices in the sugar to coat. Add more sugar as needed. The kumquat slices have a tendency to retain some moisture, which can affect the sugar-coating, so once you sugar-coat them, serve the same day or toss in sugar again before serving.

1 pound (about 37) fresh kumquats, washed

1 cup water

2 tablespoons light corn syrup

2 cups (400 grams) granulated sugar

Additional granulated sugar for coating the candied slices

# planning ahead

Everyone loves miniatures,
and almost everything can
be done in advance

Whether you cater on a regular basis, bake professionally, or simply entertain occasionally, you will find that everyone loves to be served miniatures. They are perfect for a congenial group of ten, for a celebrating crowd of one hundred, or as accompaniments to a restaurant's regular desserts. For most miniatures, almost everything can be done in advance: mixing the doughs, baking them, even decorating them to a great extent.

These procedures are designed to make efficient use of your time. The suggestions apply to the recipes in this book as well as to your own.

Keep score.

➤ When I plan to bake any more than three different miniature recipes for a large event, I draw up a simple chart to organize the process. First, I list the recipes I have chosen to bake. Then, along the top of the page, I create three thin columns, headed D, B, and A, for Dough, Baked, and Assembled. Each time I have completed one of these three crucial steps for a particular recipe, I make a check in the appropriate column next to its name. I often find it easier to bake assembly-line fashion, doing all the mixing of the dough first, then all the baking, then the assembly and decoration, rather than going from start to finish on one miniature at a time.

On the other half of my sheet of paper I write a list of specific tasks I need to complete in order to create the miniatures. The list includes the fillings and glazes I need to make and special techniques, such as peeling or blanching nuts and fruits or tempering chocolate. These items get crossed off as they are completed.

Prep early.

➤ Gather and measure ingredients for all the miniatures you plan to make at one time. You can even do this the day before mixing them. Be sure to label setups to distinguish each miniature recipe.

Mix several doughs at one time.

➤ After organizing the setups, mix one dough after another. When ingredients for doughs are similar, instead of washing bowls, wipe them thoroughly with paper towels to avoid unnecessary clean-ups.

Form doughs into circles, rolls, logs, and/or brick shapes ahead of time to bake later.

➤ For example, roll out dough between two sheets of waxed paper to form circles as recipes specify. Stack circles on baking sheet and store as recipes specify. Take time to label and date each dough.

Use time-saving techniques to shape dozens of miniatures quickly and simply.

➤ Whenever possible, bake on parchment. It's reusable, and baking sheet clean-up is minimal.

➤ To flatten balls of dough on a baking sheet uniformly at once, evenly space dough balls on the sheet, flour the underside of another baking sheet with similar or identical dimensions, and press down gently but firmly on balls.

➤ Carefully lift the top baking sheet.

➤ A cookie press or a pastry bag fitted with a decorative tip shapes cookies quickly, easily, and uniformly.

- Miniatures made from bar cookies or sheet cakes allow you to make dozens at once.

- Spread batter over a plastic stencil (see page 123) to form miniature shapes quickly and uniformly.

- To form dozens of tartlet shells at once, see Caramel Carmenitas (page 207), Garnet Tartlets (page 210), and Rose Tartlets (page 212). The method for each is different and is quicker than pressing dough in tins with fingertips, one at a time, as for Chocolate Starlets (page 186).

- Roll pastry or cookie doughs thinly, cut shapes such as 2-inch rounds for tartlets, and store in plastic containers with tight-fitting lids and plastic wrap between layers to keep shapes apart. Freeze until needed.

Streamline baking.

- To bake many batches of miniatures and make the best use of your time, try a baking relay system: Line four baking sheets with parchment just to fit. Set miniatures on each sheet of parchment, ready to bake. When one batch comes from the oven, lift the parchment with that batch to a cooling rack. Immediately place another parchment-lined baking sheet of unbaked dough in the oven.

  You usually need only four sheets for any baking relay, since most baking sheets are cool enough to handle in 10 to 15 minutes. One or two baking sheets are in the oven, while the others are cooling.

Use decorative touches like the professionals.

- Applying a streusel to cookies before baking, as in Cornmeal Batons (page 76), shortcuts decorating. A baked-on garnish saves time and decorates without any additional handling for glazing or piping later.

➤ Prefabricated decorations, such as Buttercream Bees (page 287), are invaluable. Such planning ahead frees you to finish other miniatures.

➤ Stencils make it possible to brush a dash of design and color over each miniature, decorating quickly and easily, as for Pecan Strudel (page 260).

➤ Use perfect pecan halves, as in Little Gems (page 53).

➤ To make sandwich cookies look neat and finished, flip cookies baked-bottom-side up on a tray. Dot each with jelly and sandwich a plain cookie on top, as in Apricot Medals (page 58).

➤ To make miniatures appear neat and trim, press nuts with fingertips into melted white chocolate to secure them in place, as for Java Sticks (page 54).

Store miniatures wisely.

➤ When stacking miniatures, select storage containers in which they fit snugly with little air space between them and the lid. Otherwise, the air stales the miniatures and affects their taste. Take care that lids fit tightly too.

➤ Store decorated miniatures in jelly-roll pans and cover with aluminum foil or select shallow cardboard boxes, such as cake boxes or shirt boxes, and line with foil. The smaller the air space between the miniatures and the lid, the better the flavors are contained, keeping miniatures tasting their best.

➤ When stacking miniatures in containers, place sheets of plastic or aluminum foil between layers to prevent breakage.

Develop a baker's timetable.

➤ Set up a countdown to the serving day: Draw a simple chart on graph paper to organize yourself. Across the top, form columns by writing "Several weeks before" (fill in actual dates), "Two to three weeks ahead," etc. Down the side, write the names of the miniatures you select. Fill in your timetable as each recipe specifies.

➤ Several weeks ahead: Prepare and freeze doughs.

➤ Two to three weeks ahead: Bake, wrap securely and store.

➤ Up to two days ahead: Bake miniatures from doughs and batters.

➤ Day ahead or on the serving day: Decorate and store.

Adopt smart miniature planning.

*How many miniatures to serve per person?*

Count on three per person, unless miniatures are the only dessert you're offering. Then the number is raised to five or six per person. Keep in mind that the larger the assortment, the more you have to bake. People love to taste at least one of each type of miniature.

*How many cookies in a batch?*

When you need to determine how many cookies to expect from any cookie dough, use the following procedure.

➤ Mix the dough, then weigh the entire batch and record the weight on the recipe.

➤ Shape several cookies just as the recipe specifies. Place just enough shaped cookies on the scale to register 1 ounce; record that number next to the dough's total weight.

➤ Multiply the number of shaped cookies in an ounce by the dough's total weight in ounces. For example, the Little Gems dough (page 53) weighs 22 ounces. Five cookies register 1 ounce on the scale; therefore, the recipe's yield is 110 cookies, a little over 9 dozen.

➤ Dough rolled between sheets of waxed paper to form circles, as with the Drei Augen (page 56), is calculated the same way. Find the weight of each rolled-out circle, then cut out cookies until you have an ounce. Remember, you must reroll and cut the scraps in order for your calculation to be correct.

*How many pastries from a dough?*

You can estimate about how many tartlets, turnovers, or other shapes from any pastry dough if you use the method described above.

*Learn how to form dough circles consistently the same size from a specific recipe.*

When I need a large quantity of cookies, I multiply a favorite reliable cookie recipe. Here's a quick way to roll dough circles:

➤ First make the single recipe. Weigh the dough and make a note of the weight on the recipe.

➤ As the recipe specifies, divide the dough before rolling it. Weigh just one portion and mark that weight on the recipe.

➤ Roll out that portion between two sheets of waxed paper just the shape and thickness that the recipe specifies.

➤ Measure diameter and mark that on the recipe.

Now you can multiply any favorite recipe, and roll portions of dough one after the other quickly and easily. Just refer to your notes on the recipe for the weight of a single portion. Roll each portion to the correct diameter, and you can be sure it is exactly the size the recipe specifies.

quick miniatures
reference

These categories come in
handy when you plan to
make a number of different
miniatures

To help you select which recipes to make, I have separated the miniature recipes into categories based on the method used to form them. Next to each one is its size, shape, and page. Texture is indicated only for cookies, since the textures of pastries, cakes, and candies are familiar. These categories will come in handy when you plan to make a number of different miniatures. When I bake more than one or two kinds of miniatures, I make sure to provide a variety of shapes, textures, and flavors—and perhaps even a miniature with a touch of folly.

REFERENCE CHARTS NEXT PAGE ➤

## MINIATURE COOKIES

| ROLLED/CUTOUT | SIZE/SHAPE | TEXTURE | PAGE |
|---|---|---|---|
| harlequins | 1½" star | shortbread | 51 |
| drei augen | 1½" sandwich | shortbread | 56 |
| apricot medals | 1¾" sandwich | shortbread | 58 |
| pineapple pockets | 1½" flattened cone | shortbread | 60 |
| chocolate chip swirls | 1½" round | shortbread | 62 |
| lemon sunflowers | 1½" petal | shortbread | 86 |
| spicy twin thins | 1½" star-shaped sandwich | spicy shortbread | 139 |
| bittersweet gingersnaps | 1½" x 2" rectangle | spicy miniatures | 141 |
| springerle | 1½" x 2" rectangle | spicy chewy | 149 |
| speculaas | 1½" round | spicy shortbread | 152 |
| lebkuchen circles | 1" round | spicy chewy | 156 |
| biberli | 1½" rectangle | spicy chewy | 158 |
| tiffany rings | 1½" round | chocolate shortbread | 180 |
| chocolate coins | 1¼" round | chocolate shortbread | 183 |
| chocolate candy-cane cookies | 1½" round | chocolate miniatures | 196 |

## MINIATURE COOKIES

| BAR | SIZE/SHAPE | TEXTURE | PAGE |
|---|---|---|---|
| gianduja cubes | 1½" square | chewy | 93 |
| panforte di siena | 1½" square | chewy | 97 |
| glazed almond weave | 1" x 2½" stick | chewy | 101 |
| viennese triangles | 1" triangle | chewy | 103 |
| pecan diamonds | 1½" diamond | chewy | 105 |
| florentine squares | 1½" square | crispy | 114 |
| pains d'amande | 1½" square | spicy chewy | 143 |

## MINIATURE COOKIES

| DROP | SIZE/SHAPE | TEXTURE | PAGE |
| --- | --- | --- | --- |
| almond confetti | 1½" wafer | shortbread | 88 |
| tuiles | 1½" disk | crispy | 113 |
| black walnut genoise wafers | 1¾" round sandwich | crispy | 116 |
| cognac wafers | 1" round sandwich | crispy | 120 |
| cigarettes | 1½" roll | crispy | 122 |
| nougatine cones | 1½" cone | crispy | 124 |
| miniature krumkake | 2" cone | crispy | 126 |
| chocolate fringe cups | 1¾" cup | crispy | 132 |
| chantilly fans | 1½" wedge | crispy | 134 |
| chocolate pistachio cigarettes | 1½" roll | chocolate crispy | 192 |
| dutch chocolate minicakes | 1½" minicakes | chocolate chewy | 198 |

## MINIATURE COOKIES

| HAND-FORMED | SIZE/SHAPE | TEXTURE | PAGE |
| --- | --- | --- | --- |
| little gems | 1½" round | shortbread | 53 |
| pistachio buttons | 1½" round | shortbread | 90 |
| sweet seashells | 1⅛" x 1¾" scallop | shortbread | 64 |
| chevron twists | 1½" spiral | shortbread | 70 |
| almond teardrops | 1½" teardrop | shortbread | 72 |
| macadamia crescents | 1½" crescent | shortbread | 74 |
| cornmeal batons | 1½" stick | shortbread | 76 |
| autumn acorns | 1½" acorn | shortbread | 80 |
| hahnpfeffernüsse | 1" ball | spicy chewy | 147 |
| chrabeli | 1½" leaf | spicy chewy | 151 |
| double kisses | 1½" kiss | chocolate shortbread | 166 |
| chocolate thimbles | 1½" cases | chocolate crispy | 168 |

## MINIATURE COOKIES

### REFRIGERATOR

| | SIZE/SHAPE | TEXTURE | PAGE |
|---|---|---|---|
| shortbread cameos | 1⅓" x 1¾" oval | shortbread | 49 |
| cocos | 1¼" round | shortbread | 66 |
| daddy long legs | 2" stick | shortbread | 84 |
| lemon-laced gingersnaps | 1½" round | spicy crispy | 154 |
| white blossom circles | 1½" round | chocolate shortbread | 188 |
| cocoa cavaliers | 1½" triangle | chocolate shortbread | 190 |

## MINIATURE COOKIES

### PIPED

| | SIZE/SHAPE | TEXTURE | PAGE |
|---|---|---|---|
| java sticks | 1½" stick | shortbread | 54 |
| peanut butter petal cookies | 1½" 5-petal flower | shortbread | 68 |
| maple butterballs | 1¼" spherical sandwich | shortbread | 78 |
| mimosa rosettes | 1½" rosette | shortbread | 82 |
| meringue bubbles | 1¼" round | chewy | 95 |
| macaroon trios | 1½" rounded triangle | chewy | 99 |
| swiss japonais | 1¾" round | chewy | 107 |
| ladies' wafers | 1½" round | crispy | 118 |
| crispy corkscrews | 2" spiral | crispy | 128 |
| champagne biscuits | 3" finger | crispy | 130 |
| sesame spice chips | 1½" round | spicy crispy | 145 |
| chocolate macaroons | 1½" round sandwich | chocolate chewy | 163 |
| chocolate shadows | 1½" round | chocolate shortbread | 194 |

## MINIATURE COOKIES

### COOKIE STRIPS

| | SIZE/SHAPE | TEXTURE | PAGE |
|---|---|---|---|
| neapolitan wedges | 1" wedge | chocolate shortbread | 171 |

## MINIATURE PASTRIES

| FLAKY MINIATURES | SIZE/SHAPE | PAGE |
| --- | --- | --- |
| sweet cheese puffs | 1½" puff | 236 |
| pumpkin pastries | 1½" round | 238 |
| eccles tarts | 1" x 2" barquette | 240 |
| heartovers | 1½" half heart | 242 |
| shreveshire tarts | 1" x 2" oval | 244 |
| eva deutsch's almond slices | 1" slice | 246 |
| four-star rugelach | 1½" crescent | 249 |
| cinnamon twists | 2" stick | 250 |
| sweet ravioli | 1½" square | 252 |
| california rolls | 1¼" roll | 254 |
| dried fruit pastry strips | 1" x 2" slice | 255 |
| flaky windmills | 1½" pinwheel | 258 |
| pecan strudel | ½" slice | 260 |
| miniature caramel cream vol-au-vents | 1½" round | 262 |
| fig pastry rolls | ½" slice | 264 |
| florentine pastry strips | 1" x 2" rectangle | 269 |
| streusel pastry strips | 1" x 2" rectangle | 271 |
| phyllo accordions | 2" roll | 273 |
| flaky cheesecake turnovers | 1½" triangle | 275 |

## MINIATURE PASTRIES

| TARTLET MINIATURES | SIZE/SHAPE | PAGE |
| --- | --- | --- |
| chocolate tulips | 1½" round | 178 |
| chocolate starlets | 1½" round | 186 |
| caramel carmenitas | 2½" barquette | 207 |
| garnet tartlets | 1½" round | 210 |
| rose tartlets | 1½" oval | 212 |
| double chocolate tartlets | 1½" round | 214 |
| chocolate cherry chaps | 1½" round | 216 |
| mazarine tartlets | 1½" round | 217 |
| lemon meringue tartlets | 1½" round | 219 |
| raspberry lemon tartlets | 1½" round | 221 |
| scheherazade tartlets | 1½" round | 222 |
| jade buttercups | 1½" round | 224 |
| poirettes | 1½" round | 226 |
| lemon drops | 1½" round | 228 |
| swiss bettinas | 1½" round | 230 |
| midas cups | 1½" round | 231 |

## MINIATURE CAKES

| CAKE MINIATURES | SIZE/SHAPE | PAGE |
| --- | :---: | :---: |
| hedgehogs | 1½" pet | 174 |
| pistachio petits fours | 1½" triangle | 283 |
| honey bee minicakes | 2" stick | 286 |
| parisers | 1¼" domed round | 289 |
| calypso minirolls | 2" roll | 292 |
| dominoes | 1" x 2" rectangle | 294 |
| jewel fruit prisms | 1" square | 296 |
| s'more squares | 1½" square | 298 |
| miniature fruit meringues | 1" square | 299 |
| polka dot minicakes | 1½" round | 300 |
| chocolate-pistachio tigrés | 2" round | 303 |
| punsch cakelets | 1½" square | 305 |

## MINIATURE CANDIES

| MINIATURE SWEETS | SIZE/SHAPE | PAGE |
| --- | :---: | :---: |
| toffee butter crunch | 1½" square | 319 |
| candied almond clusters | 1½" round | 322 |
| truffle lollipops | 1¼" round | 324 |
| golden caramels | ½" square | 326 |
| candied lady apples | 2" round | 328 |
| blood orange jellies | 1" square or round | 329 |
| chocolate wafers | 1½" round | 330 |
| five-spice marshmallows | 1½" round | 332 |
| raspberry jellies | 1" square or round | 334 |
| candied kumquat circles | ½" round | 336 |

Most of the miniatures can be
made in advance and stored

Storage is the final key to beautiful and delicious miniatures. Proper storing and freezing methods preserve the quality and freshness of miniatures by maintaining their correct textures, thereby maintaining their correct tastes.

The following chart lists, by texture, the best storing and freezing methods for all the miniatures in this book. Most of the miniature doughs can be made in advance and stored unbaked. Since fillings and decorations are the most perishable parts of miniatures, it is often a good idea to bake cookies, pastries, or cakes, store until close to serving time, and then add the finishing touches.

Miniatures that require a filling keep longer unfilled, because most often the filling is quite perishable, as with cream cheese mixtures, or apt to stale quickly, as with frangipanes, and because a filled miniature, as with fresh fruit and whipped cream, given time to sit may become soggy.

Whether decorations are perishable, like whipped cream, lemon curd, and fresh fruit, or nonperishable, like jellies and sugar glazes, their appearance becomes less attractive with age. For example, jelly loses its shine, and a sugar or chocolate glaze also will become less shiny and fresh-looking. In short, the less adorned a baked good is, the longer it will keep. Use the chart to plan your baking, perhaps freezing a dough until an opportune moment, baking on a quiet weeknight, then decorating the day you plan to serve the miniatures.

A note about the recommended containers for storing miniatures of different textures: Airtight sturdy plastic containers keep moisture in so that miniatures remain chewy, while airtight metal containers keep moisture out so that crispy miniatures retain their texture. Though this is especially relevant for storing miniatures at room temperature, they may be frozen in these containers also.

Proper defrosting is just as important as proper wrapping and labeling. Transfer from the freezer individual packages of dough, such as Sour Cream Pastry (page 235), or an assortment of stacked dough circles, such as Drei Augen (page 56) and Almond Teardrops (page 72), that are already on a baking sheet directly to the refrigerator at least 8 hours before using. This gives the doughs time to defrost gradually without absorbing excess moisture.

To defrost already baked miniatures, remove labeled containers from the freezer and leave out until they reach room temperature. You can keep most miniatures in the container until serving. If you're going to decorate them further, remove them to a shallow container with a cover.

I advise bakers to store decorated miniatures in a single layer, because there is no point in going to the trouble of making your creations beautiful if you are going to risk smudging the sticky or shiny ones or crushing the delicate ones under the weight of the others. To store in one layer, place the miniatures in a jelly-roll pan, then cover with aluminum foil. A cake box or similarly shaped cardboard box is also spacious enough to hold a single layer of filled, assembled, or decorated miniatures before serving.

# freezing and storing chart*

| | DOUGH OR BATTER 3 DAYS TO 1 MONTH | BAKED, UNFILLED 1 WEEK TO 1 MONTH | BAKED, FILLED† 1 WEEK TO 10 DAYS | ASSEMBLED AND DECORATED 1 TO 2 DAYS |
|---|---|---|---|---|
| SHORTBREAD | Refrigerator or freezer | Airtight metal container Room temperature or freezer | Airtight metal container or cake box Room temperature or freezer | Airtight metal container or cake box Room temperature or refrigerator |
| CHEWY | | Sturdy plastic container Room temperature or freezer | Sturdy plastic container Room temperature or freezer | Sturdy plastic container or cake box Room temperature or refrigerator |
| CRISPY | | Airtight metal container Room temperature only | Airtight metal container Room temperature only | Airtight metal container or cake box Room temperature only |
| SPICY SHORTBREAD | Refrigerator or freezer | Airtight metal container Room temperature or freezer | Airtight metal container or cake box Room temperature or freezer | Airtight metal container or cake box Room temperature or refrigerator |
| SPICY CHEWY | | Sturdy plastic container Room temperature or freezer | Sturdy plastic container Room temperature or freezer | Sturdy plastic container or cake box Room temperature only |
| SPICY CRISPY | | Airtight metal container Room temperature only | Airtight metal container Room temperature only | Airtight metal container or cake box Room temperature only |
| CHOCOLATE SHORTBREAD | Refrigerator or freezer | Airtight metal container Room temperature or freezer | Airtight metal container or cake box Room temperature or freezer | Airtight metal container or cake box Room temperature or refrigerator |

| | DOUGH OR BATTER<br>3 DAYS TO 1 MONTH | BAKED, UNFILLED<br>1 WEEK TO 1 MONTH | BAKED, FILLED†<br>1 WEEK TO 10 DAYS | ASSEMBLED AND DECORATED<br>1 TO 2 DAYS |
|---|---|---|---|---|
| CHOCOLATE<br>CHEWY | | Sturdy plastic container<br>Room temperature<br>or freezer | Sturdy plastic container<br>Room temperature<br>or freezer | Sturdy plastic container<br>or cake box<br>Room temperature only |
| CHOCOLATE<br>CRISPY | | Airtight metal container<br>Room temperature only | Airtight metal container<br>Room temperature only | Airtight metal container<br>or cake box<br>Room temperature only |
| TARTLET | Refrigerator or freezer | Airtight metal container<br>Room temperature<br>or freezer | Airtight metal container<br>or cake box<br>Room temperature,<br>refrigerator, or freezer | Cake box<br>Room temperature<br>or refrigerator |
| FLAKY | Refrigerator or freezer | Airtight metal container:<br>room temperature<br>Sturdy plastic container:<br>freezer | Cake box<br>Room temperature,<br>refrigerator, or freezer | Cake box<br>Room temperature<br>or refrigerator |
| CAKE | | Cake box<br>Room temperature<br>or freezer, well wrapped | Cake box<br>Room temperature,<br>refrigerator, or freezer | Cake box<br>Room temperature<br>or refrigerator |

*General storage guide. Please refer to recipe for specifics.*
†*If filling is perishable or contains moisture, as from fresh fruit, whipped cream, or buttercream, refrigerate.*

# index

## A

Almonds
  Almond Cake, 300
  Almond Confetti, 88–89
  Almond Filling, 217
  Almond-Hazelnut Filling, 246
  Almond Paste Frangipane, 226
  Almond Paste Frangipane Filling, 178
  Almond Paste Streusel, 190
  Almond Teardrops, 72–73
  Biberli, 158–59
  Candied Almond Clusters, 322–23
  Chocolate Coins, 183–85
  Chocolate Frangipane Filling, 214–15
  Chocolate Macaroons, 163–65
  Chocolate Marzipan Filling, 183–84
  Chocolate Tulips, 178–79
  Cocoa Cavaliers, 190–91
  Cranberry Almond Cake, 301
  Dacquoise, 93
  Dominoes, 294–95
  Double Chocolate Tartlets, 214–15
  Drei Augen, 56–57
  Eva Deutsch's Almond Slices, 246–47
  Flaky Cheesecake Turnovers, 275–76
  Florentine Pastry Strips, 269–70
  Florentine Squares, 114–15
  Gianduja Cubes, 93–94
  Gianduja Filling, 93–94
  Glazed Almond Weave, 101–2
  Honey Bee Minicakes, 286–88
  Japonais Meringue, 107
  Lebkuchen Circles, 156–57
  Limoges Petits Fours, 302
  Macaroon Trios, 99–100
  Mazarine Tartlets, 217–18
  Pains d'Amande, 143–44
  Panforte di Siena, 97–98
  Pistachio Petits Fours, 283–85
  Pistachio Silk Buttercream, 283–84
  Poirettes, 226–27
  Polka Dot Minicakes, 300–302
  Praline, 108
  Speculaas, 152–53
  splitting, 157
  Swiss Japonais, 107–10
  Truffle Lollipops, 324–25
  Tuiles, 113
  Viennese Triangles, 103–4

Anise seeds
  Chrabeli, 151
  Springerle, 149–50
Apples
  Apple Filling, 252–53
  Candied Lady Apples, 328
  Fresh Quince Filling, 253
  Sweet Ravioli, 252–53
Apricot jam
  Apricot Medals, 58–59
  Dominoes, 294–95
  Four-Star Rugelach, 249
  Poirettes, 226–27
  Punch Balls, 307
  Punch Cakelets, 305–7
  Punch Filling, 305
  Sweet Seashells, 64–65
Apricots, dried
  Apricot-Pistachio Filling, 242
  Apricot Pockets, 61
  California Rolls, 254
  Heartovers, 242–43
  Pistachio Buttons, 90
Autumn Acorns, 80–81

## B

Biberli, 158–59
Bittersweet Gingersnaps, 141–42
Black Walnut Genoise Wafers, 116–17
Blitz Puff Pastry, 266–68
  Florentine Pastry Strips, 269–70
  Streusel Pastry Strips, 271–72
Blood Orange Jellies, 329
Butter, clarifying, 274
Butter Cake, 294
  Dominoes, 294–95
  Jewel Fruit Prisms, 296–97
  Miniature Fruit Meringues, 299
Buttercream, 171–72
  Caramel Pecan Buttercream, 207–8
  Chocolate Silk Buttercream, 289
  Cognac Buttercream Filling, 120–21
  Honey Silk Buttercream, 286
  Lemon Curd Buttercream, 224
  Pistachio Silk Buttercream, 283–84
  Praline Buttercream, 108–9
  Rum Silk Buttercream, 174–75

## C

Cakes
  Almond Cake, 300
  Butter Cake, 294
  Calypso Minirolls, 292–93
  Chocolate-Pistachio Tigrés, 303–4
  Cranberry Almond Cake, 301
  cutting, 279–80
  Dominoes, 294–95

Dutch Chocolate Minicakes, 198
Genoise Sheet Cake, 283
Honey Bee Minicakes, 286–88
Jewel Fruit Prisms, 296–97
Limoges Petits Fours, 302
Miniature Fruit Meringues, 299
mixing, 279
Parisers, 289–91
Pistachio Petits Fours, 283–85
Polka Dot Minicakes, 300–302
Punsch Balls, 307
Punsch Cakelets, 305–7
S'More Squares, 298
Swiss Tea Cakes, 293
California Rolls, 254
Calypso Minirolls, 292–93
Candies
  Blood Orange Jellies, 329
  Candied Almond Clusters, 322–23
  Candied Cranberries, 222
  Candied Kumquat Circles, 336
  Candied Lady Apples, 328
  Chocolate Wafers, 330–31
  Dark Chocolate Caramels, 326
  Dark Chocolate Truffles, 324
  equipment, 312
  Five-Spice Marshmallows, 332–33
  Golden Caramels, 326–27
  Raspberry Jellies, 334–35
  Raspberry Truffles, 325
  Toffee Butter Crunch, 319–21
  Truffle Lollipops, 324–25
Candy-Cane Cookies, Chocolate, 196–97

Caramel Carmenitas, 207–9
Caramel Cream, 228
Caramel Filling, 292
Caramelized Sugar, 86
Caramel Pecan Buttercream, 207–8
Champagne Biscuits, 130–31
Chantilly Fans, 134–35
Cherries
  Chocolate Cherry Chaps, 216
  Chocolate Wafers, 330–31
Chevron Twists, 70–71
Chocolate. See also White chocolate
  Bittersweet Gingersnaps, 141–42
  Black Walnut Genoise Wafers, 116–17
  Candied Almond Clusters, 322–23
  Chocolate Butter, 195
  Chocolate Butter Glaze, 212–13, 222
  Chocolate Candy-Cane Cookies, 196–97
  Chocolate Caramel Cream, 231
  Chocolate Cherry Chaps, 216
  Chocolate Chip Swirls, 62–63
  Chocolate Coins, 183–85
  Chocolate Frangipane Filling, 214–15
  Chocolate Fringe Cups, 132–33
  Chocolate Ganache Cream, 178–79
  Chocolate Honey Ganache Glaze, 186–87
  Chocolate Macaroons, 163–65
  Chocolate Marzipan Filling, 183–84
  Chocolate Miniature Tartlet Pastry, 214
  Chocolate Pistachio Cigarettes, 192–93
  Chocolate-Pistachio Tigrés, 303–4
  Chocolate Shadows, 194–95
  Chocolate Silk Buttercream, 289

Chocolate Starlets, 186–87

Chocolate Thimbles, 168–70

Chocolate Tulips, 178–79

Chocolate Wafers, 330–31

Cocoa Cavaliers, 190–91

Dark Chocolate Caramels, 326

Dark Chocolate Fruit Glaze, 216

Dark Chocolate Ganache, 68–69, 163, 165, 303–4

Dark Chocolate Glaze, 300–301

Dark Chocolate Satin Glaze, 104, 175–76, 286–87, 289–90, 294–95

Dark Chocolate Truffles, 324

Dominoes, 294–95

Double Chocolate Tartlets, 214–15

Double Kisses, 166–67

Dutch Chocolate Minicakes, 198

European Chocolate Glaze, 184

Faux-Tempered Chocolate, 141–42

Florentine Squares, 114–15

Gianduja Cubes, 93–94

Gianduja Filling, 93–94

Glossy Chocolate Ganache Glaze, 171–72

Hedgehogs, 174–77

Honey Bee Minicakes, 286–88

melting, 313–14

Meringue Bubbles, 95–96

Midas Cups, 231

Milk Chocolate Suede Glaze, 180–81

Neapolitan Wedges, 171–73

Parisers, 289–91

Peanut Butter Petal Cookies, 68–69

Polka Dot Minicakes, 300–302

Punsch Balls, 307

Raspberry Truffles, 325

Rose Tartlets, 212–13

Scheherazade Tartlets, 222–23

S'More Squares, 298

tempering, 168–69, 314–16

Tiffany Rings, 180–82

Toffee Butter Crunch, 319–21

Truffle Lollipops, 324–25

Viennese Triangles, 103–4

White Blossom Circles, 188–89

Chrabeli, 151

Cigarettes, 122–23

Cigarettes, Chocolate Pistachio, 192–93

Cinnamon Sugar, 250

Cinnamon Twists, 250

Citron

Hahnpfeffernüsse, 147–48

Lebkuchen Circles, 156–57

Cocoa Cavaliers, 190–91

Coconut

Cocos, 66–67

Cognac

Cognac Buttercream Filling, 120–21

Cognac Sugar Glaze, 118–19, 156–57

Cognac Wafers, 120–21

Ladies' Wafers, 118–19

Cones

Miniature Krumkake, 126–27

Nougatine Cones, 124–25

Cookie doughs

mixing, 33–40

refrigerator, 45

shaping, 40–45

Cookies

Almond Confetti, 88–89

Almond Teardrops, 72–73

Apricot Medals, 58–59

Apricot Pockets, 61

Autumn Acorns, 80–81

Biberli, 158–59

Bittersweet Gingersnaps, 141–42

Black Walnut Genoise Wafers, 116–17

Champagne Biscuits, 130–31

Chantilly Fans, 134–35

Chevron Twists, 70–71

Chocolate Candy-Cane Cookies, 196–97

Chocolate Chip Swirls, 62–63

Chocolate Coins, 183–85

Chocolate Fringe Cups, 132–33

Chocolate Macaroons, 163–65

Chocolate Pistachio Cigarettes, 192–93

Chocolate Shadows, 194–95

Chocolate Starlets, 186–87

Chocolate Thimbles, 168–70

Chocolate Tulips, 178–79

Chrabeli, 151

Cigarettes, 122–23

Cocoa Cavaliers, 190–91

Cocos, 66–67

Cognac Wafers, 120–21

Cornmeal Batons, 76–77

Crispy Corkscrews, 128–29

Daddy Long Legs, 84–85

Double Kisses, 166–67

Drei Augen, 56–57

Dutch Chocolate Minicakes, 198

Florentine Squares, 114–15

Gianduja Cubes, 93–94

Glazed Almond Weave, 101–2

Hahnpfeffernüsse, 147–48

Harlequins, 51–52

Hedgehogs, 174–77

Java Sticks, 54–55

Ladies' Wafers, 118–19

Lebkuchen Circles, 156–57

Lemon-Laced Gingersnaps, 154–55

Lemon Sunflowers, 86–87

Little Gems, 53

Macadamia Crescents, 74–75

Macaroon Trios, 99–100

Maple Butterballs, 78–79

Meringue Bubbles, 95–96

Mimosa Rosettes, 82–83

Miniature Krumkake, 126–27

Neapolitan Wedges, 171–73

Nougatine Cones, 124–25

Pains d'Amande, 143–44

Panforte di Siena, 97–98

Peanut Butter Petal Cookies, 68–69

Pecan Diamonds, 105–6

Pineapple Pockets, 60–61

Pistachio Buttons, 90

Sesame Spice Chips, 145–46

Shortbread Cameos, 49–50

Speculaas, 152–53

Spicy Twin Thins, 139–40

Springerle, 149–50

Sweet Seashells, 64–65

Swiss Japonais, 107–10

Tiffany Rings, 180–82

Tuiles, 113

   Viennese Triangles, 103–4

   White Blossom Circles, 188–89

Corkscrews, Crispy, 128–29

Cornmeal Batons, 76–77

Cottage cheese

   California Rolls, 254

   Cinnamon Twists, 250

   Cottage Cheese Dough, 248

   Four-Star Rugelach, 249

Cranberries

   Candied Cranberries, 222

   Cranberry Almond Cake, 301

   Scheherazade Tartlets, 222–23

Cream cheese

   Cream Cheese Filling, 236

   Cream Cheese Pastry, 251

   Creamy Hazelnut Filling, 210–11

   Dried Fruit Pastry Strips, 255–56

   Flaky Cheesecake Turnovers, 275–76

   Garnet Tartlets, 210–11

   Pumpkin Cream Cheese Filling, 238

   Pumpkin Pastries, 238–39

   Sweet Cheese Puffs, 236–37

   Sweet Ravioli, 252–53

Creaming, 35–39

Creams

   Caramel Cream, 228

   Chocolate Caramel Cream, 231

   Chocolate Ganache Cream, 178–79

   Engadiner Cream, 230

Creamy Hazelnut Filling, 210–11

Crispy Corkscrews, 128–29

Cups, Chocolate Fringe, 132–33

Currant jelly

   Garnet Tartlets, 210–11

   Limoges Petits Fours, 302

   Mazarine Tartlets, 217–18

   Punsch Cakelets, 305–7

Currants, dried

   Dried Currant Filling, 244

   Dried Fruit Pastry Strips, 255–56

   Four-Star Rugelach, 249

   Ladies' Wafers, 118–19

   Shreveshire Tarts, 244–45

## D

Dacquoise, 93

Daddy Long Legs, 84–85

Dark Chocolate Caramels, 326

Dark Chocolate Fruit Glaze, 216

Dark Chocolate Ganache, 68–69, 163, 165, 303–4

Dark Chocolate Glaze, 300–301

Dark Chocolate Satin Glaze, 104, 175–76, 286–87, 289–90, 294–95

Dark Chocolate Truffles, 324

Defrosting, 353

Dominoes, 294–95

Double Chocolate Tartlets, 214–15

Double Kisses, 166–67

Drei Augen, 56–57

Dried Currant Filling, 244, 255

Dried Fruit Filling, 240

Dried Fruit Pastry Strips, 255–56

Dutch Chocolate Minicakes, 198

## E

Eccles Tarts, 240–41
Engadiner Cream, 230
Equipment, 15–23, 312
European Chocolate Glaze, 184
Eva Deutsch's Almond Slices, 246–47

## F

Faux-Tempered Chocolate, 141–42
Figs
    Double Chocolate Tartlets, 214–15
    Fig Filling, 264
    Fig Pastry Rolls, 264–65
Fillings. *See also* Buttercream; Creams
    Almond Filling, 217
    Almond-Hazelnut Filling, 246
    Almond Paste Frangipane, 226
    Almond Paste Frangipane Filling, 178
    Apple Filling, 252–53
    Apricot-Pistachio Filling, 242
    Caramel Filling, 292
    Chocolate Frangipane Filling, 214–15
    Chocolate Marzipan Filling, 183–84
    Cognac Buttercream Filling, 120–21
    Cream Cheese Filling, 236
    Creamy Hazelnut Filling, 210–11
    Dried Currant Filling, 244, 255
    Dried Fruit Filling, 240
    Fig Filling, 264
    Fresh Plum Filling, 253
    Fresh Quince Filling, 253
    Gianduja Filling, 93–94
    Lemon Custard Filling, 221
    Maple Cream Filling, 78
    Maple Pecan Filling, 70–71
    Pecan Filling, 260
    Pineapple Filling, 60
    Pumpkin Cream Cheese Filling, 238
    Punsch Filling, 305
    Whipped Cream Filling, 212–13
Five-Spice Marshmallows, 332–33
Flaky Cheesecake Turnovers, 275–76
Flaky Windmills, 258–59
Florentine Pastry Strips, 269–70
Florentine Squares, 114–15
Fluffy Meringue, 219, 299
Four-Star Rugelach, 249
Freezing, 352–55
Fresh Plum Filling, 253
Fresh Quince Filling, 253
Fruit, dried. *See also* individual fruits
    Dried Fruit Filling, 240
    Dried Fruit Pastry Strips, 255–56
    Eccles Tarts, 240–41
    Panforte di Siena, 97–98
Fruit, fresh. *See also* individual fruits
    Mazarine Tartlets, 217–18
    Miniature Fruit Meringues, 299

## G

Ganache
    Chocolate Ganache Cream, 178–79
    Chocolate Honey Ganache Glaze, 186–87
    Dark Chocolate Ganache, 68–69, 163,
        165, 303–4
    Glossy Chocolate Ganache Glaze, 171–72
    White Chocolate Ganache, 188–89
Garnet Tartlets, 210–11
Genoise Sheet Cake, 283
    Calypso Minirolls, 292–93
    Honey Bee Minicakes, 286–88
    Parisers, 289–91
    Pistachio Petits Fours, 283–85
    Swiss Tea Cakes, 293
Gianduja Cubes, 93–94
Gianduja Filling, 93–94
Gingersnaps
    Bittersweet Gingersnaps, 141–42
    Lemon-Laced Gingersnaps, 154–55
    Glazed Almond Weave, 101–2
Glazes. *See also* Buttercream;
    Ganache; Icings
    Chocolate Butter Glaze, 212–13, 222
    Chocolate Honey Ganache Glaze, 186–87
    Cognac Sugar Glaze, 118–19, 156–57
    Dark Chocolate Fruit Glaze, 216
    Dark Chocolate Glaze, 300–301
    Dark Chocolate Satin Glaze, 104,
        175–76, 286–87, 289–90, 294–95
    European Chocolate Glaze, 184
    Faux-Tempered Chocolate, 141–42
    Glossy Chocolate Ganache Glaze, 171–72
    Honey Butter Glaze, 273–74
    Jelly Glaze, 51–52
    Lemon Sugar Glaze, 159
    Milk Chocolate Suede Glaze, 180–81
    Sugar Glaze, 51–52, 58–59
    White Chocolate Glaze, 300

Glossy Chocolate Ganache Glaze, 171–72
Golden Caramels, 326–27
Graham crackers
    S'More Squares, 298

## H

Hahnpfeffernüsse, 147–48
Harlequins, 51–52
Hazelnuts
    Almond-Hazelnut Filling, 246
    Autumn Acorns, 80–81
    Chantilly Fans, 134–35
    Creamy Hazelnut Filling, 210–11
    Daddy Long Legs, 84–85
    Dutch Chocolate Minicakes, 198
    Eva Deutsch's Almond Slices, 246–47
    Garnet Tartlets, 210–11
    Gianduja Cubes, 93–94
    Gianduja Filling, 93–94
    Nougatine Cones, 124–25
    Panforte di Siena, 97–98
    Praline, 108
    removing skins from, 135
    Swiss Japonais, 107–10
    toasting, 320
    Toffee Butter Crunch, 319–21
Heartovers, 242–43
Heavy Cream Flaky Pastry, 257
    Fig Pastry Rolls, 264–65
    Flaky Windmills, 258–59
    Miniature Caramel Cream Vol-au-Vents,
      262–63
    Pecan Strudel, 260–61

Hedgehogs, 174–77
Honey, 106
    Chocolate Honey Ganache Glaze, 186–87
    Glazed Almond Weave, 101–2
    Honey Bee Minicakes, 286–88
    Honey Butter Glaze, 273–74
    Honey Silk Buttercream, 286
    Pecan Diamonds, 105–6
    Phyllo Accordions, 273–74

## I

Icings. *See also* Buttercream;
    Ganache; Glazes
    Lemon Icing, 154–55
    Pfeffernüsse Icing, 147–48
    Royal Icing, 171–72, 175–76,
      258, 294–95
Ingredients, 24–26

## J

Jade Buttercups, 224–25
Japonais Meringue, 107
Java Sticks, 54–55
Jellies and jams
    Apricot Medals, 58–59
    Chocolate Cherry Chaps, 216
    Dominoes, 294–95
    Drei Augen, 56–57
    Four-Star Rugelach, 249
    Garnet Tartlets, 210–11
    Jelly Glaze, 51–52
    Limoges Petits Fours, 302

Little Gems, 53
Mazarine Tartlets, 217–18
Poirettes, 226–27
Punsch Balls, 307
Punsch Cakelets, 305–7
Punsch Filling, 305
Sweet Seashells, 64–65
Viennese Triangles, 103–4
Wine Jelly, 296
Jellies (candies)
    Blood Orange Jellies, 329
    Raspberry Jellies, 334–35
Jewel Fruit Prisms, 296–97

## K

Kiwi
    Jade Buttercups, 224–25
Krumkake, Miniature, 126–27
Kumquat Circles, Candied, 336

## L

Ladies' Wafers, 118–19
Lady Apples, Candied, 328
Lebkuchen Circles, 156–57
Lemon
    Biberli, 158–59
    Jade Buttercups, 224–25
    Lemon Curd, 219, 228
    Lemon Curd Buttercream, 224
    Lemon Custard Filling, 221
    Lemon Drops, 228–29
    Lemon Gelée, 224

Lemon Icing, 154–55

Lemon-Laced Gingersnaps, 154–55

Lemon Meringue Tartlets, 219–20

Lemon Sugar Glaze, 159

Lemon Sunflowers, 86–87

Punsch Balls, 307

Punsch Cakelets, 305–7

Punsch Filling, 305

Raspberry Lemon Tartlets, 221

Limoges Petits Fours, 302

Little Gems, 53

# M

Macadamia Crescents, 74–75

Macaroons

Chocolate Macaroons, 163–65

Macaroon Trios, 99–100

Making ahead, 339–44

Maple syrup and sugar

Maple Butterballs, 78–79

Maple Cream Filling, 78

Maple Pecan Filling, 70–71

Tiffany Rings, 180–82

Marshmallows

Five-Spice Marshmallows, 332–33

S'More Squares, 298

Marzipan

Chocolate Coins, 183–85

Chocolate Marzipan Filling, 183–84

Dominoes, 294–95

European Chocolate Glaze, 184

Mazarine Tartlets, 217–18

Meringue

Fluffy Meringue, 219, 299

Japonais Meringue, 107

Lemon Meringue Tartlets, 219–20

Meringue Bubbles, 95–96

Miniature Fruit Meringues, 299

Midas Cups, 231

Milk Chocolate Suede Glaze, 180–81

Mimosa Rosettes, 82–83

Miniature Caramel Cream Vol-au-Vents, 262–63

Miniature Fruit Meringues, 299

Miniature Krumkake, 126–27

Miniature Tartlet Pastry, 205–6

Molasses

Lemon-Laced Gingersnaps, 154–55

Sesame Spice Chips, 145–46

# N

Neapolitan Wedges, 171–73

Nougatine Cones, 124–25

Nuts. *See also* individual nuts

grinding and chopping, 16–17

measuring, 16

toasting, 125

# O

Oranges

Blood Orange Jellies, 329

Calypso Minirolls, 292–93

Punsch Balls, 307

Punsch Cakelets, 305–7

Punsch Filling, 305

# P

Pains d'Amande, 143–44

Panforte di Siena, 97–98

Parisers, 289–91

Pastries

California Rolls, 254

Caramel Carmenitas, 207–9

Chocolate Cherry Chaps, 216

Cinnamon Twists, 250

Double Chocolate Tartlets, 214–15

Dried Fruit Pastry Strips, 255–56

Eccles Tarts, 240–41

Eva Deutsch's Almond Slices, 246–47

Fig Pastry Rolls, 264–65

Flaky Cheesecake Turnovers, 275–76

Flaky Windmills, 258–59

Florentine Pastry Strips, 269–70

Four-Star Rugelach, 249

Garnet Tartlets, 210–11

Heartovers, 242–43

Jade Buttercups, 224–25

Lemon Drops, 228–29

Lemon Meringue Tartlets, 219–20

Mazarine Tartlets, 217–18

Midas Cups, 231

Miniature Caramel Cream Vol-au-Vents, 262–63

Pecan Strudel, 260–61

Phyllo Accordions, 273–74

Poirettes, 226–27

Pumpkin Pastries, 238–39

Raspberry Lemon Tartlets, 221

Rose Tartlets, 212–13

Scheherazade Tartlets, 222–23
Shreveshire Tarts, 244–45
Streusel Pastry Strips, 271–72
Sweet Cheese Puffs, 236–37
Sweet Ravioli, 252–53
Swiss Bettinas, 230
Pastry doughs
 Blitz Puff Pastry, 266–68
 Chocolate Miniature Tartlet Pastry, 214
 Cottage Cheese Dough, 248
 Cream Cheese Pastry, 251
 Heavy Cream Flaky Pastry, 257
 Miniature Tartlet Pastry, 205–6
 mixing, 201–2
 rolling, 202
 Sour Cream Pastry, 235
 Yogurt Pastry, 235
Peanut butter
 Double Kisses, 166–67
 Peanut Butter Petal Cookies, 68–69
Pears
 Poirettes, 226–27
Pecans
 Caramel Pecan Buttercream, 207–8
 Chevron Twists, 70–71
 Little Gems, 53
 Maple Pecan Filling, 70–71
 Pecan Diamonds, 105–6
 Pecan Filling, 260
 Pecan Strudel, 260–61
 Phyllo Accordions, 273–74
Pfeffernüsse Icing, 147–48

Phyllo dough
 Flaky Cheesecake Turnovers, 275–76
 Phyllo Accordions, 273–74
 working with, 274, 276
Pineapple
 Pineapple Filling, 60
 Pineapple Pockets, 60–61
Pine nuts
 Hedgehogs, 174–77
 Macaroon Trios, 99–100
Pistachios
 Apricot-Pistachio Filling, 242
 Apricot Pockets, 61
 blanching shelled, 285
 California Rolls, 254
 Chocolate Pistachio Cigarettes, 192–93
 Chocolate-Pistachio Tigrés, 303–4
 Heartovers, 242–43
 Pistachio Buttons, 90
 Pistachio Petits Fours, 283–85
 Pistachio Silk Buttercream, 283–84
 Spicy Twin Thins, 139–40
Plum Filling, Fresh, 253
Poirettes, 226–27
Polka Dot Minicakes, 300–302
Pomegranates
 removing seeds from, 223
 Scheherazade Tartlets, 222–23
Praline, 108
 Praline Buttercream, 108–9
 Praline Powder, 109
Puff pastry. See Blitz Puff Pastry

Pumpkin
 Pumpkin Cream Cheese Filling, 238
 Pumpkin Pastries, 238–39
Punsch Balls, 307
Punsch Cakelets, 305–7
Punsch Filling, 305

Q
Quince Filling, Fresh, 253

R
Raspberries and raspberry jam
 Punsch Cakelets, 305–7
 Raspberry Jellies, 334–35
 Raspberry Lemon Tartlets, 221
 Raspberry Truffles, 325
 Viennese Triangles, 103–4
Rose Tartlets, 212–13
Royal Icing, 171–72, 175–76, 258, 294–95
Rugelach, Four-Star, 249
Rum Silk Buttercream, 174–75

S
Scheherazade Tartlets, 222–23
Sesame seeds
 Phyllo Accordions, 273–74
 Sesame Spice Chips, 145–46
Shortbread Cameos, 49–50
Shreveshire Tarts, 244–45
S'More Squares, 298

Sour cream
 Almond Confetti, 88–89
 Eccles Tarts, 240–41
 Eva Deutsch's Almond Slices, 246–47
 Heartovers, 242–43
 Miniature Krumkake, 126–27
 Pumpkin Pastries, 238–39
 Shreveshire Tarts, 244–45
 Sour Cream Pastry, 235
 Sweet Cheese Puffs, 236–37
Speculaas, 152–53
Spicy Twin Thins, 139–40
Springerle, 149–50
Stencils, 123
Storage, 22, 342, 352–55
Strawberry jam
 Mazarine Tartlets, 217–18
Streusel, 76, 271
 Almond Paste Streusel, 190
 Streusel Pastry Strips, 271–72
Strudel, Pecan, 260–61
Sugar, Caramelized, 86
Sugar Glaze, 51–52, 58–59
Sweet Cheese Puffs, 236–37
Sweet Ravioli, 252–53
Sweet Seashells, 64–65
Swiss Bettinas, 230
Swiss Japonais, 107–10
Swiss Tea Cakes, 293

T

Tarts and tartlets. *See* Pastries
Tiffany Rings, 180–82
Tigrés, Chocolate-Pistachio, 303–4
Toffee Butter Crunch, 319–21
Truffles
 Dark Chocolate Truffles, 324
 Raspberry Truffles, 325
 Truffle Lollipops, 324–25
Tuiles, 113
Turnovers, Flaky Cheesecake, 275–76

V

Viennese Triangles, 103–4
Vol-au-Vents, Miniature Caramel Cream,
 262–63

W

Walnuts
 Black Walnut Genoise Wafers, 116–17
 Chocolate Starlets, 186–87
 Dried Fruit Filling, 240
 Eccles Tarts, 240–41
 Engadiner Cream, 230
 Four-Star Rugelach, 249
 Java Sticks, 54–55
 Panforte di Siena, 97–98
 Phyllo Accordions, 273–74
 Swiss Bettinas, 230
Whipped Cream Filling, 212–13
White Blossom Circles, 188–89

White chocolate
 Champagne Biscuits, 130–31
 Java Sticks, 54–55
 Limoges Petits Fours, 302
 Pistachio Buttons, 90
 Polka Dot Minicakes, 300–302
 Spicy Twin Thins, 139–40
 White Blossom Circles, 188–89
 White Chocolate Ganache, 188–89
 White Chocolate Glaze, 300
Windmills, Flaky, 258–59
Wine
 Jewel Fruit Prisms, 296–97
 Wine Jelly, 296

Y

Yogurt Pastry, 235

# table of equivalents*

## LIQUID AND DRY MEASURES

| U.S. | Metric |
|---|---|
| ¼ teaspoon | 1.25 milliliters |
| ½ teaspoon | 2.5 milliliters |
| 1 teaspoon | 5 milliliters |
| 1 tablespoon (3 teaspoons) | 15 milliliters |
| 1 fluid ounce (2 tablespoons) | 30 milliliters |
| ¼ cup | 60 milliliters |
| ⅓ cup | 80 milliliters |
| 1 cup | 240 milliliters |
| 1 pint (2 cups) | 480 milliliters |
| 1 quart (4 cups, 32 ounces) | 960 milliliters |
| 1 gallon (4 quarts) | 3.84 liters |
| 1 ounce (by weight) | 28 grams |
| 1 pound | 454 grams |
| 2.2 pounds | 1 kilogram |

## OVEN TEMPERATURES

| Fahrenheit | Celsius | Gas |
|---|---|---|
| 250 | 120 | ½ |
| 275 | 140 | 1 |
| 300 | 150 | 2 |
| 325 | 160 | 3 |
| 350 | 180 | 4 |
| 375 | 190 | 5 |
| 400 | 200 | 6 |
| 425 | 220 | 7 |
| 450 | 230 | 8 |
| 475 | 240 | 9 |
| 500 | 260 | 10 |

## LENGTH MEASURES

| U.S. | Metric |
|---|---|
| ⅛ inch | 3 millimeters |
| ¼ inch | 6 millimeters |
| ½ inch | 12 millimeters |
| 1 inch | 2.5 centimeters |

*The exact equivalents in these tables have been rounded for convenience.